Constituent Order in Language and Thought

Traditionally, due to the availability of technology, psycholinguistic research has focused mainly on Western languages. However, this focus has recently shifted toward a more diverse range of languages, whose structures often throw into question many previous assumptions in syntactic theory and language processing. Based on a case study in field-based comparative psycholinguistics, this pioneering book is the first to explore the neurocognition of endangered "object-before-subject" languages, such as Kaqchikel and Seediq. It draws on a range of methods – including linguistic fieldwork, theoretical linguistic analysis, corpus research, questionnaire surveys, behavioural experiments, eye tracking, event-related brain potentials, functional magnetic resonance imaging, and near-infrared spectroscopy – to consider preferred constituent orders in both language and thought, examining comprehension as well as production. In doing so, it highlights the importance of field-based cross-linguistic cognitive neuroscientific research in uncovering universal and language-particular aspects of the human language faculty, and the interaction between language and thought.

MASATOSHI KOIZUMI is Professor of Linguistics and Brain Science at Tohoku University, Japan. His research interests include grammatical theory and neurocognition of language. He is currently engaged in field-based cognitive neuroscience research on understudied languages.

Constituent Order in Language and Thought

A Case Study in Field-Based Psycholinguistics

Masatoshi Koizumi
Tohoku University, Japan

CAMBRIDGE
UNIVERSITY PRESS

Shaftesbury Road, Cambridge CB2 8EA, United Kingdom

One Liberty Plaza, 20th Floor, New York, NY 10006, USA

477 Williamstown Road, Port Melbourne, VIC 3207, Australia

314–321, 3rd Floor, Plot 3, Splendor Forum, Jasola District Centre, New Delhi – 110025, India

103 Penang Road, #05–06/07, Visioncrest Commercial, Singapore 238467

Cambridge University Press is part of Cambridge University Press & Assessment, a department of the University of Cambridge.

We share the University's mission to contribute to society through the pursuit of education, learning and research at the highest international levels of excellence.

www.cambridge.org
Information on this title: www.cambridge.org/9781108926096

DOI: 10.1017/9781108915571

© Masatoshi Koizumi 2023

This publication is in copyright. Subject to statutory exception and to the provisions of relevant collective licensing agreements, no reproduction of any part may take place without the written permission of Cambridge University Press & Assessment.

First published 2023
First paperback edition 2025

A catalogue record for this publication is available from the British Library

ISBN 978-1-108-84403-1 Hardback
ISBN 978-1-108-92609-6 Paperback

Cambridge University Press & Assessment has no responsibility for the persistence or accuracy of URLs for external or third-party internet websites referred to in this publication and does not guarantee that any content on such websites is, or will remain, accurate or appropriate.

In memory of Hideyuki Hirano

Contents

List of Figures		*page* x
List of Tables		xv
Preface		xvii
List of Abbreviations		xx

1 Introduction   1
   1.1 Word Order Preference   2
   1.2 Origins of Word Order Preference   3
   1.3 Outline of the Book   8

2 Kaqchikel Mayan   15
   2.1 Kaqchikel and the Mayan Family   15
   2.2 Typological Basics   16
   2.3 Word Order   19

3 Word Order Preference in Sentence Comprehension I: Behavioral Studies   23
   3.1 Previous Studies   23
   3.2 Competing Hypotheses   24
   3.3 Predictions   26
   3.4 Processing Load   26
   3.5 Effects of Animacy   29
   3.6 General Discussion   31
   3.7 Conclusion   34

4 Word Order Preference in Sentence Comprehension II: fMRI Studies   36
   4.1 Brain Primer   37
   4.2 Functional Brain Measurement   37
   4.3 Previous fMRI Studies on Word Order Processing   39
   4.4 Neural Substrates for Word Order Processing in Kaqchikel   44
   4.5 Conclusion   48

5 Word Order Preference in Sentence Comprehension III: ERP Studies without Context   49
   5.1 Previous ERP Studies on Word Order Processing   49

	5.2	Identifying Gap Positions	51
	5.3	Conclusion	59
6	**Word Order Preference in Sentence Comprehension IV: ERP Studies with Context**		61
	6.1	Sentence Comprehension within Context	61
	6.2	Discussion	64
	6.3	Conclusion	65
7	**Basic Word Order in Language and Natural Order of Thought**		66
	7.1	SO Preference in Basic Word Order	66
	7.2	Natural Order of Thought	70
	7.3	Conclusion	73
8	**Constituent Order Preference in Event Representation**		75
	8.1	Competing Hypotheses	75
	8.2	Order of Thought in Kaqchikel	76
	8.3	Conclusion	84
9	**Word Order Preference in Sentence Production I: Production Frequency**		86
	9.1	Previous Studies	86
	9.2	Competing Hypotheses	86
	9.3	Word Order Frequency in Kaqchikel	89
	9.4	Effects of Animacy on Word Order in Syntactically Unambiguous Sentences	92
	9.5	General Discussion	93
	9.6	Conclusion	99
10	**Word Order Preference in Sentence Production II: Time Course and Cognitive Load**		101
	10.1	Introduction	101
	10.2	Time Course and Cognitive Load of Japanese Sentence Production	102
	10.3	Time Course and Cognitive Load of Kaqchikel Sentence Production	108
	10.4	General Discussion	110
	10.5	Conclusion	114
11	**Grammatical Processing and Event Apprehension**		115
	11.1	Introduction	115
	11.2	A Picture–Sentence Matching Behavioral Study	117
	11.3	A Picture–Sentence Matching fMRI Study	122
	11.4	Conclusion	125
12	**Syntactic Structure of Kaqchikel Revisited**		126
	12.1	Agreement and Hierarchical Structure in Kaqchikel	126
	12.2	A Right-Specifier Analysis	128
	12.3	A Predicate Fronting Analysis	131
	12.4	Conclusion	137

Contents ix

13 Syntax and Processing Load 141
    13.1 Kaqchikel 141
    13.2 Japanese 156
    13.3 General Discussion 161
    13.4 Conclusion 163

14 Concluding Remarks 164
    14.1 Field-Based Comparative Psycholinguistics 164
    14.2 Major Findings and Implications 165
    14.3 Future Work 165

Appendix A Spatial Frames of Reference of Kaqchikel Speakers:
    A Comparative Study with Japanese Speakers 167
Appendix B Syntax and Processing in Seediq: A Behavioral Study 185
References 204
Index 225

Figures

1.1 A schematic representation of the possible origin of SO word order preference within the Universal Cognition View. (Adapted from Kemmerer 2012 with permission.) *page* 6
2.1 Distribution of Mayan languages. Kaqchikel is number 23. (Based on Map 4 in Law 2014, with modification by Bennett, Coon, and Henderson 2016, used with permission.) 16
3.1 Histograms of the reaction times for sentences with the VOS, SVO, and VSO word orders. The error bars indicate the standard error of the mean. 28
4.1 Language-relevant brain regions and fiber tracts in the left hemisphere. (Adapted from Friederici et al. 2017 with permission.) 38
4.2 Activation of the left IFG in the comparison of OS vs. SO German sentences. (Adapted from Grewe et al. 2007 with permission.) 40
4.3 Brain regions activated more in CS than R. (Adapted from Kim et al. 2009 with permission.) 42
4.4 Brain regions activated more in CS than WL. (Adapted from Kim et al. 2009 with permission.) 43
4.5 Brain regions activated more in SS than CS. (Adapted from Kim et al. 2009 with permission.) 43
4.6 Activated brain regions while processing the VOS (A) and SVO (B) word orders relative to the null task condition. (Adapted from Koizumi and Kim 2016 with permission.) 46
4.7 Brain regions more activated for SVO than VOS. (Adapted from Koizumi and Kim 2016 with permission.) 47
5.1 Design of the task used in the experiment. 51
5.2 Electrode locations of the International 10–20 system for EEG recording (downloaded from Wikimedia Commons, May 16, 2022). The letters F, T, C, P, and O stand for the frontal, temporal, central, parietal, and occipital array, respectively. A and Fp identify the earlobes and frontal polar sites,

List of Figures   xi

respectively. Even numbers (2, 4, 6, 8) refer to electrode positions on the right hemisphere, and odd numbers (1, 3, 5, 7) refer to those on the left hemisphere. 53

5.3 The grand average ERPs for the third phrase of SVO and VOS (i.e., the O of SVO and the S of VOS). The dotted line indicates the SVO condition, and the solid line indicates the VOS condition. The X-axis represents time, with marks representing 100 ms. The Y-axis represents voltage, ranging from –5 to 5 μV. Negativity is plotted upward. The topographical voltage maps represent the mean of the difference calculated as SVO minus VOS for every 100 ms from 300 to 800 ms. (Adapted from Yano, Yasunaga, and Koizumi 2017 with permission.) 56

5.4 The grand average ERPs for the third phrase of VSO and VOS. The dotted line indicates the VSO condition, and the solid line indicates the VOS condition. The X-axis represents time, with marks representing 100 ms. The Y-axis represents voltage, ranging from –5 to 5 μV. Negativity is plotted upward. The topographical voltage maps represent the mean of the difference calculated as VSO minus VOS for every 100 ms from 300 to 800 ms. (Adapted from Yano, Yasunaga, and Koizumi 2017 with permission.) 57

5.5 The grand average ERPs for the second phrase of OVS and SVO. The solid line indicates the SVO condition, and the dotted line indicates the OVS condition. The X-axis represents time, with marks representing 100 ms. The Y-axis represents voltage, ranging from –5 to 5 μV. Negativity is plotted upward. The topographical voltage maps represent the mean of the difference calculated as OVS minus SVO for every 100 ms from 300 to 800 ms. (Adapted from Yano, Yasunaga, and Koizumi 2017 with permission.) 58

5.6 The grand average ERPs for the third phrase of SVO and OVS. The solid line indicates the SVO condition, and the dotted line indicates the OVS condition. The X-axis represents time, with marks representing 100 ms. The Y-axis represents voltage, ranging from –5 to 5 μV. Negativity is plotted upward. The topographical voltage maps represent the mean of the difference calculated as SVO minus OVS for every 100 ms from 300 to 800 ms. (Adapted from Yano, Yasunaga, and Koizumi 2017 with permission.) 59

6.1 Panel A: The grand averaged ERP waveforms for the third region in the SVO (O, dotted lines) and VOS (S, solid lines) word order conditions for all seventeen electrode sites.

	Negativity is plotted upward. Panel B: Voltage maps for the difference ERPs (SVO – VOS) for every 100 ms between 300 and 800 ms. (Adapted from Yasunaga et al. 2015.)	62
6.2	Panel A: The grand averaged ERP waveforms for the second region in the VSO (S, dotted lines) and VOS (O, solid lines) word order conditions for all seventeen electrode sites. Negativity is plotted upward. Panel B: The voltage maps of the difference ERPs (VSO – VOS) for every 100 ms between 300 and 800 ms. (Adapted from Yasunaga et al. 2015.)	63
7.1	The distribution of word order types in the world. Each circle represents a SOV language in (A) and a SVO language in (B). (Adapted from Dryer 2013. Available online at http://wals.info/chapter/81 [last accessed September 19, 2022].)	68
7.2	Evolution of word order. The bold lines indicate the most frequent changes caused by natural drift without diffusion, and the other lines indicate other possible changes. (Adapted from Gell-Mann and Ruhlen 2011: 17291 with permission.)	69
7.3	Historical word order changes from SOV and the two competing hypotheses.	73
8.1	Pictures with different patient animacy conditions. (Adapted from Kubo et al. 2015 with permission.)	77
8.2	Frequencies of gestures with agent–patient and patient–agent orders.	78
8.3	Effects of the animacy of the patient on the relative order of agent and patient.	79
8.4	Distribution of constituent orders.	80
8.5	Effects of patient animacy on the distribution of gesture orders (Japanese speakers).	82
8.6	Effects of patient animacy on the distribution of gesture orders (Kaqchikel speakers).	83
8.7	Effects of patient animacy on the distribution of gesture orders II (Kaqchikel speakers).	84
8.8	Effects of patient animacy on the distribution of gesture orders III (Kaqchikel speakers).	85
9.1	Pictures of different patient animacy conditions. (Adapted from Kubo et al. 2015 with permission.)	89
9.2	Word order preference in Kaqchikel in the picture description task.	91
9.3	Pictures used in the second experiment. (Adapted from Kubo et al. 2015 with permission.)	93
9.4	Effects of animacy in the picture description task.	94
9.5	A schematic model of language processing.	95

List of Figures

10.1	A schematic model of language processing.	102
10.2	(a) Locations of the probes used in NIRS measurements. (b) Schematic representation of the procedure in the present experiment. (Adapted from Takeshima et al. 2015 with permission.)	103
10.3	An example of area of interest (AOI) setting. The left AOI covers the agent area, and the right AOI covers the patient area, with the sizes of the two AOIs being comparable. (Adapted from Takeshima et al. 2015 with permission.)	105
10.4	Relative fixation time during the picture presentation for (a) canonical SOV utterances and (b) scrambled OSV utterances. The black vertical lines represent speech onset. (Adapted from Takeshima et al. 2015 with permission.)	106
10.5	Average peak concentration changes of oxyhemoglobin under the two word order conditions on channel 32, which is estimated to be in the left IFG. The error bars represent the standard errors of the means. (Adapted from Takeshima et al. 2015 with permission.)	107
10.6	Mean target advantage scores (proportion of looks to the agent minus proportion of looks to the patient) for each experimental condition. The vertical dotted lines represent the boundaries of the time windows used for statistical analyses. (Adapted from Koizumi et al. 2019.)	109
10.7	Proportion of looks to the agent/patient AOI during the picture presentation for (a) SVO and (b) VOS utterances. The black vertical lines represent speech onset. (Adapted from Koizumi et al. 2019.)	111
10.8	Average peak concentration changes of oxyhemoglobin under the four conditions in channel 29, which is estimated to be in the left IFG. The error bars represent the standard errors of the means. (Adapted from Koizumi et al. 2019.)	112
11.1	Design of the sentence–picture matching experiment. (Adapted from Yano, Yasunaga, and Koizumi 2017 with permission.)	116
11.2	Examples of the stimulus pictures depicting a transitive action with agent(s) and patient(s) used in the picture–sentence matching task. (Adapted from Kiyama et al. 2017 with permission.)	118
11.3	Accuracy rate of the picture–sentence matching task of Kaqchikel reversible sentences. Error bars indicate 95 percent confidence intervals. (Adapted from Kiyama et al. 2017 with permission.)	119

xiv   List of Figures

11.4	Reaction time of the picture–sentence matching task of Kaqchikel reversible sentences. Error bars indicate 95 percent confidence intervals. (Adapted from Kiyama et al. 2017 with permission.)	119
11.5	Plot of percentage of Spanish use in daily life and SVO preference in terms of reaction time in a picture-matching task of Kaqchikel sentences with animate objects (average of OVS, VOS, and VSO minus SVO). (Adapted from Kiyama et al. 2017 with permission.)	120
11.6	(a) Reaction times (RTs) from the onset of the picture in the picture–sentence matching and control tasks. (b) Accuracy in the picture–sentence matching and control tasks. (Adapted from Ohta et al. 2017.)	123
11.7	Regions identified by the contrast of (VOS + VSO + OVS) – SVO. (Adapted from Ohta et al. 2017.)	124
11.8	(a) Regions identified by the contrast of VSO – VOS. (b) Regions identified by the contrast of OVS – SVO. (Adapted from Ohta et al. 2017.)	124
A.1	A perceiving subject (a human) sees a ball and a car.	168
A.2	Geographic distribution of Mayan languages. (Based on Map 4 in Law 2014, with modification by Bennett, Coon, and Henderson 2016, used with permission.)	173
A.3	RELATIVE and ABSOLUTE responses to the Animal Recall Task.	176
A.4	RELATIVE and ABSOLUTE responses to the Chips Recognition Task.	177
A.5	RELATIVE and ABSOLUTE responses to the Transitive Inference Task.	178
A.6	Mean relative response ratios by native language.	180
A.7	The number of times the relative FoR was used in the Chips Recognition Task and Transitive Inference Task and the responses' correlations ($r = .399, p = .081$).	183
B.1	The mean response accuracy rates for each condition. The error bars indicate standard errors of the mean.	196
B.2	The mean response time (ms) for each condition. The error bars indicate standard errors of the mean.	197

Tables

1.1	Order of subject, object, and verb	*page* 10
2.1	Set A (ergative and genitive)	19
2.2	Set B (absolutive)	19
3.1	The averages (M) and standard deviations (SD) of time duration for word order	27
3.2	Reaction times and error rates for semantically plausible transitive sentences judged as semantically correct	28
3.3	Reaction times (ms) of sentence plausibility judgment for Kaqchikel VOS and SVO sentences with animate and inanimate objects	31
7.1	Order of subject, object, and verb I	67
7.2	Order of subject, object, and verb II	67
9.1	Distribution of word orders in Japanese (based on data published in Imamura and Koizumi 2011)	87
9.2	Distribution of word orders in Turkish (based on data published in Slobin and Bever 1982)	87
9.3	Distribution of word orders in Serbo-Croatian (based on data published in Slobin and Bever 1982)	87
9.4	Distribution of word orders in Finnish (based on data published in Hakulinen and Karlsson 1980)	87
9.5	Distribution of word orders in Italian (based on data published in Bates 1976)	88
9.6	Distribution of word orders in Greek (based on data published in Lascaratou 1989)	88
9.7	Distribution of word orders in Polish (based on data published in Siewierska 1993)	88
9.8	Distribution of four transitive constructions in Japanese (based on data published in Imamura and Koizumi 2011)	97
10.1	The means and standard deviations of utterance latency for word order conditions (M = mean, SD = standard deviation)	104
10.2	The means and standard deviations of utterance latency (ms) for word order and patient animacy conditions	108

13.1	Word-by-word predictions of the DLT for the subject-extracted RC in (8)		145
13.2	Word-by-word predictions of the DLT for the object-extracted RC in (9)		145
13.3	Predictions of the DLT for VOS in Kaqchikel		146
13.4	Predictions of the DLT for SVO in Kaqchikel		147
13.5	Predictions of the DLT for VSO in Kaqchikel		147
13.6	Predictions of the DLT for OVS in Kaqchikel		148
13.7	Predictions of the DLT for [S-NOM O-ACC V] in Japanese		158
13.8	Predictions of the DLT for [S-TOP O-ACC V] in Japanese		158
13.9	Predictions of the DLT for [O-ACC S-NOM V] in Japanese		158
13.10	Predictions of the DLT for [O-TOP S-NOM V] in Japanese		159
13.11	Ranking of relative processing cost in Kaqchikel predicted by the three factors combined		162
13.12	Ranking of relative processing costs in Japanese predicted by the three factors combined		163
A.1	Japanese and Kaqchikel speakers' responses (RELative, ABSolutive, or Others) to the three tasks		179
B.1	Summary of the statistical analysis on the response accuracy data		197
B.2	Summary of the statistical analysis on the response time data		198
B.3	The relationship between the two accounts (the Universal Saliency and the Syntactic Complexity) with respect to the processing cost, and the four sentence patterns based on voice and word order		200

Preface

In many flexible word order languages, sentences with a transitive verb (V) in which the subject (S) precedes the object (O) (SO word order = SOV, SVO, VSO) are reported to be "preferred" over those in which the opposite occurs (OS word order = OSV, OVS, VOS). For example, SO sentences are easier to process and are produced more frequently than OS sentences in Finnish, Japanese, Sinhalese, and others (Sekerina 1997; Bader and Meng 1999; Mazuka, Itoh, and Kondo 2002; Kaiser and Trueswell 2004; Tamaoka et al. 2005; Kanduboda and Tamaoka 2012). This empirical evidence of the preference for SO word order, however, is not conclusive, because it comes exclusively from SO languages, that is, languages in which SO is the most syntactically simple word order. It is, therefore, necessary to study OS languages to investigate whether or not the same preference holds as well as identify underlying factors determining word order preference in sentence comprehension and production. To this end, my colleagues and I have been conducting a research project on Kaqchikel, a Mayan language spoken in Guatemala, whose syntactically basic word order is VOS.[1]

This book assembles some of the major findings we have obtained through this project over the last decade. Most of our Kaqchikel experiments discussed in the following chapters were conducted in the central highland of Guatemala, home of the Kaqchikel people. We visited the region more than ten times with equipment such as an EEG amp and an eye tracker at hand. The several remaining experiments were carried out in Japan by inviting Kaqchikel speakers to our labs at Tohoku University and Tokyo University because they required an MRI or NIRS scanner, which are too large to transport to Guatemala. This monograph, therefore, presents a case study in field-based comparative psycholinguistics.

Core members of the project include (alphabetically, by first name) Apay Tracy Tang, Daichi Yasunaga, Filiberto Patal Majzul, Godai Saito, Hajime Ono, Hiromu Sakai, Hitoshi Goto, Jiro Gyoba, Juan Esteban Ajsivinac Sian, Jungho Kim, Katsuo Tamaoka, Keiyu Niikuni, Koichi Otaki, Koji Sugisaki, Kuniya Nasukawa, Kuniyoshi L. Sakai, Laura Rodrigo, Lolmay Pedro Oscar García Matzar, Manami Sato, Masataka Yano, Mikihiro Tanaka, Noriaki Yusa,

Riku Asaoka, Ryo Tachibana, Sachiko Kiyama, Shin'ichi Chigusa, Shinri Ohta, Takuya Kobo, Tsutomu Sakamoto, Yasuhiro Takeshima, Yoshiho Yasugi, Yuko Otsuka, and Yumi Omori. Many other people worked together with us at various stages of this research.

I want to thank the Kaqchikel speakers who contributed to our research in the two countries either as participants or collaborators, as well as Comunidad Lingüística Kaqchikel and Academia de Lenguas Mayas de Guatemala for their invaluable support. Furthermore, I am indebted to Byron Rene Escobedo Menendez, Ambassador of Guatemala to Japan, and Teruaki Nagasaki, Japanese Ambassador to Guatemala, for their help and guidance.

Portions of this work were presented at Harvard University, International Christian University, Kanda University of International Studies, Keio University, Kobe University, Kwansei Gakuin University, Mie University, Kyoto Women's University, MIT, Nagoya University, National Institute for Japanese Language and Linguistics, National Museum of Ethnology (Japan), National Tsing Hua University (Taiwan), RIKEN Center for Brain Science, Leibniz-Zentrum Allgemeine Sprachwissenschaft (ZAS), as well as a number of conferences such as the Second Formal Approaches to Mayan Linguistics, the twenty-sixth annual CUNY Sentence Processing Conference, Architecture and Mechanisms of Language Processing 2013, and the eighth Workshop on Altaic Formal Linguistics, to name just a few. I thank for numerous suggestions those who attended these events, in particular, Akira Watanabe, Barbara Lust, Colin Phillips, Danfeng Wu, Danny Fox, David Pesetsky, Edith Aldridge, Haruo Kubozono, Hiroyuki Ura, Hisashi Noda, Hisatsugu Kitahara, Hsiu-chuan Liao, Jaklin Kornfilt, Jessica Coon, Jim Huang, John Haviland, John Whitman, Judith Aissen, Junko Ito, Kaoru Horie, Kazuko Yatsushiro, Kazuko Inoue, Mineharu J. J. Nakayama, Kenneth Wexler, Martin Hackl, Michael Kenstowicz, Koichi Tateishi, Mutsumi Imai, Noam Chomsky, Nobuko Hasegawa, Nora England, Norvin Richards, Reiko Mazuka, Robert Henderson, Ryosuke Shibagaki, Sabine Iatridou, Shigeo Tonoike, Shigeru Miyagawa, Taro Kageyama, Tasaku Tsunoda, Tomoyuki Yoshida, Uli Sauerland, Yasuhiro Shirai, Yukiko Ueda, Wayne O'Neil, and Wei-tien Dylan Tsai.

The research reported here was supported in part by JSPS KAKENHI (Grant Numbers 22222001, 26580069, 15H02603, 19H05589). I am grateful to Tohoku University for granting me study leave and to the Harvard-Yenching Institute for the 2017–2018 visiting scholar fellowship, during which the first draft of this book was written. I am grateful to Elizabeth Perry, Jim Huang, Ruohong Li, Shigeru Miyagawa, Susan Scott, Lindsay Strogatz, Francesca Coppola, James Flaherty, and Tamiko Arata for their hospitality during my stay in Boston. Thanks are also due to Bethan Lee, Helen Barton, Isabel Collins, Laura Simmons, Malini Soupramanian, and the Cambridge University Press for their support.

Finally, I would like to express my appreciation to my parents, Toshiharu and Shizuka, my wife Chikako, our daughters, Minori and Megumi, and our son Morris (Irish Setter), for having been sympathetic to and supportive of my work for all these years.

NOTE

1. This is part of a larger project, which has come to be known as the FALCOHN (Field-Based Approaches to Language, Cognition, and Human Nature) project.

Abbreviations

*	ungrammatical
-	morpheme boundary
1	first person
2	second person
3	third person
A	Set A = ergative or genitive
ABS	absolutive
ACC	accusative
AV	agent voice
B	Set B = absolutive
CAU	causative
CL	classifier
DAT	dative
CP	completive
DET	determiner
ERG	ergative
GEN	genitive
GV	goal voice
IC	incompletive
NOM	nominative
pl	plural
POS	possessive
PM	plural marker
PRF	perfective
PST	past tense
sg	singular
TOP	topic
VT	transitive verb

1 Introduction

Over seven thousand languages are currently in use on this planet (Eberhard, Simons, and Fennig (Eds.) 2020). Since the nineteenth century, descriptive and theoretical linguistic research has consistently increased the range of languages (their numbers and types) it covers as research subjects. It continues to contribute toward elucidating the universality and individuality of human languages. The growing body of theories in the latter half of the twentieth century, such as generative grammar (Chomsky 1957), linguistic typology (Greenberg 1963), and cognitive linguistics (Langacker 1987), accelerated this process of elucidation.

Meanwhile, as for the processing procedure and neural basis of language in the brain, psycholinguistic research with English as its subject of study became popular after the so-called cognitive revolution of the 1950s. By the 1980s, the subject of study expanded to languages other than English, such as German and Japanese. Then, in the 1990s, advanced technologies such as magnetic resonance imaging (MRI) and magnetoencephalography (MEG) to measure brain function came into practical use, which stimulated research into the neural basis of language. However, research involving psycholinguistics and neurolinguistics, which utilize behavioral testing and functional brain measurements, has until now mainly been conducted in laboratories of some developed nations due to economic, political, technical, and other restraints. Therefore, the selection of subject languages for research is extremely biased toward those spoken in rich countries and regions (Anand, Chung, and Wagers 2011; Norcliffe, Harris, and Jaeger 2015, among others). According to Anand, Chung, and Wagers (2011), one-third of all major psycholinguistic research conducted in the world studies English, and only ten languages account for 85 percent of the research. Only fifty-seven languages have ever been the subject of these studies, including those that have been covered only once. Most of these are Indo-European languages and are so-called Subject-before-Object (SO) languages (languages where the subject precedes the object as the basic word order). As a result, many current theories of psycholinguistics and linguistic neuroscience fail to acknowledge the nature of Object-before-Subject (OS) languages (languages where the object precedes the subject as the basic word order) and treat the nature of SO languages as though it is universal to the human language. A detailed consideration of language processing stages of more diverse languages and their neural bases is essential to elucidate the universality and individuality of human language processing, as well as the full cognitive function that controls language and thought.

The research reported in this book is an attempt to fill in the gap through a series of behavioral and neuroimaging experiments on Kaqchikel Maya, an endangered OS language spoken in Guatemala, with special reference to constituent order in language and thought. It is part of a larger project, the FALCOHN (Field-Based Approaches to Language, Cognition, and Human Nature) project, which investigates other rarely studied languages from various perspectives.

1.1 Word Order Preference

Human languages differ from one another in many respects, such as phonemes, syllable structures, case-marking, basic word order, and grammatically possible word orders. The word order in some languages, such as English, is relatively fixed, while other languages, such as Japanese, allow for some variation. In many languages with flexible word orders, sentences with a transitive verb (V) in which the subject (S) precedes the object (O) (SO word orders: SOV, SVO, VSO) have been reported to have a processing advantage over sentences in which S follows O (OS word orders: OSV, OVS, VOS) (Bader and Meng 1999 for German; Kaiser and Trueswell 2004 for Finnish; Kim 2012 for Korean; Mazuka, Itoh, and Kondo 2002 and Tamaoka et al. 2005 for Japanese; Sekerina 1997 for Russian; Tamaoka et al. 2011 for Sinhalese).[1] In Japanese, for example, the SOV word order, as exemplified in (1a), is processed faster than the OSV word order, as in (1b), according to various psycholinguistic studies using sentence plausibility judgment tasks (Chujo 1983; Tamaoka et al. 2005), self-paced reading (Koizumi and Imamura 2016; Shibata et al. 2006), and eye tracking (Mazuka, Itoh, and Kondo 2002; Tamaoka et al. 2014).

(1)   a. Naomi ga   suika   o   kitta.   [SOV]
          Naomi NOM watermelon ACC cut
          "Naomi cut the watermelon."
    b. Suika   o   Naomi ga   kitta.   [OSV]
          watermelon ACC Naomi NOM cut

Neurolinguistic studies have also shown a similar SO processing preference. Functional magnetic resonance imaging (fMRI) studies have found a greater activation at the left inferior frontal gyrus (IFG) in the processing of OS word orders compared to SO word orders (Grewe et al. 2007 for German; Kim et al. 2009 and Kinno et al. 2008 for Japanese). Furthermore, studies with event-related potentials (ERPs) have revealed that, relative to SO word orders, OS word orders elicit a late positivity effect called P600 and/or (sustained) anterior negativity (Erdocia et al. 2009 for Basque; Rösler et al. 1998 for German; Hagiwara et al. 2007 and Ueno and Kluender 2003 for Japanese).

This SO preference has also been observed in sentence production, as SO orders are more frequently used than OS orders. For instance, Imamura and Koizumi (2011) report that, among Japanese transitive sentences with a nominal subject and a nominal object in the corpus of novels they studied, more than 97 percent had the SOV word order. This shows that, although Japanese is said to be "a free word order language" or "a flexible word order language," the SO order is strongly preferred to the OS order in sentence production. Higher rates of SO-ordered utterances have been reported in many other flexible languages as well (Slobin and Bever 1982 for Turkish and Serbo-Croatian; Hakulinen and Karlsson 1980 for Finnish; Bates 1976 for Italian).

A similar SO order preference has also been observed in rigid word order languages. In English, for example, object-extracted relative clauses such as (2b), in which the object precedes the subject, take longer to process and incur a higher left IFG activation than subject-extracted relative clauses such as (2a), in which the subject precedes the object (Caplan, Stanczak, and Waters 2008; King and Just 1991; Traxler, Morris, and Seely 2002; Wanner and Maratsos 1978; among many others).

(2)   a. Subject-extracted relative clause (SO order)
        [The lawyer that irritated the banker] filed a hefty lawsuit.

      b. Object-extracted relative clause (OS order)
        [The lawyer that the banker irritated] filed a hefty lawsuit.

Taken together, abundant evidence supports the claim that SO word orders are preferred to OS word orders in many of the world's languages.

1.2 Origins of Word Order Preference

The observations in the previous section bring up the question of why SO word orders should be preferred in sentence comprehension and production, along with the related empirical question of whether this preference is universal across all human languages. In the literature, a number of factors have been proposed that may affect word order preference in sentence comprehension and production.

1.2.1 Individual Grammar View

Many of the previous statements about word order preference can be classified under what we call the Individual Grammar View (IGV), which claims that SO preference is attributed to the grammatical factors of individual languages, such as syntactic complexities. According to the IGV, therefore, studies have found an SO word order preference because they have targeted SO languages.

Within each individual language, word orders beyond the syntactically basic one are derived from it through syntactic operations such as scrambling, which induces syntactic complexities. The IGV hypothesizes that a syntactically determined basic SO word order in a language is favored over other available word orders because derived OS word orders require the processing of more complex syntactic structures (see Gibson 2000; Hawkins 2004; Laka and Erdocia 2012; Marantz 2005; O'Grady 1997; Pritchett and Whitman 1995; among others). Consider the Japanese examples in (1) again, repeated here as (3).

(3) a. Naomi ga suika o kitta. [SOV]
    Naomi NOM watermelon ACC cut
    "Naomi cut the watermelon."

   b. Suika o Naomi ga kitta. [OSV]
    watermelon ACC Naomi NOM cut

Boldly simplifying for expository purposes, the sentences in (3a) and (3b) have mental representations like (4a) and (4b), respectively. Linguistic representations like these are called syntactic structures.

(4) a. [$_S$ [Naomi ga] [$_{VP}$ [suika o] kitta]]   [SOV]
      Naomi NOM watermelon ACC cut

   b. [[suika o]$_i$ [$_S$ [Naomi ga] [$_{VP}$ t_i kitta]]   [OSV]
      watermelon ACC Naomi NOM   cut

In (4a), the object *suika o* "watermelon ACC" and the verb *kitta* "cut" are grouped together to form a verb phrase (VP), which in turn is merged with the subject *Naomi ga* "Naomi NOM" to constitute a sentence. In (4b), the object has been dislocated to the head of the sentence and is grammatically associated with the phonetically empty category in the original object position, indicated by the symbol *t*. In the linguistic literature, a dislocated element like this is called an antecedent, and the associated empty category is called a trace, hence the symbol *t*. For convenience, a subscript (such as $_i$ in (4)) is used to indicate which antecedent corresponds to which trace. In psycholinguistics, the terms "filler" and "gap" are used more frequently than "antecedent" and "trace" to refer to the dislocated element and its associated empty category, respectively. Note that the syntactic structure in (4b) is more complex than the one in (4a) because the former contains a filler-gap dependency and the latter does not. Thus, when processing a sentence like (3b), the parser must associate the filler with the corresponding gap, which requires additional computational steps that are not needed in the processing of a sentence like (3a). According to a version of the IGV, this is why (3b) is more difficult to process than (3a).

1.2 Origins of Word Order Preference

English relative clauses such as those in (2), both subject-extracted and object-extracted, contain a filler-gap dependency as schematically shown in (5), with the fillers and gaps indicated by italics and underscores, respectively. The IGV would attribute the greater difficulty of processing the object-extracted relative clause to the greater distance between the filler and the gap than exists in the subject-extracted relative clause.

(5) a. Subject-extracted relative clause (SO order)
    [*the lawyer*$_i$ that___$_i$ irritated the banker] filed a hefty lawsuit

   b. Object-extracted relative clause (OS order)
    [*the lawyer*$_i$ that the banker irritated___$_i$] filed a hefty lawsuit

1.2.2 Universal Cognition View

Another class of claims posits that grammar-independent universal human cognitive factors may play a primary role in determining word order preference. We call this the Universal Cognition View (UCV), which suggests that SO word orders are preferred in all human languages, regardless of the basic word order in individual languages (Bornkessel et al. 2003; Bornkessel-Schlesewsky and Schlesewsky 2009a, 2009b; Kemmerer 2012; MacWhinney 1977; Primus 1999; Tanaka et al. 2011; among others).

Some proposals in this category are concerned with event structure. A prototypical transitive event such as "Naomi cutting a watermelon" involves a transitive action ("cutting") performed by an agent (the entity that performed the action, "Naomi") on a patient (the entity that had the action performed on it, "a watermelon"). Primus (1999) argues that the agent–patient order is preferred to the patient–agent order because the patient's involvement in an event depends on the agent (and his or her actions), rather than vice versa (see also Keenan and Comrie 1977). Bornkessel-Schlesewsky and Schlesewsky (2009a) contend that the first NP in a sentence is preferentially interpreted as the subject because language users prefer simpler intransitive events, which involve only one obligatory participant (animate or inanimate) corresponding to the subject in a sentence, to more complex transitive events, which by definition involve multiple participants corresponding to the subject and the object (see also Gibson 2000 for a related proposal). Other researchers have suggested that the temporal precedence of the agent's action over the patient's change of state is captured in an iconic or isomorphic way by the temporal precedence of the subject over the object (Croft 1991, 1998; Langacker 1991, 2008). Putting these and other related proposals together, Kemmerer (2012: 54) goes on to hypothesize that the sequential and hierarchical organization of the prototypical transitive action scenario is extracted by a part of the left IFG, the white area in the schematic of the brain in Figure 1.1.

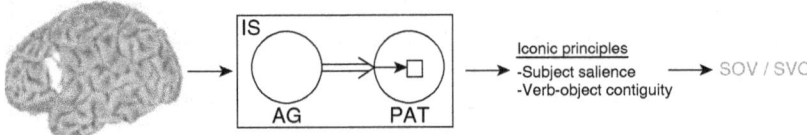

Figure 1.1 A schematic representation of the possible origin of SO word order preference within the Universal Cognition View. (Adapted from Kemmerer 2012 with permission.)

Another well-known candidate for universal cognitive factors affecting word order preference is the concept referred to variously as empathy, view point, or perspective-taking (Kuno and Kaburaki 1977; MacWhinney 1977). MacWhinney (1977: 152) suggests that speakers tend to choose the perspective most compatible with the perspective they (wish to) assume in their interactions with the world. Both speakers and listeners therefore prefer "the starting point" closest to the one compatible with their perspective. In describing the event of "Naomi cutting a watermelon," for instance, we tend to choose the perspective (closer to that) of the human agent, Naomi, rather than the perspective of the inanimate patient, a watermelon. We therefore prefer the sentence starting with "Naomi" (1a) to the sentence starting with "a watermelon" (1b), resulting in a general SO preference.

Conceptual accessibility is another notion that plays a prominent role in the discussion of constituent order in the psycholinguistic literature, defined as "the ease with which the mental representation of some potential referent can be activated in or retrieved from memory" (Bock and Warren 1985: 50); agents are conceptually more accessible than patients, animate entities are conceptually more accessible than inanimate ones, concrete entities are conceptually more accessible than abstract ones, and so on. Several studies have reported that prominent entities such as agents, animate ones, concrete ones, and prototypical ones tend to appear as sentence-initial subjects (Bock and Warren 1985; Bornkessel-Schlesewsky and Schlesewsky 2009a; Branigan, Pickering, and Tanaka 2008; Hirsh-Pasek and Golinkoff 1996; Primus 1999; Slobin and Bever 1982).

Finally, the UCV may be further supported by the fact that a vast majority of the world's languages feature one of the SO word orders as a basic word order (SOV: 50.1 percent, SVO: 38.3 percent, VSO: 8.2 percent, VOS: 2.0 per cent, OVS: 0.8 percent, OSV: 0.6 percent, Gell-Mann and Ruhlen 2011; see also Dryer 2013).

1.2.3 Relative Contribution of Grammatical Factors and Cognitive Factors

We can summarize the two views reviewed in the previous sections as follows.

(6)   Two Possible Sources of Word Order Preference in Sentence Processing

  a. Individual Grammar View
     Word order preference in sentence processing is largely attributable to grammatical factors of individual languages, such as syntactic complexity.

  b. Universal Cognition View
     Word order preference in sentence processing is largely attributable to grammar-independent human cognitive features that are universal, such as conceptual accessibility.

Note that grammatical factors and grammar-independent universal cognitive factors are not necessarily mutually exclusive. There is ample evidence that they all affect human sentence comprehension and production in one way or another, as demonstrated in numerous studies, such as those mentioned above. What has not been made clear are their relative contributions and interactions in aspects of sentence processing. Both views correctly account for the SO word order preference in sentence comprehension and production in SO languages (i.e., languages that have one of the SO word orders as a basic word order). In Japanese, for example, SOV is easier to process and more frequently used than OSV, as alluded to above, which may be because SOV is (i) the syntactically simplest word order (IGV) and/or (ii) consistent with conceptual prominence relations (UCV). Thus, it is difficult, if not impossible, to evaluate the relative strengths of these factors by solely focusing on SO languages such as Japanese. To determine which is the primary factor in the observed word order preference and how the factors interact, it is necessary to study languages for which the two views would create different predictions. In fact, in OS languages, the two positions offer opposite predictions regarding preferred order. The IGV predicts OS preference in OS languages because SO word orders have more complex syntactic structures than the syntactically basic OS word order. Thus, unlike in SO languages, OS word orders should require a lower processing cost than SO word orders in OS languages. In contrast, according to the UCV, SO preference should be observed in such languages as well because SO preference does not pertain to the syntactic characteristics of individual languages. Therefore, SO word orders would be processed more easily and used more frequently than OS word orders even in OS languages. For this reason and with these hypotheses in mind, we conducted a series of sentence processing studies on the comprehension and the production of a VOS language, Kaqchikel, a Mayan language spoken in Guatemala. In this book, we report the core results of this project and consider the relationship between language and thought, primarily focusing on constituent order preferences, by drawing on the obtained data.

1.3 Outline of the Book

In Chapter 2, we will sketch aspects of the grammar of Kaqchikel relevant to the discussions in the subsequent chapters. Kaqchikel is a head-marking and morphologically ergative language in which subjects and objects are not overtly case-marked for grammatical relations. Rather, grammatical relations are obligatorily marked on predicates, e.g., a verb with two sets of agreement morphemes, one set for a transitive subject and another for a transitive object and an intransitive subject. The word order of Kaqchikel is relatively flexible, and all of the logically possible six word orders are grammatically allowed. Among these, VOS is considered the basic word order of Kaqchikel by many Mayan language researchers (Ajsivinac Sian et al. 2004: 162; García Matzar and Rodríguez Guaján 1997: 333; Rodríguez Guaján 1994: 200; Tichoc Cumes et al. 2000: 195). For the purpose of the present study, we assume the schematic syntactic structures shown in (7), in which VOS is structurally simpler than the other orders. Because SOV and OSV are rarely used in Kaqchikel, they will not be considered.

(7) Order   Schematic syntactic structure
     VOS   [VOS]
     VSO   [[V gap$_i$ S] O$_i$]
     SVO   [S$_i$ [VO gap$_i$]]
     OVS   [O$_i$ [V gap$_i$ S]]

As we have mentioned above, SO word orders are easier to process than OS word orders in the sentence comprehension of many languages in the world. We will refer to this generalization as the SO Preference in Sentence Comprehension.

(8)   SO Preference in Sentence Comprehension
     In individual languages with flexible word order, SO word orders are easier to process than OS word orders.

In Chapters 3 to 5, we will consider the sources of this preference and whether the generalization holds true even in an OS language like Kaqchikel. According to the IGV, word order preference in sentence comprehension is largely attributable to grammatical factors of individual languages, such as syntactic complexities. In other words, a language's syntactically determined basic word order should be easier to process than other grammatically possible orders in that language. The IGV therefore predicts that, in Kaqchikel, VOS should be easier to process than SVO, VSO, or OVS. In contrast, according to the UCV, word order preference in sentence comprehension is largely attributable to grammar-independent human cognitive features that are universal, which means that SO word orders should be easier to process than OS word orders even in OS languages. Thus, the UCV predicts that, in Kaqchikel, SVO and VSO should be easier to process than VOS or OVS.

In Chapter 3, we will report two behavioral experiments with a sentence plausibility judgment task in Kaqchikel to test these predictions. In this task, Kaqchikel sentences in one of the three commonly used orders (VOS, SVO, and VSO) were presented in a random order to participants through headsets. The participants were asked to judge whether each sentence was semantically plausible and to push a YES button for correct sentences or a NO button for incorrect sentences as quickly and accurately as possible. The time from the beginning of each stimulus sentence until a button was pressed was measured as the reaction time. We found that semantically natural sentences were processed faster in the VOS order than in the SVO or VSO orders, which suggests that VOS is easier to process than SVO or VSO. These results are compatible with the prediction of the IGV, but not with the prediction of the UCV, showing that the SO preference in sentence comprehension is not fully grounded in the universal properties of human cognition; rather, processing preference may be language-specific to some extent, reflecting syntactic differences in individual languages.

In Chapter 4, we will compare brain activations in response to Kaqchikel sentences with the VOS and SVO orders, obtained using functional magnetic resonance imaging (fMRI). It is known that the left inferior frontal gyrus (IFG) of the brain exhibits enhanced activation in response to grammatically complex, demanding sentences. The fMRI experiment we conducted with Kaqchikel speakers revealed that cortical activation in the left IFG was significantly higher in response to SVO sentences than VOS sentences, which clearly shows that it is the grammatical features of individual languages, and not universal human cognitive features, that primarily modulate brain activation and determine sentence processing load.

In Chapters 5 and 6, we will investigate the time course of the processing of Kaqchikel sentences with alternative word orders. A sentence–picture matching task was employed in two experiments measuring event-related potentials (ERPs). In one of the experiments, a Kaqchikel sentence was presented aurally through a headset; afterwards, a picture was presented in the center of a screen, either matching the event described by the preceding sentence or not. Upon seeing the picture, the participants were asked to judge whether the picture was congruent with the sentence. In the other experiment, a picture was presented before the corresponding sentence. The target sentences used in these experiments were all transitive, with thematically reversible agents and patients, arranged into four word orders: VOS, VSO, SVO, and OVS. A late positive ERP component called P600 was used to examine processing loads, as P600 has been found to be elicited by sentences with a filler-gap dependency, reflecting an increased syntactic processing cost. The results of the two experiments demonstrated that SVO elicited a greater positivity (P600) than VOS, and that VSO elicited a similar posterior positivity, relative to VOS. This range of properties follows naturally from the combination of the IGV and the syntactic structures of Kaqchikel transitive sentences given in (7) above. Most importantly, the results clearly indicate that VOS is the syntactically simplest and easiest-to-process word order of the grammatically possible ones in Kaqchikel, which is in line with our previous findings, described in Chapters 3 and 4. In short, Chapters 3 to 6 present data showing that a VOS preference was observed in Kaqchikel sentence comprehension, which provides empirical support for the IGV.

In Chapter 7, we will turn our attention to basic word order in language and natural order of thought. In his seminal work, Greenberg (1963: 77) observed that, "[i]n declarative sentences with nominal subject and object, the dominant order is almost always one in which the subject precedes the object," a generalization known as Greenberg's Universal 1. Parallel to the SO Preference in Sentence Comprehension, we will refer to this as the SO Preference in Basic Word Order.

(9) SO Preference in Basic Word Order
A vast majority of the world's languages have one of the SO word orders as their basic word order.

This generalization has been firmly supported empirically by a number of subsequent works. Gell-Mann and Ruhlen (2011), for instance, observed the distribution shown in Table 1.1 of the 2,135 languages in their sample.

It is interesting to note that the distribution is heavily biased even among the three SO orders, with SOV being the most frequent, which indicates that SOV has some special status among the six possible word orders in some sense. Why should this be the case? In order to address this question, Goldin-Meadow et al. (2008) showed short animations depicting transitive events (e.g., a girl twisting a knob, a boy opening a box) to speakers of four languages (Chinese, English, Spanish [all SVO], and Turkish [SOV]). The participants were then asked to

Table 1.1 *Order of subject, object, and verb*

SO languages		OS languages	
SOV	50.1%	OSV	0.6%
SVO	38.3%	OVS	0.8%
VSO	8.2%	VOS	2.0%
SO total	**96.6%**	**OS total**	**3.4%**

Note: Calculated based on the number of languages reported in Gell-Mann and Ruhlen (2011).

1.3 Outline of the Book

describe the depicted events by using only their hands, i.e., with gestures. The speakers of all four languages dominantly used the agent–patient–action order in their gestures, regardless of the basic word order of their languages. Similar results have also been obtained in a number of subsequent studies (Futrell et al. 2015; Gibson et al. 2013; Hall, Mayberry, and Ferreira 2013; Langus and Nespor 2010). Goldin-Meadow et al. (2008: 9167) took these results to suggest that the agent–patient–action order reflects the natural sequencing of an event representation and that developing languages use it as the default pattern, thus displaying an SOV word order.[2]

Although this and other studies in gesture production have claimed that the agent–patient order is the universal preference when humans think about events and describe them nonverbally, the studies have only assessed speakers of languages in which the subject precedes the object in the basic word order (i.e., SO languages). Such limited evidence is not sufficient to conclude that all humans universally perceive the world in the agent–patient order, and it cannot help us disentangle whether the apparent preference for agent–patient sequences is the result of universal cognitive factors or the influence of the word order of SO languages. In order to disentangle these two possibilities (i.e., the UCV and the IGV), it is crucial to examine speakers of a language in which the object precedes the subject in the basic word order. In Chapter 8, we will report on a gesture production experiment we conducted with Kaqchikel speakers similar to Goldin-Meadow et al. (2008), finding that Kaqchikel speakers dominantly produced agent–patient gestures. Therefore, agent–patient ordering does seem to be a universal preference for event description, which is in line with the UCV as well as the results of previous studies.

In Chapter 9, we will discuss the SO preference observed in the domain of language production, i.e., that sentences with SO orders are more frequently produced than sentences with OS orders in many languages.

(10)   SO Preference in Sentence Production
        In individual languages with flexible word order, SO word orders are more frequently used than OS word orders.

Although the language production mechanism is often assumed to be universal, the range of languages investigated so far is typologically quite limited. We conducted a sentence production experiment with a picture description task to clarify word order selection in Kaqchikel. In this experiment, participants verbally described the target pictures with a simple sentence. Speakers of Kaqchikel had a general preference for producing the SVO order over the VOS order. This is consistent with the prediction of the UCV, but not with that of the IGV. Therefore, the SO word order might be a universal preference in sentence production, which is in line with the results of previous studies.

The experimental studies on Kaqchikel reviewed so far suggest that the cognitive load during sentence comprehension is primarily determined by grammatical processes operating on linguistic representations, whereas word order selection in sentence production more faithfully reflects conceptual processing at the stage of event apprehension and preverbal message construction. In particular, agent-first orders are likely to be selected over others because of the conceptual saliency of agents. If this conjecture is on the right track, we would expect that the cognitive load during sentence production is higher for SVO sentences than for VOS sentences because the production of a sentence surely includes, as its central part, the construction of linguistic representations, and the grammatical processes involved in this are presumably similar to those involved in the comprehension of a parallel sentence, although there may be some differences. In Chapter 10, we will report on an experiment to verify this prediction. In this experiment, we asked participants to describe, using Kaqchikel sentences, the events depicted in pictures shown on a display. The interval between the onset of the picture presentation and the starting point of the participant's utterance was recorded as utterance latency. The participants' neural activations during sentence production were measured using near-infrared spectroscopy (NIRS). The results of utterance latency analyses revealed that the latency was significantly smaller in the SVO word order than in the VOS order, which is consistent with our conclusion from Chapter 9 that SVO is more frequently used than VOS partly because of the conceptual saliency of the subject. As for brain activation, the participants showed significantly higher peak values in the SVO word order than the VOS, consistent with the expectation mentioned above. The results of this experiment support the conclusion that, although Kaqchikel speakers preferentially use the SVO word order because of the saliency of the subject, SVO sentences require more processing resources than VOS sentences both in comprehension and in production.

In Chapter 11, we will discuss some task-dependent effects on word order preference. Different tasks activate different aspects of cognitive processes in the brain. We show that the picture–sentence matching task facilitates the processing of SVO in comparison with the other orders in Kaqchikel, at least partially because of the saliency of agentive concepts accelerating memory retrieval. We also show that Kaqchikel speakers who use Spanish in daily life tend to process Kaqchikel sentences in the SVO and VSO orders more quickly.

In Chapter 12, we will consider the syntactic structure of Kaqchikel sentences in more detail than in Chapter 2. There are multiple syntactic routes to the VOS order. Different VOS languages may have different syntactic structures. There are two major proposals regarding how Mayan VOS word order is grammatically obtained: a right-specifier analysis (Aissen 1992) and a predicate fronting analysis (Coon 2010). We propose in this chapter that

Kaqchikel, and possibly Chol as well, derive the VOS order through a right-specifier route, rather than a predicate fronting route.

In Chapter 13, we will observe how representative theories of sentence processing costs fare in accounting for the relative difficulties among Kaqchikel sentences with different word orders. The relative processing costs associated with Kaqchikel transitive sentences with the four different word orders are correctly predicted by the Hierarchical Distance Hypothesis (Hawkins 2004; O'Grady 1997), whereas the relative processing costs associated with the corresponding four transitive constructions in Japanese are correctly predicted by the Linear Distance Hypothesis (Gibson 1998, 2000). However, the relative processing costs in these languages are also consistent with the assumption that they are shaped by the combined effects of the three factors: production frequency, linear distance, and hierarchical distance, suggesting the cognitive uniformity of the human parser.

Finally, we will conclude in Chapter 14.

The Appendices supplement the studies reported in the main chapters, of the relationships between language and thought, in two different ways. In Appendix A, we will elucidate the spatial frames of reference of Kaqchikel and Japanese speakers from a comparative-psycholinguistic perspective. In Appendix B, we will discuss syntax and processing in Seediq (Taiwan, Austronesian), another VOS language, to investigate to what extent our findings from Kaqchikel apply to other OS languages.

Many of our own studies discussed in this book have already been published as journal articles. They were, however, written at different times with different research questions. Some of the conclusions drawn there even appear to be contradictory to each other. In this book, we will attempt to put them together and give them a uniform and coherent interpretation to achieve a better understanding of the relationship between language and thought. Thus, the purposes of the studies, the interpretations of the data, and the conclusions stated in this book are not necessarily the same as those of the original papers.

In order to make this monograph accessible to a wider readership, the detailed statistics of our experimental results will not be reported in the text; interested readers are referred to the original articles. Instead, expressions such as "statistical analyses show," "the difference is significant," and so on will be used where the statistical significance level is set at .05 ($p < .05$), unless otherwise noted.

NOTES

1. The notions of grammatical relations, such as subject and object, are known to be problematic in many respects (Comrie 1989; Primus 1999). Only for the sake of exposition do we tentatively assume the following definitions in this book: the

subject is the more agent-like argument in a transitive clause, and the object is the more patient-like argument in a transitive clause. These definitions may be inadequate for symmetrical voice languages such as Seediq discussed in Appendix B, for which a configurational approach may fare better. Importantly, our final conclusions can be stated without reference to these labels.

2. The basic constituents of a sentence, i.e., the subject, object, and verb, bear some relation R to each other in the mental representation (i.e., syntactic structure) of that sentence. R is systematically mapped onto the temporal precedence relation holding between the externalized linguistic expressions corresponding to the three units: *subject > object > verb*, for example. R itself need not be a temporal precedence relation. In this book, I use the term "word order" ambiguously to refer to (i) R and (ii) the temporal precedence relation. What R is in fact remains one of the central issues in linguistics and is briefly addressed in Chapter 12.

Similarly, the basic elements of an event, the agent, patient, and action, bear some relation R′ to each other in the nonverbal mental representation of that event. R′ is mapped onto the temporal precedence relation between the gestures corresponding to the three units: *agent > patient > action*, for example. Again, R′ need not be a temporal precedence relation. We use the term "order of thought" ambiguously to refer to (i) R′ and (ii) the temporal precedence relation. What R′ is and what determines/affects R′ are discussed in Chapters 7 to 11.

2 Kaqchikel Mayan

In this chapter, we will provide background information on Kaqchikel, a language of the Mayan family, which is necessary to understand the subsequent discussions in this book.

2.1 Kaqchikel and the Mayan Family

The Mayan family comprises of about thirty languages primarily spoken in Guatemala, Mexico, and Belize. Kaqchikel, previously spelled "Cakchiquel," is a language of the K'ichean branch of the Mayan family (see (1) below). It is used by approximately half a million speakers in Guatemala, mostly in the highlands between Guatemala City and Lake Atitlán (Brown, Maxwell, and Little 2006: 2; England 2003: 733; Richards 2003: 60; Tay Coyoy 1996: 55; see also García Matzar, Cotzajay, and Tuiz 1999; Simons and Fennig 2017) (Figure 2.1). Many Kaqchikel speakers are bilingual, Spanish being their other language, although one can still easily find monolingual Kaqchikel speakers.

(1) A Possible Classification of Mayan Languages
    a. **Huastecan**: Wastek, Chicomuceltec [extinct]
    b. **Yukatekan**: Yukatek, Lakantun; Itza', Mopan
    c. **Greater Tseltalan**:
        i. **Cholan**: Ch'orti', Cholti [extinct]; Chontal, Chol
        ii. **Tseltalan**: Tzotzil, Tseltal
    d. **Greater Q'anjob'alan**:
        i. **Chujean**: Tojolabal, Chuj
        ii. **Q'anjob'alan**: Mocho (Motocintlec); Jakaltek, Akatek, Q'uanjob'al
    e. **K'ichean-Mamean** (or Eastern Mayan):
        i. **Mamean**: Ixil, Awakatek; Mam, Teco
        ii. **K'ichean**: Sipakapense, Sakapultek, Tz'utujil, *Kaqchikel*, K'ichee'; Poqomam, Poqomchi'; Uspantek; Q'eqchi'

                    (Adapted from Campbell and Kaufman 1985: 188)

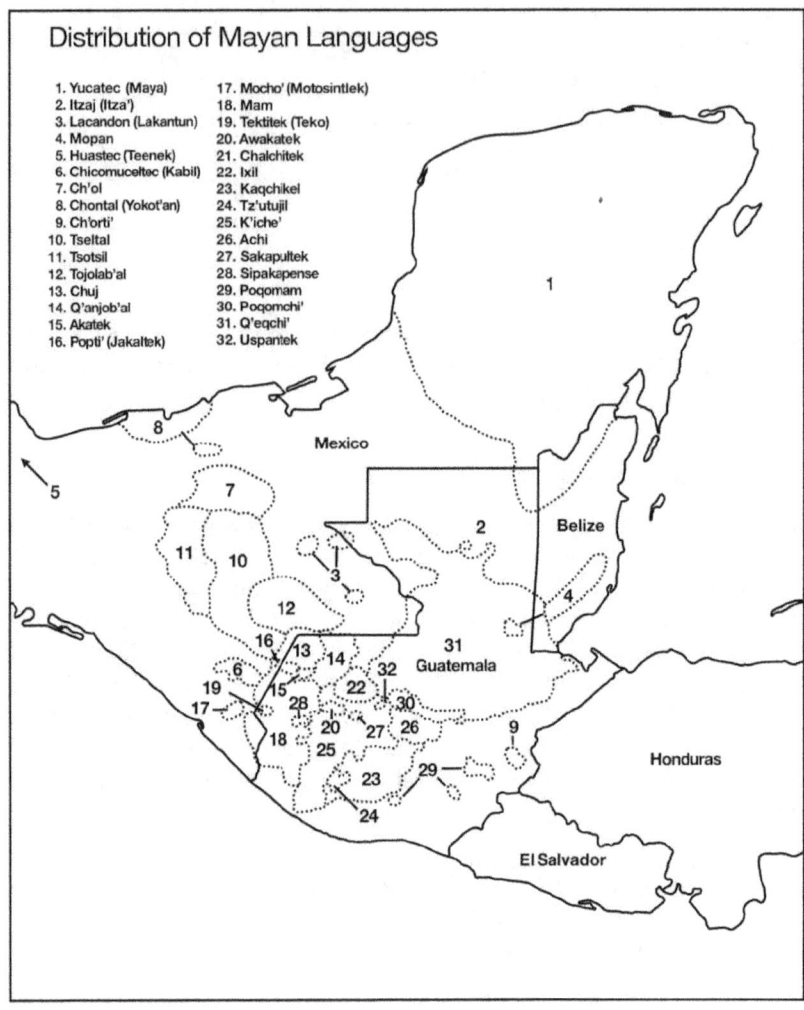

Figure 2.1 Distribution of Mayan languages. Kaqchikel is number 23. (Based on Map 4 in Law 2014, with modification by Bennett, Coon, and Henderson 2016, used with permission.)

2.2 Typological Basics

Like other Mayan languages, Kaqchikel is a head-marking and morphologically ergative language. Subjects and objects are not overtly case-marked for grammatical relations; rather, grammatical relations are obligatorily marked on

2.2 Typological Basics

the predicate with two sets of agreement morphemes, one denoting a transitive subject and the other denoting a transitive object and an intransitive subject.

The world's languages differ with respect to the morphology of marking grammatical relations. Some languages, called dependent-marking, encode grammatical relations via case-marking on nominals (Nichols 1986). In Japanese, for example, the subjects of transitive and intransitive verbs are marked with the nominative case marker *ga*, while the objects of transitive verbs are marked with the accusative case marker *o*, as shown in (2). In Tongan, the ergative case marker *'e* is used for transitive subjects, while the absolutive case marker *'a* occurs with intransitive subjects and transitive objects, as shown in (3).

(2) Japanese
    a. Minori ga sakana o tabe-ta.
       Minori NOM fish ACC eat-PST
       "Minori ate a fish."

    b. Minori ga warat-ta.
       Minori NOM laugh-PST
       "Minori laughed."

(3) Tongan
    a. Na'e lau 'e Sione 'a e tohi.
       PST read ERG Sione ABS REF book
       "Sione read a book."

    b. Na'e 'alu 'a Sione ki Tonga.
       PST go ABS Sione to Tonga
       "Sione went to Tonga."

(Otsuka 2005a: 345)

Although Japanese and Tongan are both dependent-marking languages, they differ in how they morphologically align the three core arguments, i.e., transitive subjects (hereafter A), transitive objects (O), and intransitive subjects (S). In Japanese, A and S are grouped together and marked by *ga*, and O is singled out with *o*. Languages with this type of alignment are called accusative or nominative-accusative languages. The case for A and S in such languages is referred to as nominative (NOM), and the case for O is named accusative (ACC). In Tongan, however, S and O appear in the same case, and A is assigned a different case. Languages with this type of alignment are called ergative or ergative-absolutive languages. The case for A in such languages is called ergative (ERG), and the case for S and O is referred to as absolutive (ABS). These two alignment systems may be schematized as in (4).

(4) Ergative   Accusative

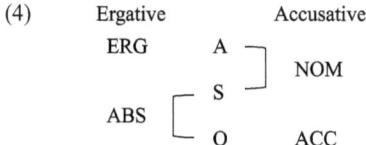

In contrast to dependent-marking languages such as Japanese and Tongan, grammatical relations in head-marking languages are expressed via agreement on predicates (Nichols 1986). In the following Palauan examples, the agreement marker *ng-* cross-references the transitive subject (A) and the intransitive subject (S), whereas *-ii* is the agreement morpheme cross-referencing the object (O).

(4) Palauan
    a. Ng mo kol-ii a bobai *pro*.
       3sg= AUX.FUT eat.PF-3sgO DET papaya he
       "He is going to eat (up) the papaya."

    b. Ng merael a chais er a beluu.
       3sg= go DET news PREP DET area
       "A rumor is going around."

(Nuger 2010: 45, 85)

Note that the same agreement morpheme is used for A and S, and a different one is used for O, demonstrating the accusative alignment. Thus, Palauan may be considered a head-marking accusative language. Following the same terminology, Japanese is a dependent-marking accusative language, and Tongan is a dependent-marking ergative language.

Finally, Kaqchikel is a head-marking ergative language. Grammatical relations are obligatorily marked on predicates with two sets of person/number morphemes, which have been traditionally called Set A and Set B in Mayan linguistics. Set A corresponds to ergative (transitive subjects) and genitive (possessors) marking, and Set B corresponds to absolutive (transitive objects and intransitive subjects) marking. The order of the morphemes is [Aspect-ABS-Verb stem] for intransitive verbs and [Aspect-ABS-ERG-Verb stem] for transitive verbs.[1] Some examples of the morphological ergativity of Kaqchikel are given in (5) (see Larsen and Norman 1979 for Mayan ergativity in general).

(5) a. *Y-e'-oq'*
      IC-ABS3pl-cry
      "They cry."

    b. *Y-e'-in-to'*
      IC-ABS3pl-ERG1sg-help
      "I help them."

    c. *Y-i-ki-to'*
      IC-ABS1sg-ERG3pl-help
      "They help me."

Note that the third-person plural morpheme for the intransitive subject in (5a) is *e'*, which is identical to the morpheme for the transitive object in (5b), rather than the morpheme for the transitive subject in (5c), which is *ki*.

Table 2.1 *Set A (ergative and genitive)*

Person	Singular		Plural	
	Pre-vocalic	Pre-consonantal	Pre-vocalic	Pre-consonantal
1st	inw-/w-	in-/nu-	q-	qa-
2nd	aw-	a-	iw-	i-
3rd	r-	ru-	k-	ki-

Table 2.2 *Set B (absolutive)*

Person	Singular		Plural	
	Pre-vocalic	Pre-consonantal	Pre-vocalic	Pre-consonantal
1st	in-	i-	oj-	oj-
2nd	at-	a-	ix-	ix-
3rd	Ø-	Ø-	e'-	e-

The forms of Set A and Set B are displayed in Tables 2.1 and 2.2, respectively.

As noted above, the possessive (i.e., genitive) Set A forms are generally identical to the ergative Set A forms except in the first-person singular, where the ergative form is *in(w)-* and the possessive form is *nu-/w-*.

2.3 Word Order

In Kaqchikel, as in other Mayan languages, nominal arguments need not be overtly expressed if their contents are recoverable from context. In other words, Kaqchikel is a pro-drop language. Each expression in (5) above may therefore function as an independent utterance with appropriate context. When nominal arguments are overtly expressed, Kaqchikel allows for different grammatical word orders, as do many other Mayan languages. The word order of most Mayan languages is predicate-initial in pragmatically neutral contexts (Aissen 1992; England 1991). According to García Matzar and Rodríguez Guaján (1997) and others, the basic word order of Kaqchikel in unmarked discourse is VOS, as exemplified in (6a), with neither the subject nor the object topicalized or focused (Ajsivinac Sian et al. 2004:162; García Matzar and Rodríguez Guaján 1997: 333; Rodríguez Guaján 1994: 200; Tichoc Cumes et al. 2000: 195). VSO is also possible for semantically nonreversible sentences, as in (6b), although VOS is still favored in such cases according to our consultants.

(6) a. X-Ø-u-chöy   ri   chäj   ri   ajanel.   [VOS]
CP-ABS3sg-ERG3sg-cut DET pine.tree DET carpenter

b. X-Ø-u-chöy   ri   ajanel   ri   chäj.   [VSO]
CP-ABS3sg-ERG3sg-cut DET carpenter DET pine.tree
"The carpenter cut the pine tree."

In cases like (7a) and (7b), where the sentence is semantically reversible, a VOS interpretation is overwhelmingly favored (even though a VSO interpretation is still possible).

(7) a. X-Ø-r-oqotaj   ri   me's   ri   tz'i'.
CP-ABS3sg-ERG3sg-run.after DET cat DET dog
"The dog ran after the cat."

b. X-Ø-r-oqotaj   ri   tz'i'   ri   me's.
CP-ABS3sg-ERG3sg-run.after DET dog DET cat
"The cat ran after the dog."

It is possible to topicalize the subject by moving it in front of the verb, as exemplified in (8a) (García Matzar and Rodríguez Guaján 1997: 334). Similarly, the object may be fronted as a topic, as shown in (8b) (García Matzar and Rodríguez Guaján 1997: 335).[2]

(8) a. Ri ajanel x-Ø-u-chöy   ri chäj.   [SVO]
DET carpenter CP-ABS3sg-ERG3sg-cut DET pine.tree
"The carpenter cut the pine tree."

b. Ri chäj x-Ø-u-chöy   ri ajanel.   [OVS]
DET pine.tree CP-ABS3sg-ERG3sg-cut DET carpenter
"The carpenter cut the pine tree."

All possible word orders other than VOS are thus pragmatically and syntactically marked.

Furthermore, adjuncts can also be topicalized to the left of the verb, giving rise to a derived word order as in (9). When certain types of adjuncts (locative, instrumental, etc.) are preposed, the particle *wi* is inserted in the post-verbal position, as illustrated in (9b) (García Matzar and Rodríguez Guaján 1997: 349; Matsumoto 2016; cf. also Yasugi 2005).

(9) a. Aninäq x-Ø-u-b'in-isa-j   la ak'wal la achi
rapidly CP-ABS3sg-ERG3sg-walk-CAU-VT DET girl DET man
"The man made the girl walk rapidly." (Tichoc Cumes et al. 2000: 228)

b. Wawe' Iximche' n-Ø-u-b'än   wi ri r-ochoch
here Iximche' IC-ABS3sg-ERG3sg-do WI DET POS3sg-house
ri a Waqi' Kej.
DET CL Waqi' Kej
"Here in Iximche', Waqi' Kej builds his house."
(García Matzar and Rodríguez Guaján 1997: 354)

2.3 Word Order

It is thus clear that the preverbal position is not the dedicated subject position in Kaqchikel.

For these and other reasons, many Mayan language researchers consider the syntactically determined basic word order of modern Kaqchikel to be VOS (Ajsivinac Sian et al. 2004: 162; García Matzar and Rodríguez Guaján 1997: 333; Rodríguez Guaján 1994: 200; Tichoc Cumes et al. 2000: 195).[3] This conclusion is consistent with Aissen's (1992) proposal that VOS is the base-generated order in Mayan. Although there is still debate on the precise syntactic structures of Mayan languages, for the purpose of the present study it is sufficient to initially assume, for Kaqchikel transitive sentences with different word orders, the schematic syntactic structures shown in (10), in which VOS is structurally simpler than the other orders (cf. Aissen 1992; England 1991; Imanishi 2014; Preminger 2011; Tada 1993; for concise overviews of Mayan grammars, see Bennett 2016 (phonology); Coon 2016 (morphosyntax); and Henderson 2016 (semantics); for a more comprehensive survey of the Mayan languages, see Aissen, England, and Maldonado 2017).[4]

(10) | Order | Schematic syntactic structure
 | VOS | [VOS]
 | VSO | [[V gap$_i$ S] O$_i$]
 | SVO | [S$_i$ [VO gap$_i$]]
 | OVS | [O$_i$ [V gap$_i$ S]]

We will discuss Kaqchikel clause structure in more detail in Chapter 12.[5]

NOTES

1. Unless otherwise noted, the description of Kaqchikel grammar in this chapter, including its word order preference, is based on our fieldwork with our three consultants, Lolmay Pedro Oscar García Matzar (Chimaltenango), Juan Esteban Ajsivinac Sian (Patzicía), and Filiberto Patal Majzul (Patzún).
2. When a transitive subject undergoes some types of movement to the pre-verbal position, such as *wh*-movement and focus movement, ergative agreement does not appear on the verb and a special morpheme suffixes to the stem, a construction commonly termed Agent Focus (AF). We will not be concerned with AF in this book. All transitive sentences with the SVO word order used in our experimental studies reported in the subsequent chapters have canonical transitive agreement. For AF, see, among others, Preminger (2014), Heaton and O'Grady (2016), and Watanabe (2017).
3. The results of a study of word order acquisition in Kaqchikel (Sugisaki et al. 2012) suggest that Kaqchikel-speaking three-year-old children know that VOS is the unmarked order in their language. Moreover, William Norman (at a talk at the Taller Maya/Mayan Workshop in San Cristóbal de las Casas, Chiapas, Mexico in 1977, as discussed in Larsen 1988: 333f) argues that the basic word order is VOS in K'iche', a Mayan language closely related to Kaqchikel, a conclusion supported by Pye's (1992) observation that K'iche' children acquire the VOS order early on.

Some researchers have suggested that Kaqchikel is currently shifting to an SVO language under the influence of Spanish (Brown, Maxwell, and Little 2006; England 1991, 2003; Garzon et al. 1998; see also Clemens 2013; Imanishi 2014, 2020). For example, England (1991: 472) writes that "Kaqchikel is the language of the K'ichean branch that is perhaps the most insistent on SVO order today." However, SVO was already used frequently before the language had contact with Spanish (Rodríguez Guaján 1989 quoted in England 1991; García Matzar and Rodríguez Guaján 1997: 334). We will come back to this issue in the following chapters.
4. According to García Matzar and Rodríguez Guaján (1997), SOV and OSV are also grammatically allowed in Kaqchikel. However, because these two word orders are rarely used, we will not consider them in this study.
5. For the syntax of verb initial languages more generally, see Carnie and Guilfoyle (Eds.) (2000) and Chung (2017), for example.

3 Word Order Preference in Sentence Comprehension I: Behavioral Studies

In this chapter, we will consider the nature of word order preference in sentence comprehension, drawing on evidence from behavioral experiments.

3.1 Previous Studies

In many languages with flexible word orders, word orders where the subject precedes the object (SO orders) have a processing advantage over those where the object precedes the subject (OS orders). In terms of behavioral indices, Tamaoka et al. (2005), for example, have observed that Japanese readers take less time to judge whether a sentence makes sense when it has the SOV word order than when it has the OSV word order. Shorter reading times for SOV sentences than OSV sentences in Japanese have also been reported using self-paced reading and eye-tracking methodologies (Imamura and Koizumi 2008; Mazuka, Itoh, and Kondo 2002; Tamaoka et al. 2014). Even if the referent of the object is mentioned in the immediately preceding sentence, thereby making the OSV word order conform with the information-structural requirement that "words in a sentence be arranged in such a way that those that represent old, predictable information come first, and those that represent new, unpredictable information come last" (Kuno 1978: 54), OSV still takes longer to process than SOV in Japanese (Koizumi and Imamura 2016). Similarly, in Finnish, SVO sentences are processed faster than OVS sentences even when an appropriate context is provided for the latter (Hyönä and Hujanen 1997; Kaiser and Trueswell 2004). Parallel results have been reported for many other languages (see Hemforth 1993 for German; Sekerina 1997 for Russian; Tamaoka et al. 2011 for Sinhalese; Kim 2012 for Korean; among many others). In terms of neurophysiological indices, functional magnetic resonance imaging (fMRI) studies have found that the left inferior frontal gyrus exhibits enhanced activation during the processing of OS word orders compared to SO word orders (Grewe et al. 2007 for German; Kim et al. 2009 and Kinno et al. 2008 for Japanese). Moreover, event-related potential (ERP) studies of the brain have observed P600 and/or (sustained) anterior negativity for OS orders relative to SO orders (Rösler et al. 1998 for German; Hagiwara et al. 2007 and Ueno and

Kluender 2003 for Japanese; Erdocia et al. 2009 for Basque). Taken together, abundant evidence supports the claim that SO word orders are less difficult to process than OS word orders in many of the world's languages. We will refer to this generalization as the SO Preference in Sentence Comprehension.

(1) SO Preference in Sentence Comprehension
In individual languages with flexible word order, SO word orders are easier to process than OS word orders.

3.2 Competing Hypotheses

As we have seen in the previous section, SO word orders are preferred to OS word orders in the sentence comprehension of many languages in the world. The question that follows is why this should be the case and, relatedly, whether this preference is universal or language-specific. In the psycholinguistic literature, a number of suggestions have been made regarding the factors affecting word order preference in sentence comprehension. As mentioned in Section 1.2 of Chapter 1, these may be divided into two broad groups: the Individual Grammar View (IGV) and the Universal Cognition View (UCV).

The IGV posits that the grammatical factors of individual languages, such as syntactic complexity, are what primarily determines word order preference in each language (see Gibson 1998, 2000; Hawkins 2004; Marantz 2005; O'Grady 1997; Pritchett and Whitman 1995, among others). A basic intuition behind this view is expressed succinctly and clearly in the following passage from Marantz (2005: 439).

All other things being equal, the more complex a representation – the longer and more complex the linguistic computations necessary to generate the representation – the longer it should take for a subject to perform any task involving the representation and the more activity should be observed in the subject's brain in areas associated with creating or accessing the representation and with performing the task.

Something along this line is assumed either implicitly or explicitly in virtually all studies in cognitive (neuro)science. As far as we know, all theories of linguistic complexity, including Pritchett and Whitman's (1995) Representational Theory of Complexity, Gibson's (2000) Dependency Locality Theory, and Hawkins's (2004) Minimize Domains, converge in predicting that, all other things being equal, sentences involving an instance of syntactic movement are more difficult to process than their counterparts without such movement. In particular, a language's syntactically simplest, basic word order is easier to process than other grammatically possible, but syntactically more complex derived word orders in the language. Thus, according to the IGV, SO word orders were found to be preferred

3.2 Competing Hypotheses

in previous studies because they were the syntactically basic word orders in the target languages.

(2)   Individual Grammar View [Processing Load]
   Sentence processing load is largely attributable to grammatical factors of individual languages, such as syntactic complexity.

In contrast, according to the UCV, the SO preference in comprehension is largely attributable to human cognitive features that are universal and independent of the grammar of particular languages (Bornkessel-Schlesewsky and Schlesewsky 2009a, 2009b; Kemmerer 2012; Tanaka et al. 2011, to mention just a few proponents). Event structure, perspective-taking, and conceptual saliency, for instance, have all been suggested as universal feature candidates (cf. Bock and Warren 1985; Bornkessel-Schlesewsky and Schlesewsky 2009a; Branigan, Pickering, and Tanaka 2008; Hirsh-Pasek and Golinkoff 1996; Primus 1999; Slobin and Bever 1982). The UCV thus leads to the expectation that SO word orders have a lower processing load regardless of the basic word order in any individual language, which is consistent with what has been reported in the literature so far.

(3)   Universal Cognition View [Processing Load]
   Sentence processing load is largely attributable to grammar-independent human cognitive features that are universal, such as conceptual accessibility.

Note that grammatical factors and grammar-independent universal cognitive factors are not necessarily mutually exclusive. There is ample evidence that they all affect human sentence processing in one way or another, as demonstrated in numerous studies, such as those mentioned above. What has not been made clear are their relative contributions and interactions in aspects of sentence processing. Both views correctly account for the SO word order preference in sentence comprehension in SO languages. In Japanese, for example, SOV is easier to process than OSV, which may be because SOV is (i) the syntactically basic word order (IGV) and/or (ii) an SO order (UCV). However, the sentence processing studies conducted so far have all targeted SO languages, except for a few recent ones (e.g., Clemens et al. 2015; Norcliffe, Harris, and Jaeger 2015). Hence, it remains unclear whether the SO word order preference is a reflection of the basic word orders in individual languages or more universal human cognitive features. To evaluate the relative strengths of these factors and determine which is primary for the observed word order preference, it is necessary to examine languages for which the two theories offer different predictions, namely, languages in which the object precedes the subject in the syntactically basic word order (OS languages). We thus turn to an OS language, Kaqchikel.

3.3 Predictions

As mentioned in Section 2.3 of Chapter 2, Kaqchikel's syntactically basic word order is VOS, but SVO and VSO are also grammatically possible and commonly used (Ajsivinac Sian et al. 2004). The latter two are derived from VOS through syntactic movements, as schematically shown in (4).

(4) Order   Syntactic representation
     VOS   [VOS]
     VSO   [[V gap$_i$ S] O$_i$]
     SVO   [S$_i$ [VO gap$_i$]]

Given these structures, the following predictions can be made about processing load in the comprehension of Kaqchikel sentences. If the preference for SO word orders shown by speakers of SO languages is mainly caused by the syntactic structure of the individual languages' basic word orders, as suggested by the IGV, VOS sentences in Kaqchikel should incur a lower processing load than VSO or SVO sentences. On the other hand, if SO word orders incur a lower processing load than OS orders regardless of the grammar of particular languages, as suggested by the UCV, then Kaqchikel VOS sentences should incur a greater processing load than the other two. In order to test these predictions, we conducted an experiment with a sentence plausibility judgment task.

3.4 Processing Load

3.4.1 Methods

Data from twenty-two native speakers of Kaqchikel were analyzed in this study.[1] The target sentences used in the experiment were so-called non-reversible transitive sentences, which contain a definite animate subject, a definite inanimate object, and an action verb. They were all semantically natural, grammatical sentences, and were arranged into three of the possible and common word orders (VOS, VSO, SVO), as shown in (5).

(5) a. [VOS] *X-Ø-u-chöy*   *ri*   *chäj*   *ri*   *ajanel*
CP-ABS3sg-ERG3sg-cut DET pine.tree DET carpenter
"The carpenter cut the pine tree."

b. [VSO] *X-Ø-u-chöy*   *ri*   *ajanel*   *ri*   *chäj*
CP-ABS3sg-ERG3sg-cut DET carpenter DET pine.tree

c. [SVO] *Ri*   *ajanel*   *x-Ø-u-chöy*   *ri*   *chäj*
DET carpenter CP-ABS3sg-ERG3sg-cut DET pine.tree

We created 108 target sentences with thirty-six distinct lexical sets such as those in (5). Additionally, we created thirty-six sets of (i.e., a total of 108)

3.4 Processing Load

Table 3.1 *The averages (M) and standard deviations (SD) of time duration for word order*
(Adapted from Koizumi et al. 2014 with permission)

Word order	Whole sentence (ms)		Before third phrase (ms)	
	M	SD	M	SD
VOS	3,002	469	1,948	317
SVO	3,006	468	1,893	274
VSO	3,001	470	1,897	298

Abbreviations: *M* = mean; *SD* = standard deviation.

transitive sentences that were grammatical but not semantically natural (e.g., #*Xuch'äj ri kaq'ïq' ri xta Selfa* "Miss Selfa washed the air"). The seventy-two sets, consisting of 216 sentences, half semantically natural and half not, were distributed among three lists using a Latin square procedure. Sixty semantically plausible and implausible filler sentences were then added to each list. Each participant was assigned one of the three lists so that she or he would not hear multiple lexically matched sentences.

The sentences were recorded by a male native speaker of Kaqchikel and were edited using Praat (Boersma and Weenink 2010). After the editing, all the test items were judged as natural in terms of prosody by our native Kaqchikel consultants. There were no significant differences between the word orders in terms of time between the onset and offset of the sentence or between the onset of the sentence and the onset of the third phrase (i.e., the S of VOS or the O of SVO/VSO) (Table 3.1).

A sentence plausibility judgment task (e.g., Caplan, Chen, and Waters 2008) was administered using E-Prime (version 2.0, Psychology Software Tools). In this task, the stimulus sentences were presented in a random order to the participants through headsets. The participants were asked to judge whether each sentence was semantically plausible and to push a YES button for correct sentences or a NO button for incorrect sentences as quickly and accurately as possible. The time from the beginning of each stimulus sentence until a button was pressed was measured as the reaction time.

For data compilation and statistical analysis, readers are referred to the original article (Koizumi et al. 2014).

3.4.2 Results and Discussion

The results of the experiment are summarized in Table 3.2 and Figure 3.1. Statistical analyses showed that VOS sentences (3,403 ms) were processed

Table 3.2 *Reaction times and error rates for semantically plausible transitive sentences judged as semantically correct (Adapted from Koizumi et al. 2014 with permission)*

Word order	Reaction time (ms)		Error rate (%)	
	M	SD	M	SD
VOS	3,403	673	10.61	30.85
SVO	3,559	663	7.58	26.51
VSO	3,601	674	22.90	42.10

Abbreviations: *M* = mean; *SD* = standard deviation.

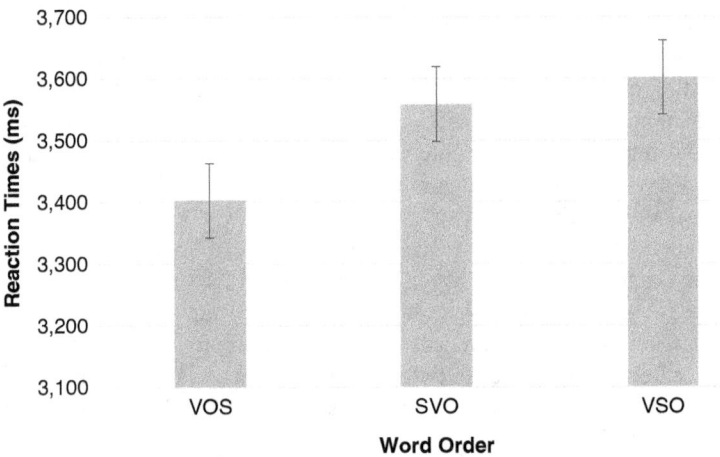

Figure 3.1 Histograms of the reaction times for sentences with the VOS, SVO, and VSO word orders. The error bars indicate the standard error of the mean.

faster than SVO sentences (3,559 ms) and VSO sentences (3,601 ms). No significant difference was found between SVO and VSO processing time. In terms of error rates, VSO was higher than VOS and SVO, and the latter two were comparable.

These results suggest that VOS is easier to process than SVO or VSO, which is compatible with the prediction of the IGV, but not with the prediction of the UCV. This shows that, in Kaqchikel, the OS word order VOS is preferred to the SO word orders SVO and VSO, which provides evidence that the SO Preference in Sentence Comprehension is not fully grounded in the universal properties of human cognition. Although this finding does not deny the existence of universal factors in the SO preference, it certainly demonstrates that the grammatical factors of individual languages have a relatively larger influence on sentence processing load. Based on this result, we argue that the SO Preference in Sentence Comprehension may not reflect a universal aspect of human languages; rather, processing preference may be language-specific to some extent, reflecting syntactic differences in individual languages.

A possible caveat concerns the use of semantically non-reversible sentences in this study. As explained above, all the target sentences consisted of an animate subject and inanimate object, so the subject and object were not comparable in terms of animacy. It is well known that the effects of animacy are omnipresent in various aspects of language (e.g., Silverstein 1976). Thus, the conclusion above might hold only of non-reversible sentences, and it may not be extendable to semantically reversible sentences, in which both the subject and object are animate entities. To test this possibility, we conducted a follow-up study with both reversible and non-reversible sentences.

3.5 Effects of Animacy

3.5.1 Methods

Data from twenty-four participants were analyzed in this study.[2] The target sentences were eighty pairs of semantically natural transitive sentences with the VOS and SVO word orders. Half of the pairs had an animate object, and the other half had an inanimate object; the subject was always animate. In order to morpho-syntactically differentiate subject and object, half of the sentences contained a singular subject and plural object, and the other half contained a plural subject and singular object. That is, there were four types of sentences in terms of the combination of animacy (animate/inanimate) and number (singular/plural) of subject and object, as exemplified in (6) through (9).

(6) Singular animate subject and plural inanimate object
   a. [VOS] *X-e-ru-pïs   ri   taq lej   ri   ch'utitata'.*
             CP-ABS3pl-ERG3sg-wrap DET PM   tortilla DET   uncle
             "The uncle wrapped the tortillas."

   b. [SVO] *Ri   ch'utitata' x-e-ru-pïs   ri   taq lej.*
             DET   uncle   CP-ABS3pl-ERG3sg-wrap DET PM   tortilla

(7) Plural animate subject and singular inanimate object
   a. [VOS] *X-Ø-ki-jiq'aj   ri   jub'ül pom   ri   taq ajawa'.*
             CP-ABS3sg-ERG3pl-breath DET fragrant incense DET   PM   lords
             "The lords breathed the fragrant incense."

(8) b. [SVO] Ri   taq   ajawa'   x-Ø-ki-jiq'aj   ri   jub'ül
            DET   PM   lords   CP-ABS3sg-ERG3pl-breath DET fragrant
            pom
            incense

(8)   Singular animate subject and plural animate object
        a. [VOS] X-e-ru-kajij   ri   taq   yuqüy b'aq ri   cholonel.
                 CP-ABS3pl-ERG3sg-annoy   DET   PM   bone-setter DET speaker
                 "The speaker annoyed the bone-setters."

        b. [SVO] Ri   cholonel   x-e-ru- kajij   ri   taq   yuqüy b'aq.
                 DET   speaker   CP-ABS3pl-ERG3sg-annoy DET   PM   bone-setter

(9)   Plural animate subject and singular animate object
        a. [VOS] X-Ø-ki-köl   ri   achijilom   ri   taq   ixjayilom.
                 CP-ABS3sg-ERG3pl-save   DET   husband   DET   PM   wife
                 "The wives saved the husband."

        b. [SVO] Ri   taq   ixjayilom   x-Ø-ki-köl   ri   achijilom.
                 DET   PM   wife   CP-ABS3sg-ERG3pl-save   DET   husband

These target sentences were combined with semantically plausible and implausible filler sentences. They were then counterbalanced and categorized into three groups according to word order.

All the stimulus sentences were recorded by a male native speaker of Kaqchikel, and all the test items were judged as natural in terms of prosody by our native Kaqchikel consultants. The difference in the duration of VOS sentences (M = 3,274 ms) and SVO sentences (M = 3,274 ms) was not significant.

The procedure was the same as in the experiment described in the previous section.

3.5.2   Results and Discussion

There was no significant difference between the conditions in terms of error rates. Table 3.3 shows the means and standard deviations of reaction times for the correctly judged semantically plausible target sentences. The effect of word order was significant, but the effect of object animacy and the interaction were not significant. The results indicated that SVO sentences (M = 3,938 ms, SD = 650 ms) took longer to process than VOS sentences (M = 3,847 ms, SD = 658 ms) regardless of object animacy.

To summarize, in order to explore the processing load of transitive sentences in the two most commonly used word orders in Kaqchikel (i.e., VOS and SVO) with reference to the animacy of the object, we conducted an experiment with a sentence plausibility judgment task. The results showed that VOS was processed faster than SVO regardless of the animacy of the object; that is, the

Table 3.3 *Reaction times (ms) of sentence plausibility judgment for Kaqchikel VOS and SVO sentences with animate and inanimate objects*

Word order	Animate object		Inanimate object	
	M	SD	M	SD
VOS	3,856	597	3,839	715
SVO	3,911	585	3,964	706

Abbreviations: M = mean; SD = standard deviation.

sentence processing load was not significantly affected by the animacy of the object. Rather, syntactic features played a more prominent role in parsing, a result consistent with the IGV.

3.6 General Discussion

We reviewed two Kaqchikel sentence processing studies and tested the predictions of the IGV and UCV. The results revealed that, in Kaqchikel, the VOS word order was processed faster than SVO and VSO regardless of the animacy of the object, thereby supporting the IGV. On the basis of this result, we argue that the SO preference in sentence comprehension observed in previous studies is not a universal feature of all languages; rather, processing preference may be language-specific to some extent, reflecting syntactic differences in individual languages.

The Individual Grammar View [Processing Load] in (2) above states that sentence processing load is largely attributable to grammatical factors of individual languages. In particular, for the sake of concreteness, we assume that all else being equal, a language's syntactically simplest basic word order is easier to process than other grammatically possible but syntactically more complex derived word orders in the language. Let us refer to this particular version of the IGV as the syntactic complexity hypothesis. Given this and the syntactic analyses of Kaqchikel sentences shown in (4), repeated here as (10), VOS should incur a lower processing load than VSO and SVO. This prediction was borne out, as we have seen in the previous sections.

(10) Order Syntactic representation
      VOS   [VOS]
      VSO   [[V gap$_i$ S] O$_i$]
      SVO   [S$_i$ [VO gap$_i$]]

In other words, we interpret the results of the two experiments reviewed above as follows: In Kaqchikel, VOS is easier to process than VSO/SVO because VOS is syntactically simpler than VSO/SVO.

However, one may view this difference in processing load between VOS on the one hand and SVO/VSO on the other as being attributable to the ergative nature of Kaqchikel. In typological work, it is customary to distinguish between marked and unmarked cases (Primus 1999). The unmarked case is the case that generally surfaces on the sole argument of an intransitive verb in a given language. In nominative-accusative languages, the nominative case is unmarked, and the accusative case is marked. The intransitive subject and transitive subject are case-marked in nominative, and the transitive object is singled out, being case-marked in accusative. In ergative-absolutive languages, the absolutive case is unmarked, and the ergative case is marked. The intransitive subject and transitive object are case-marked in absolutive, and the transitive subject alone is case-marked in ergative. The ergative and accusative tend to be marked overtly, while the absolutive and nominative often appear with zero marking.

(11)   Case markedness

	Unmarked case	Marked case
Accusative languages:	nominative	accusative
Ergative languages:	absolutive	ergative

Given the notion of case markedness in (11), it appears possible to uniformly describe the word order preferences in both Kaqchikel and SO languages, as stated in (12) (Polinsky et al. 2012; Primus 1999).[3]

(12)   Case-Markedness Hypothesis
Unmarked-before-marked case orders (e.g., nom-acc, abs-erg)
are easier to process than
marked-before-unmarked case orders (e.g., acc-nom, erg-abs).

According to the case-markedness hypothesis, in Japanese, for example, a nominative-accusative language, SOV is easier to process than OSV because the former is an unmarked(nominative)-before-marked(accusative) case order, whereas the latter is a marked-before-unmarked case order. In the same vein, in Kaqchikel, an ergative language, VOS is preferred to SVO/VSO because VOS is an unmarked(absolutive)-before-marked(ergative) case order, in contrast to SVO/VSO, which follows the opposite order.[4] If the case-markedness hypothesis turns out to be correct, we are still in support of the IGV because case marking is a core grammatical property of individual languages. The battle is now within the IGV between the case-markedness hypothesis and the syntactic complexity hypothesis. Below, we present three pieces of evidence in favor of the syntactic complexity hypothesis against the case-markedness hypothesis.

3.6 General Discussion

3.6.1 Basque

Erdocia et al. (2009) conducted a self-paced reading study in Basque, a language isolate. Basque is an ergative SOV language with a relatively free word order. They compared canonical SOV sentences such as (13a) and non-canonical OSV sentences such as (13b), in which the subjects are marked with the ergative marker -*k*, and the objects bear no overt case ending, indicating they are in absolutive.

(13) a. Emakume-a-k gizon-a ikusi du
 woman-the-ERG man-the seen has
 "The woman has seen the man."

 b. Gizon-a emakume-a-k ikusi du
 man-the woman-the-ERG seen has
 "The woman has seen the man."

(Erdocia et al. 2009)

Since OSV is syntactically more complex than SOV, the syntactic complexity hypothesis predicts that OSV sentences should take longer to read than SOV sentences. In contrast, the case markedness hypothesis leads us to expect that S-ERG O-ABS V, in which the marked ergative NP precedes the unmarked absolutive NP, should be more difficult to process than O-ABS S-ERG V, in which the absolutive NP precedes the ergative NP. The reading experiment by Erdocia et al. (2009) revealed that SOV sentences were processed significantly faster than OSV sentences. This result is consistent with the syntactic complexity hypothesis but not with the case markedness hypothesis.

3.6.2 Tongan

Another argument against the case markedness hypothesis comes from Tongan. Tongan is an Austronesian language of the Polynesian branch. It is an ergative language with VSO being the syntactically basic word order. It is possible to derive the VOS word order by scrambling (Otsuka 2005b, 2005c).

(14) a. VSO
 Na'e fili 'e Sione 'a Pila.
 PST choose ERG Sione ABS Pila
 "Sione chose Pila."

 b. VOS
 Na'e fili 'a Pila 'e Sione.
 PST choose ABS Pila ERG Sione
 "Sione chose Pila."

(Otsuka 2005b)

The syntactically canonical V S-ERG O-ABS order should be easier to process than the syntactically derived non-canonical V O-ABS S-ERG order according to the syntactic complexity hypothesis, whereas the opposite is the case given the case markedness hypothesis.

Tamaoka et al. (2021) conducted two behavioral experiments, one with the lexical maze task (Forster, Guerrera, and Elliot 2009) and one with the sentence plausibility judgment task. The results of the two experiments converged in showing that VSO was processed faster than VOS, in support of the syntactic complexity hypothesis.

3.6.3 Japanese

Japanese is a nominative-accusative SOV language, with OSV being another possible word order. As we have seen several times by now, the subject of a typical transitive sentence in Japanese is marked by the nominative case marker *ga* and the object by the accusative case marker *o*. In some stative sentences, however, the object is case-marked in nominative and the subject is marked in dative by *ni*, as exemplified by the potential sentences in (15).

(15) a. S-DAT O-NOM V
Kenzi   ni   tyuugokugo ga   yom-e-ru   daroo-ka
Kenzi   DAT   Chinse   NOM   read-can-PRS MOD-Q
"Can Kenzi read Chinese?"

b. O-NOM S-DAT V
Tyuugokugo ga$_i$ Kenzi   ni   t$_i$ yom-e-ru   daroo-ka
Chinese   NOM   Kenzi   DAT   read-can-PRS MOD-Q
"Can Kenzi read Chinese?"

Since the unmarked case in Japanese is nominative,[5] and the dative is a marked case, (15a) should be more difficult to process than (15b) if the processing preference is driven by surface case considerations. Conversely, if syntactic structure is the primary factor determining the processing costs of different word orders, (15b) should incur additional processing costs compared to (15a). Tamaoka et al. (2005) performed a reading experiment with a sentence plausibility judgment task to test these divergent predictions. They found that (15a) was processed faster than (15b), which is again consistent with the version of the IGV based on syntactic complexity but not the one based on case orders.

3.7 Conclusion

We started out with two possible scenarios: the IGV and the UCV. According to the IGV, transitive sentences with different word orders are processed based on

3.7 Conclusion

the syntactic configuration, which would predict in Kaqchikel that word orders other than VOS should be associated with extra processing cost due to the presence of a filler-gap dependency. In contrast, on the UCV the processing of alternative word orders considers cognitive features of event participants, not their grammatical functions, and VOS should therefore be more difficult to process than SVO and VSO. The results of the two Kaqchikel experiments confirmed the IGV. We have also seen in Section 3.6 that although a variant of the IGV based on case markedness is consistent with the Kaqchikel data reported in this chapter, it fails to account for a wider range of empirical facts, including the processing preferences observed in ergative SO languages such as Basque and Tongan.

NOTES

1. This section is based on Koizumi et al. (2014).
2. This section is based on Kiyama et al. (2013).
3. As far as the discussion here is concerned, the distinction between unmarked and marked cases is equivalent to the distinction between independent and dependent cases in the sense of Marantz (1991, 2000). Thus, the case-markedness hypothesis in (12) amounts to saying that independent-before-dependent case order is easier to process than dependent-before-independent case order.
4. As Kaqchikel is a head-marking rather than dependent-marking language, nominal arguments are not overtly case-marked. The ergative-absolutive distinction is expressed by verb agreement instead of case marking.
5. The case used for the sole argument of an intransitive verb is nominative in Japanese.

4 Word Order Preference in Sentence Comprehension II: fMRI Studies

We saw in Chapter 3 that Kaqchikel sentences in the VOS word order were processed faster than those in the SVO or VSO order. This suggests that, in Kaqchikel, the OS order VOS is easier to process than SVO and VSO, both of which are SO orders. Based on this result, we concluded that the SO order preference in sentence comprehension may not be universal; rather, processing load in sentence comprehension may be greatly affected by the syntactic nature of the individual language.

We will now expand on these behavioral studies by examining brain activations during the processing of Kaqchikel sentences with different word orders. As we will review in Sections 4.3 and 5.1, an SO preference in sentence comprehension has been observed not only in previous behavioral studies but also in those with functional brain measurements, such as functional magnetic resonance imaging (fMRI) and electroencephalogram (EEG). In this chapter, we consider whether the elevated neural activities that are frequently observed for OS word orders relative to SO word orders are primarily due to individual grammatical factors or universal cognitive factors by comparing Kaqchikel sentences with different word orders.

Functional brain measurements are potentially more informative than behavioral experiments because, while data obtained via the latter are basically unidimensional (e.g., reaction times), data obtained via the former are multidimensional, including not only information about the strength of the signals but also where in the brain and at what time they occur. This enables us to identify qualitatively different aspects of linguistic knowledge and sentence processing that might be reflected in the activations of different neural substrates with different time courses.

We will discuss an fMRI experiment in Section 4.4 and EEG experiments in Chapters 5 and 6. Before that, in the next two sections we will briefly go over some background knowledge about the human brain and functional brain measurements that will be necessary for understanding the subsequent discussions.

4.1 Brain Primer

The brain is the center of the human nervous system, containing more than one hundred billion neurons. It consists of three major parts: the cerebrum, the cerebellum, and the brain stem. The cerebrum is the largest part of the human brain, associated with higher brain functions such as thought, action, and language, and is therefore the center of attention in most studies of cognitive neuroscience of language. The cerebellum is located behind the cerebrum and primarily controls the coordination and control of voluntary movement, although it also plays a role in higher functions such as language. The brain stem connects the rest of the brain to the spinal cord, which runs down the neck and back, regulating vital functions such as breathing, consciousness, and body temperature.

The cerebrum has two hemispheres: the left and the right. In general, the right hemisphere receives sensations from and controls the movement of the left side of the body, and the left hemisphere does the same for the right side of the body. The hemispheres are divided into four sections called lobes: the frontal lobe, the parietal lobe, the occipital lobe, and the temporal lobe. The frontal lobe is associated with reasoning, planning, speech, movement, emotions, and problem-solving. The parietal lobe is associated with the perception of stimuli and the recognition of the movement and orientation of objects. The occipital lobe is related to visual processing. Finally, the temporal lobe plays roles in the perception and recognition of auditory stimuli, in memory, and in speech.

Language is a complex cognitive system consisting of various submodules. The neural substrates of language, therefore, involve various brain regions that are interconnected, forming a complex network. Major language-relevant brain regions and fiber tracts are schematically shown in Figure 4.1. The processing of syntactic structures in particular involves a left frontotemporal neural network with two distinct brain regions: (i) Broca's area in the inferior frontal gyrus (IFG) and (ii) Wernicke's area in the posterior superior temporal cortex (pSTC) (Grodzinsky, Pieperhoff, and Thompson 2021).[1] For recent reviews of neural networks for sentence comprehension and production, see Friederici (2017), Friederici et al. (2017), Grodzinsky, Pieperhoff, and Thompson (2021), and Walenski et al. (2019), as well as the following review papers published in *Science* 366: Hagoort (2019), Jarvis (2019), Pylkkänen (2019), and Scott (2019).

4.2 Functional Brain Measurement

Functional brain measurements observe electromagnetic impulses or changes to blood flow resulting from heightened brain activity under specific

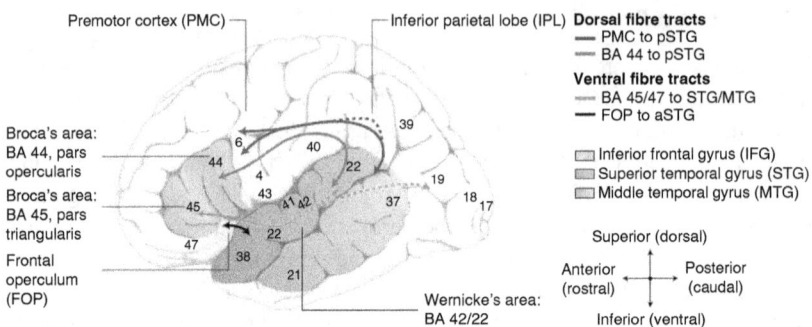

Figure 4.1 Language-relevant brain regions and fiber tracts in the left hemisphere.
(Adapted from Friederici et al. 2017 with permission.)

conditions. The brain is made up of about one hundred billion neurons, and neuronal activity is an electrical process. The electrical activity of active neurons in the brain produces electrical currents that spread through the head. Although the electrical potential produced by a single neuron is very small, many neurons activating together produce electrical potentials large enough to be recorded by electrodes placed on the scalp. The record of these electrical signals (i.e., voltage differences) is referred to as an electroencephalogram (EEG). An EEG provides a continuous recording of overall brain activity. EEG components that are time-locked to a specific event, such as the presentation of a word, are called event-related potentials (ERPs). Each ERP component reflects brain activation associated with one or more mental operations. As ERPs provide a precise time resolution (in milliseconds), they are suitable for studying the time course of brain activity. Moreover, the electrical currents inside the head produce magnetic fields that can be measured above the scalp surface with a magnetoencephalogram (MEG).

Within the domain of language processing, particular ERP components have been identified as reflecting phonological, semantic, and syntactic processes. For example, the N400 is a centroparietally distributed negativity at around 400 ms after the onset of a stimulus. It is considered to reflect lexical-semantic processes and is observed both at the word and at the sentence level. The N400 is often followed by a positive wave called a late positive component (LPC), which is an index of the retrieval of episodic memory and elaborative processes. A left anterior negativity between 150 and 300 ms reflects online syntactic and morphosyntactic processes. The P600 is a centroparietally distributed positivity at around 600 ms, traditionally associated with difficulties in syntactic processing such as gap-filling parsing and syntactic reanalysis.

However, P600 effects are also observed in some cases of semantic anomaly. This suggests that P600 reflects more general processing difficulty or that several types of P600 exist, each reflecting a distinct underlying process (see Chapter 5 for further discussion of P600).

Magnetic resonance imaging (MRI) is a way of obtaining pictures of various parts of the brain using magnetic fields and radio-frequency energy. MRI can be used to examine brain anatomy (structural MRI) and brain function (functional MRI, fMRI). Both types of MRI provide high spatial resolution. However, unlike electrophysiological techniques such as EEG and MEG, fMRI does not directly detect neural activity, but rather detects the changes in blood oxygenation that occur in response to neural activation. Neural events happen in milliseconds, but the blood oxygenation changes that they induce are spread out over several seconds, making fMRI's temporal resolution relatively limited.

Near-infrared spectroscopy (NIRS) also measures cerebral hemodynamic responses in relation to neural activity, utilizing near-infrared light to measure changes in blood oxy- and deoxy-hemoglobin concentrations in the brain as well as total blood volume changes in various regions of the cerebral cortex. NIRS can determine activity in specific regions of the brain by continuously monitoring blood hemoglobin level but, as with other hemodynamic techniques such as fMRI, NIRS does not provide a good temporal resolution.

4.3 Previous fMRI Studies on Word Order Processing

Studies using fMRI have found that there is a greater activation of the left inferior frontal gyrus (IFG, see Figure 4.1) during the processing of OS word orders than SO word orders (Bornkessel-Schlesewsky, Schlesewsky, and von Cramon 2009; Grewe et al. 2007; and Meyer et al. 2012 for German; Caplan, Stanczak, and Waters 2008; Santi and Grodzinsky 2010; and Thompson et al. 2010 for English; Kim et al. 2009 and Kinno et al. 2008 for Japanese). Grewe et al.'s (2007) fMRI study on German sentence processing, for example, reported significant activation in the left IFG for OS sentences in contrast to SO sentences (Figure 4.2), interpreting this as support for a linearization principle that stipulates that subjects encoding agents typically precede objects encoding patients (see also Bornkessel-Schlesewsky and Schlesewsky 2009a, 2009b).

Based on these and other findings, Kemmerer (2012) suggests that the SO word order reflects the most natural way of linearizing and nesting the core conceptual components of actions in Broca's area regardless of the syntactic nature of any individual language.

In the next section, we report a sentence comprehension experiment using fMRI to measure the cortical activations of Kaqchikel speakers. To provide

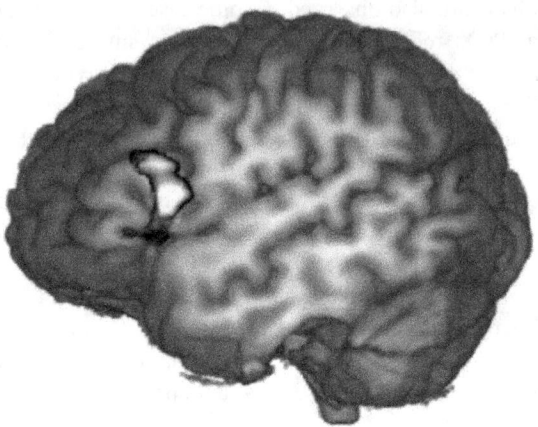

Figure 4.2 Activation of the left IFG in the comparison of OS vs. SO German sentences.
(Adapted from Grewe et al. 2007 with permission.)

a basis for comparison, in the remainder of this section, we will discuss a parallel study we had previously conducted with Japanese speakers, that is, Kim et al. (2009). Kim et al. (2009) conducted an experiment using fMRI to examine brain activity during Japanese sentence comprehension. Thirty-six native speakers of Japanese participated in the experiment, all of whom were right-handed. The handedness survey was based on the Edinburgh Handedness Inventory (Oldfield 1971). It is known that the majority of right-handed people (about 95 percent) mainly process languages in their left hemisphere (left hemisphere language dominance), while many left-handed people process languages in their right hemisphere or use both hemispheres equally. Since it is not possible to conduct an analysis properly when data on people with different dominant hemispheres are combined, participants in language experiments on brain function measurements are often limited to right-handed people.

Kim et al. (2009) compared brain activities under the following four conditions: canonical sentence condition (CS), scrambled sentence condition (SS), word list condition (WL), and rest condition (R). Sample stimuli used in the CS, SS, and WL conditions are shown below.

(1) Canonical sentence condition
  a. Correct SOV sentences
   obasan   ga   yoozi   o   tasuke-ta
   woman   NOM   baby   ACC   save-PST
   "The woman saved the baby."

4.3 Previous fMRI Studies on Word Order Processing

      b. Incorrect SOV sentences
          kangohu ga   petto o   yotot-ta.
          nurse   NOM pet   ACC employ-PST
          "The nurse employed the pet."

(2)   Scrambled sentence condition (SS)
      a. Correct OSV sentences
          yoozi o   obasan   ga   tasuke-ta.
          baby ACC woman   NOM save-PST
          "The woman saved the baby."

      b. Incorrect OSV sentences
          petto o   kangohu ga   yatotta.
          pet   ACC nurse   NOM employ-PST
          "The nurse employed the pet."

(3)   Word list condition (WL)
      a. Correct word lists
          hahaoya ga   keikan ga   sinyuu ga
          mother   NOM police NOM friend NOM

      b. Incorrect word lists
          narabe-ta   sagasi-ta   narabe-ta
          arrange-PST search-PST arrange-PST

Under CS, we presented Japanese transitive sentences in the canonical word order (SOV) one by one at the center of the screen. Participants judged whether the sentences were semantically natural and pressed the Yes or No button (sentence plausibility judgment task). Under SS, transitive sentences in the scrambled word order (OSV) were presented, and a sentence plausibility judgment task was performed in the same manner as under CS. Under WL, we used the same set of words as those under CS and SS. To prevent the presented character strings from forming sentences, only three noun phrases with the nominative case particle *ga*, only three noun phrases with the accusative case particle *o*, or only three verbs in their past tense form were presented on the screen. We asked the participants to judge whether the screen contained two identical nouns or verbs and to answer by pressing buttons. Under R, no language stimulus was used; participants observed the plus sign ("+") presented in the center of the screen.

    The regions of the brain showing higher activation under CS than under R are shown in Figure 4.3. Signals of brain activities measured under CS contain components that reflect, for example, the brain activities for sustaining life that are unrelated to language tasks, in addition to brain activities for sentence comprehension and correct/wrong judgment. Therefore, it is not possible to know which part subserves the activities for language processing by looking only at brain activation under CS. To remove activation unrelated to

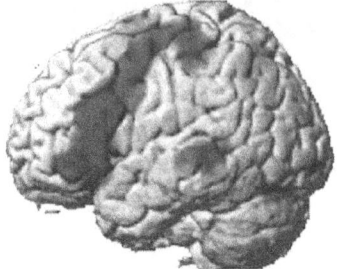 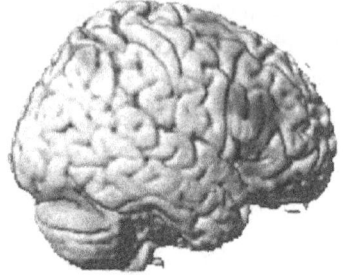

Figure 4.3 Brain regions activated more in CS than R. (Adapted from Kim et al. 2009 with permission.)

language tasks, we subtracted R activation from CS activation and analyzed the remaining brain activation. As described above, in research using fMRI, the subtraction method is used to extract data on brain activities suitable for research purposes.

In Figure 4.3, activation was observed in broad areas of the left and right cerebral hemispheres, and it can be observed that various abilities and processes are necessary to understand sentences. Comparison of the left and right hemispheres shows that the left hemisphere has a wider activated area and a higher degree of activation. This reflects that (for the majority of people) language processing is left-hemisphere dominant. The activation observed in the lower part of the left hemisphere from the occipital lobe to the temporal lobe (particularly the region called the fusiform gyrus at the base of the temporal lobe, which is not visible in the figure) reflects the processing of letters and word forms. Additionally, activation of the motor area (posterior frontal lobe) and the somatosensory cortex (anterior parietal lobe) of the left hemisphere reflects the task of moving the fingers of the right hand (to press the Yes or No button in response to a task).

Figure 4.4 shows regions where there is higher activation under CS than under WL. Since all the brain activation associated with recognizing words, judging whether they meet the conditions, and pressing the button was subtracted, the dark-colored areas in Figure 4.4 can be considered to reflect sentence-level processing (combining words to build a syntactic structure and calculating the meaning based on the syntactic structure). No activation was observed in the right hemisphere, indicating that left-hemisphere dominance is evident in sentence-level processing. In the left hemisphere, activation was observed in the inferior frontal gyrus of the frontal lobe and the superior and mid temporal gyrus of the temporal lobe. These areas are places where activation is observed in various language tasks, and damage by illness or injury

4.3 Previous fMRI Studies on Word Order Processing   43

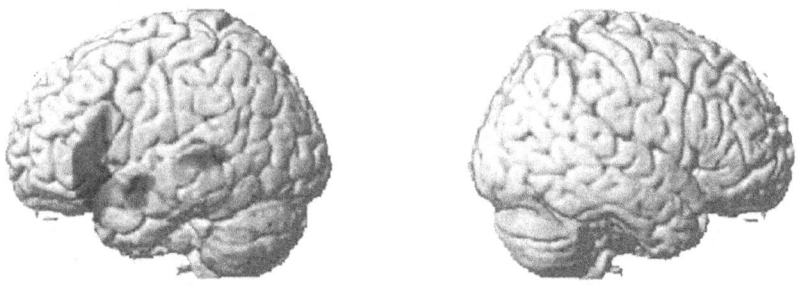

Figure 4.4 Brain regions activated more in CS than WL.
(Adapted from Kim et al. 2009 with permission.)

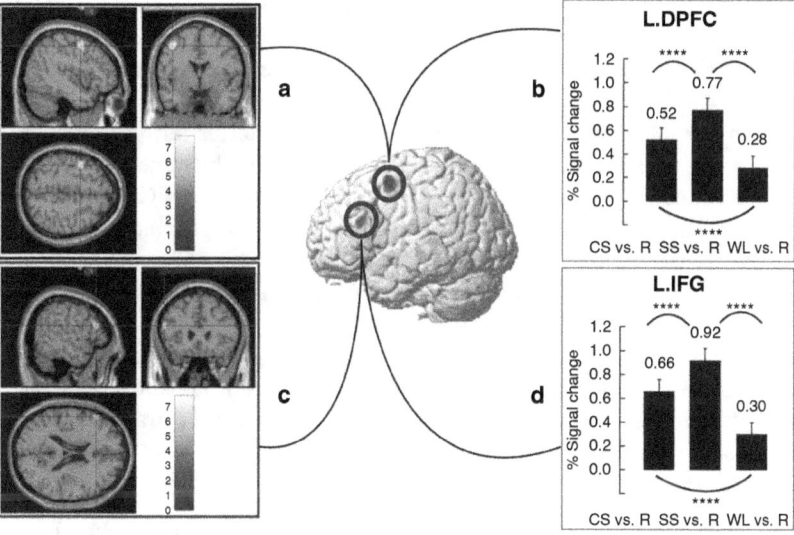

Figure 4.5 Brain regions activated more in SS than CS.
(Adapted from Kim et al. 2009 with permission.)

impairs the comprehension and production of language. For this reason, it has long been called the language center.

Where, then, does the scrambling process take place in the brain? Figure 4.5 shows the places where the activation was greater under SS than under CS; no activation was higher under CS than under SS. The left dorsolateral prefrontal cortex (upper cluster in Figure 4.5) and the left IFG (lower cluster in Figure 4.5) showed higher activation under SS than under CS. This suggests that these two areas play important roles in understanding scrambled sentences. It is known that the activation of the left dorsolateral prefrontal cortex increases when the level of task difficulty and loads on verbal working memory increase. This may play a part in the function of retaining the object at the beginning of sentences in working memory until encountering the gap position associated with it when understanding scrambled sentences. On the other hand, the left IFG is sometimes called the grammar center (Sakai 2005) and is considered to contribute more directly to syntactic processing. This may contribute to the process of integrating the information of the object held in working memory into the gap position (inserting a trace into the syntactic structure).

While Kim et al. (2009) used the sentence plausibility judgment task, Kinno et al. (2008) measured and compared brain activity for basic word order sentences and scrambled sentences when performing picture–sentence matching tasks. The picture–sentence matching task involves presenting a picture and a sentence on the screen at the same time and determining whether the contents of the picture and the sentence match. As a result of the experiment, higher activation was observed in three regions – the left IFG, the left dorsolateral prefrontal cortex, and the posterior left superior temporal gyrus – under the scrambled sentence condition than under the canonical sentence condition. Of these three regions, the left IFG and the left dorsolateral prefrontal cortex are the places where higher activation was observed under the scrambled sentence condition than under the canonical sentence condition by Kim et al. (2009). Furthermore, it has been reported that damage to the left IFG impairs the understanding of sentences involving word order conversion (Grodzinsky and Santi 2008; Hagiwara 1993; Hagiwara and Caplan 1990; Kinno et al. 2009). From the above evidence, the left inferior frontal gyrus is considered to play a central role in the processing of word order conversion.

4.4 Neural Substrates for Word Order Processing in Kaqchikel

We used fMRI to examine cortical activations during the processing of Kaqchikel sentences with VOS and SVO orders.[2] As noted above, the syntactically basic word order in Kaqchikel is VOS, and SVO is a derived word order. Given this, the Individual Grammar View would predict higher left IFG activation in the SVO condition than in the VOS condition, whereas the Universal Cognition View would posit the opposite expectation. In particular, we evaluate Kemmerer's (2012) suggestion that the SO word order preference reflects the most natural way of linearizing and nesting the core conceptual components of actions in a brain region called Broca's area (i.e., the left IFG).

4.4.1 Methods

Data from sixteen right-handed, healthy Kaqchikel native speakers with normal hearing were analyzed in this study. Handedness was evaluated using the Edinburgh Handedness Inventory (Oldfield 1971). All participants were living in Guatemala when they traveled to Japan to participate in this study.

The target items used in this experiment were semantically natural, grammatical, transitive sentences (i.e., "correct sentences") arranged into the VOS and SVO word orders. Either the subject or the object was singular, and the other was plural, as exemplified in (4) and (5).

(4) a. [VOS] *X-e-ru-pi's*   *ri*   *taq*   *lej*   *ri*   *ch'utitata'.*
CP-ABS3pl-ERG3sg-wrap   DET   PM   tortilla   DET   uncle
"The uncle wrapped the tortillas."

    b. [SVO] *Ri*   *ch'utitata'*   *x-e-ru-pi's*   *ri*   *taq*   *lej.*
DET   uncle   CP-ABS3pl-ERG3sg-wrap   DET   PM   tortilla

(5) a. [VOS] *X-Ø-ki-jiq'aj*   *ri*   *jub'ül*   *pom*   *ri*   *taq*
CP-ABS3sg-ERG3pl-breath   DET   fragrant   incense   DET   PM
ajawa'.
man
"The men breathed the fragrant incense."

    b. [SVO] *Ri*   *taq*   *ajawa'*   *x-Ø-ki-jiq'aj*   *ri*   *jub'ül*
DET   PM   man   CP-ABS3sg-ERG3pl-breath   DET   fragrant
pom.
incense

Fifty-two pairs of target sentences were created. Additionally, twenty-four pairs of grammatical but not semantically natural sentences were arranged into each of the two word orders. All seventy-six sentence pairs, consisting of 152 sentences, were counterbalanced and then categorized into two groups according to word order. All the stimulus sentences were recorded by a male native Kaqchikel speaker and were edited in Praat. All the edited sentences were judged as natural in terms of prosody by our native Kaqchikel consultants. The difference between the duration of VOS sentences ($M = 3{,}456$ ms, $SD = 360$) and that of SVO sentences ($M = 3{,}434$ ms, $SD = 347$) was not significant.

The total number of stimuli was divided into two sessions with seventy-six stimuli each. The stimuli were presented to participants in an event-related design in two sessions. Each session consisted of three conditions: verb-object-subject order (VOS), subject-verb-object order (SVO), and null task (N). The 152 stimuli were equally distributed across the two task conditions (VOS and SVO). There were fifty-two semantically plausible ("correct") transitive sentences and twenty-four semantically implausible ("incorrect") transitive sentences in each session, except for the N condition, in which the participant made no response. During the experiment, participants wore headphones and stayed in supine positions inside the MRI scanner. The participants listened to the stimulus sentences in a random order through the headphones. They were required to judge whether each sentence was semantically plausible by pushing a YES button or a NO button as quickly and accurately as possible.

The data were acquired with a 3.0 Tesla MRI scanner (Philips Achieva Quasar Dual, Philips Medical Systems, Best, the Netherlands) while conducting the sentence comprehension tasks. Readers are referred to Koizumi and Kim (2016) for detailed explanation of image acquisition and data analyses.

4.4.2 Results and Discussion

We identified similar activations in the left IFG and the left middle temporal gyrus in the VOS and SVO conditions (Figure 4.6). This suggests that most cognitive processes involved in the comprehension of SVO sentences are also involved in the comprehension of VOS sentences.

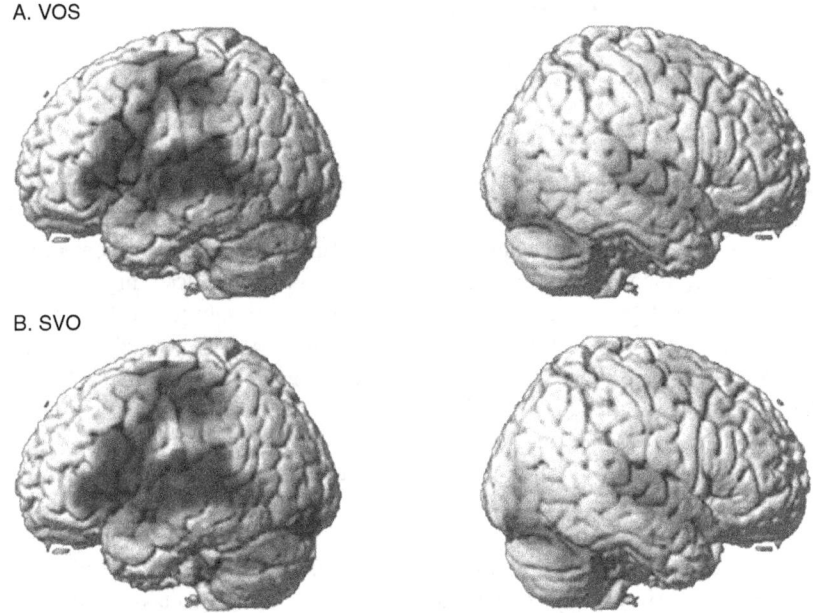

Figure 4.6 Activated brain regions while processing the VOS (A) and SVO (B) word orders relative to the null task condition.
(Adapted from Koizumi and Kim 2016.)

4.4 Neural Substrates for Word Order Processing in Kaqchikel

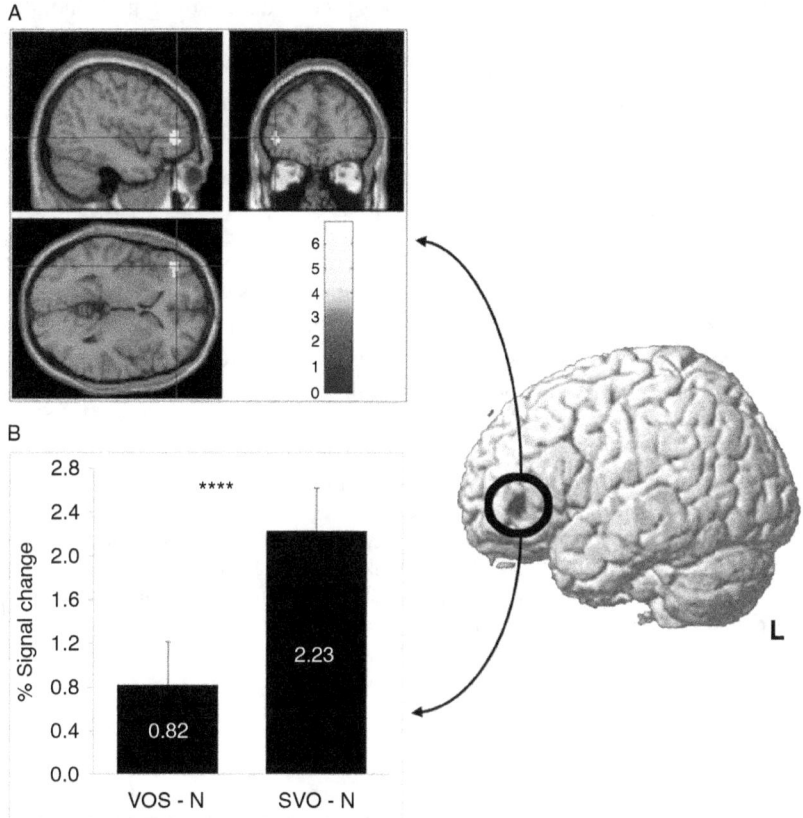

Figure 4.7 Brain regions more activated for SVO than VOS. (Adapted from Koizumi and Kim 2016.)

A direct comparison of the SVO and VOS data showed that cortical activation in the left IFG was significantly higher in the SVO condition than in the VOS condition (Figure 4.7). There was no significant activation in the reverse comparison. Relative to the VOS condition, the SVO condition elicited activation in a region in the left IFG close to the border with the left middle frontal gyrus. Activation in this area has been reported for non-canonical (OS) word order against canonical (SO) word order in previous studies in English as well (Caplan et al. 2000; Rogalsky, Matchin, and Hickok 2008; Waters et al. 2003; see Walenski et al. 2019 for a review). Thus, the higher cortical activation of the SVO condition in Kaqchikel clearly shows that it is the grammatical features of individual languages, not universal human cognitive features, that primarily modulate brain activations and determine sentence processing load, which agrees with the Individual Grammar View's prediction. On the other hand, the Universal Cognition View's prediction that SO word orders should be easier to process than OS word orders regardless of the basic word order of any individual language is not borne out by these experimental results from Kaqchikel.

4.5 Conclusion

Parallel to the results of the behavioral experiments reported in the previous chapter, the present fMRI experiment revealed that VOS sentences are easier to process than SVO sentences in Kaqchikel. This fact is consistent with the hypothesis that the syntactically basic word order in each language is the easiest to process among the grammatically possible word orders in that language.

NOTES

1. The left anterior temporal lobe has also been implicated in basic sentence composition (Brennan et al. 2012; Brennan and Pylkkänen 2012, 2017).
2. This section is based on Koizumi and Kim (2016), which is licensed under a Creative Commons Attribution 4.0 International License.

5 Word Order Preference in Sentence Comprehension III: ERP Studies without Context

The studies on the processing of Kaqchikel sentences reported in the previous two chapters found that semantically plausible sentences in the VOS order were processed faster and associated with less cortical activations than those in the SVO or VSO order. This suggests that VOS, an OS order, is preferred to SVO and VSO, both SO orders, in Kaqchikel sentence comprehension. Based on these results, we concluded that SO Preference in Sentence Comprehension may not be universal.

A remaining question has to do with the time course of sentence processing. These experiments measured reaction times and brain activations when understanding sentences, and although these data reflect the processing load of a sentence as a whole, they convey little information about the time course of sentence processing. Based on this, we cannot determine whether processing load increased in the expected sentence regions at the expected times. In order to overcome this difficulty, we recorded event-related potentials (ERPs) while Kaqchikel speakers listened to sentences with different word orders, which enabled us to investigate the time course of parsing. This experiment (presented in Section 5.2) employed a sentence–picture matching task in which a Kaqchikel sentence was aurally presented through a headset, followed by a picture presented in the center of a computer screen in front of the participant. The participant was to judge whether the meaning of the sentence was congruent with the content of the picture.

5.1 Previous ERP Studies on Word Order Processing

As mentioned in Section 4.2, a late positive component of ERPs called P600 is related to processing difficulties primarily due to syntactic complexity. Consider the examples in (1). The embedded clause in (1b) is initiated with the interrogative pronoun *who*, which has been moved from the object position of the embedded verb *imitated*, creating a filler-gap dependency that does not exist in (1a).

(1) a. Emily wondered whether the performer in the concert had imitated a pop star for the audience's amusement.

b. Emily wondered who the performer in the concert had imitated for the audience's amusement.

In a seminal study, Kaan et al. (2000) observed that, compared with (1a), (1b) elicited a P600 at the embedded verb (*imitated*), which, being transitive, is a good indication of the presence of an upcoming gap position associated with the filler *who*. This P600 can be interpreted as a reflection of the increased cognitive load incurred by the additional processes necessary to integrate the filler into the gap position.

Similar late positive effects have been observed in flexible word order languages for sentences with an OS word order relative to parallel sentences with an SO word order (Erdocia et al. 2009 for Basque; Matzke et al. 2002 and Rösler et al. 1998 for German; Hagiwara et al. 2007, Ueno and Kluender 2003, and Yano and Koizumi 2018 for Japanese). As a concrete example, consider the ERP study by Ueno and Kluender (2003), which compared canonical SOV sentences like (2a) and non-canonical OSV sentences like (2b) in Japanese.

(2) Ano jimotono shinbun ni yoruto ...
the local newspaper to according ...

a. S adv OV:
sono inochishirazuno bokenka ga toto sore o
the reckless adventurer NOM finally that ACC
mitsuketa-ndesu-ka.
discovered-POL-Q
"According to the local newspaper, did the reckless adventurer finally discover that?"

b. OS adv V:
sore o$_i$ sono inochishirazuno bokenka ga toto ___$_i$
that ACC the reckless adventurer NOM finally
mitsuketa-ndesu-ka.
discovered POL-Q

Ueno and Kluender found a P600 effect at the subject and the pre-gap adverb position in (2b) relative to (2a), interpreting these results by assuming that the parser needed to syntactically integrate the scrambled object with its original position, which was reflected in the P600 effects. The successive P600 effects may be due to a temporal ambiguity of the original position of the filler. If the parser actively attempts to fill a gap (Active Filler Strategy; Frazier and Clifton 1989), it should perform a gap-filling parsing at the subject first and do so again at the adverb after detecting a final gap position.

5.2 Identifying Gap Positions

We investigated the time course of the processing of Kaqchikel sentences with alternative word orders, paying particular attention to P600.[1]

5.2.1 Methods

Sixteen native speakers of Kaqchikel participated in the experiment. All participants were classified as right-handed based on the Edinburgh Handedness Inventory (Oldfield 1971) and all of them had normal or corrected-to-normal vision. None of the participants had a history of neurological disorders.

A sentence–picture matching task was employed in this experiment. In this task, a Kaqchikel sentence was first presented aurally through a headset. While listening to a sentence, participants were asked to gaze at the fixation presented in the center of a monitor and not to blink or move while an electroencephalogram (EEG) was recorded. After the sentence was heard, a picture was presented in the center of the screen, either matching the event described by the preceding sentence or not. Upon seeing the picture, the participants were asked to judge whether the picture was congruent with the sentence and then to press a YES or NO button to record their judgment (Figure 5.1).

The target sentences used in this experiment were all transitive, with thematically reversible agents and patients. They were arranged into four word orders: VOS, VSO, SVO, and OVS. Recall that these four word orders are associated with different syntactic structures in Kaqchikel, as shown in (3).

(3) Order   Schematic syntactic structure
     VOS   [VOS]
     VSO   [[V gap$_i$ S] O$_i$]
     SVO   [S$_i$ [VO gap$_i$]]
     OVS   [O$_i$ [V gap$_i$ S]]

In constructing the target sentences, the following six verbs, commonly used in Kaqchikel, were employed: *ch'äy* "hit," *jik'* "pull," *nïm* "push," *oyoj* "call," *pixab* "bless," and *xib'ik* "surprise." The agents and patients were familiar color

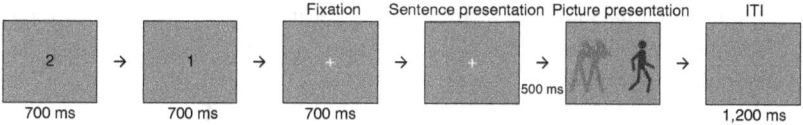

Figure 5.1 Design of the task used in the experiment.
(Adapted from Yano, Yasunaga, and Koizumi 2017 with permission.)

terms describable in Kaqchikel: *käq* "red," *xar* "blue," *säq* "white," and *q'ëq* "black." Either the subject or the object of each sentence was pluralized so that they were morpho-syntactically disambiguated by the agreement marking of the verb. Half of the sentences contained a singular subject and plural object, and the other half contained a plural subject and singular object. Some examples are shown in (4).

(4) a. X-Ø-k-oyoj ri xar ri taq käq. [VOS]
CP-ABS3sg-ERG3pl-call DET blue DET PM red
"The reds called the blue."

b. X-Ø-k-oyoj ri taq käq ri xar. [VSO]
CP-ABS3sg-ERG3pl-call DET PM red DET blue

c. Ri taq käq x-Ø-k-oyoj ri xar. [SVO]
DET PM red CP-ABS3sg-ERG3pl-call DET blue

d. Ri xar x-Ø-k-oyoj ri taq käq. [OVS]
DET blue CP-ABS3sg-ERG3pl-call DET PM red

The sentences were recorded by a male native speaker of Kaqchikel. After the editing, all the test items were judged to be natural in terms of prosody by our native Kaqchikel consultants. There was no significant difference between the word orders in terms of time between the onset and offset of the sentence. The stimulus onset asynchrony (SOA) between the first and second phrases (i.e., the duration of Region 1) and the SOA between the second and third phrases (i.e., the duration of Region 2) were greater than 900 ms in all four conditions. Thus, it can be safely assumed that EEG signals up to approximately 900 ms after the onset of each phrase were not affected by the input of the subsequent phrase. Phrases directly compared with each other were comparable and not significantly different in duration. In particular, there was no main effect of the word order of the four conditions on the duration of the third region.

A total of 192 sentences with four word orders (forty-eight items per condition) and corresponding pictures were used. In half of the trials the sentences were congruent with the pictures, and in the other half they were not. The incongruent pictures depicted an event with a different agent (e.g., *The blacks called the blue*), a different patient (e.g., *The reds called the black*), the agent and patient reversed (e.g., *The blue called the reds*), or the incorrect action (e.g., *The reds pushed the blue*). The stimuli were presented in a random order to the participants such that they could not anticipate correct responses during the auditory presentation.

The EEG for the sentences was recorded from seventeen Ag-AgCl electrodes located at Fz, Cz, Pz, F7, F8, F3, F4, T7, T8, C3, C4, P7, P8, P3, P4, O1, and O2, according to the International 10–20 system (Jasper 1958) (Figure 5.2).

5.2 Identifying Gap Positions

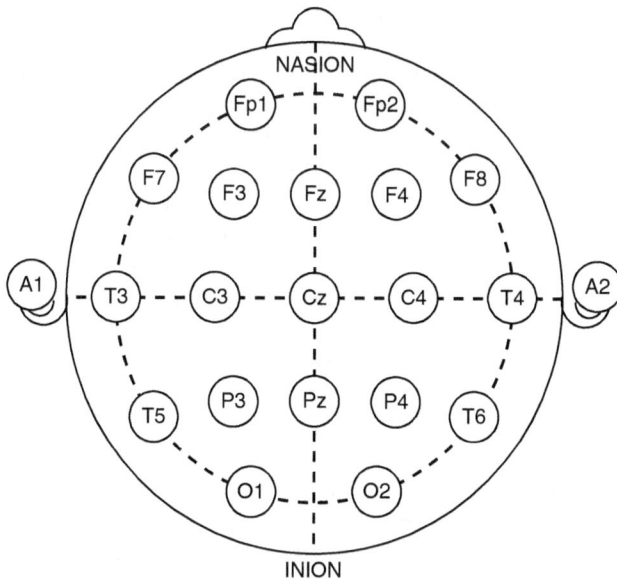

Figure 5.2 Electrode locations of the International 10–20 system for EEG recording (downloaded from Wikimedia Commons, May 16, 2022). The letters F, T, C, P, and O stand for the frontal, temporal, central, parietal, and occipital array, respectively. A and Fp identify the earlobes and frontal polar sites, respectively. Even numbers (2, 4, 6, 8) refer to electrode positions on the right hemisphere, and odd numbers (1, 3, 5, 7) refer to those on the left hemisphere.

The linked earlobe served as a reference. Readers are referred to Yano, Yasunaga, and Koizumi (2017) for a detailed explanation of electrophysiological data analysis.

5.2.2 Predictions

The P600 effect, a late positive ERP component, was used to examine processing loads. It has been observed that the P600 is elicited by the filler-gap integration cost, distributed over the scalp with a posterior focus. This effect is robust and is often observed across types of difficulty with processing loads against dependency formation (Kaan et al. 2000), types of languages (Yang, Charles, and Liu 2010 for Chinese; Hagoort and Brown 2000 for Dutch; Hagiwara et al. 2007 for Japanese), and various methodological factors, such as modality of the stimulus (i.e., visual or auditory). A P600 effect is also observed for syntactically anomalous sentences (e.g., *The hungry guests helped himself to the food*; Osterhout and

Holcomb 1992; Osterhout and Mobley 1995), thematically violated sentences (e.g., *For breakfast the eggs would only eat toast and jam*; Kuperberg et al. 2003), and picture–sentence mismatches (e.g., *The triangle stands in front of the square*, after a picture of a triangle behind a square; Vissers et al. 2008) (see Bornkessel-Schlesewsky and Schlesewsky 2009b for a more general review). However, only grammatical sentences were used and analyzed in the present study. In addition, although grammatically non-preferred continuation (i.e., a garden-path sentence) also elicits a P600 effect, our experimental sentences did not include such continuation, requiring a revision of the initial phrasing (e.g., *The man is painting the house and the garage is already finished*; Kaan and Swaab 2003a, 2003b). Therefore, the P600 effect observed in the present experiment is considered to only reflect an increased syntactic processing cost due to a gap-filling process.

The sets of words used for S and O were identical across the four conditions so that the ERPs elicited by them could be directly compared. On the other hand, the words for V were different from those for S and O in a number of relevant respects, including meaning, grammatical category, production frequency, and the number of phonemes and morphemes. As these factors affect the distribution and amplitudes of ERPs (e.g., Bornkessel-Schlesewsky and Schlesewsky 2009b), ERPs elicited by S or O were not compared with those elicited by V. In summary, the following comparisons were of interest: VOS versus SVO in the third phrase, VSO versus VOS in the second and third phrases, and SVO versus OVS in the second and third phrases.

According to the Individual Grammar View (IGV), syntactic complexities matter in sentence processing. If SVO involves a filler-gap dependency in Kaqchikel, as schematically shown in (3) above, we would predict P600 to be elicited in the third phrase, where the parser is supposed to associate the dislocated S with the original gap position in comparison to VOS. For the same reason, VSO should also elicit a P600 effect compared to VOS in the third phrase, reflecting the increased cost of integrating an O with the gap site. As for the comparison between SVO and OVS, the first region should not differ because the participants would not have been able to determine whether the first NP is S or O before receiving agreement information in the second phrase. In the second phrase of the OVS sentence, the parser is expected to associate the O with the gap following V, which is not the case in the SVO sentence. Thus, OVS would show a greater P600 amplitude than SVO. In the third region, however, SVO would elicit a P600 effect compared to OVS because the parser would encounter the gap site at this region. These predictions of the IGV are summarized in (5).

5.2 Identifying Gap Positions

(5) Predictions of the Individual Grammar View

    a. SV**O** vs. VO**S**

$$S_i \quad V \quad [O \; \_\_{}_i \quad \Leftarrow P600$$
$$V \quad O \quad S\,]$$

    b. VS**O** vs. VO**S**

$$V \; \_\_{}_i \; S \quad [O_i \quad \Leftarrow P600$$
$$V \quad\quad O \quad S\,]$$

    c. S**V**O vs. O**V**S

$$S_i \; [V \quad\quad\;]O \; \_\_{}_i \quad$$
$$O \; [V \; \_\_{}_i]S \quad \Leftarrow P600$$

    d. SV**O** vs. OV**S**

$$S_i \quad V \quad [O \; \_\_{}_i \quad \Leftarrow P600$$
$$O_i \quad V \; \_\_{}_i \; S\,]$$

The Universal Cognition View (UCV), however, would predict that VOS and OVS should induce an increased processing load compared to SVO or VSO, as summarized in (6).

(6) Predictions of the Universal Cognition View

    {VOS, OVS} <= P600
    {VSO, SVO}

5.2.3 Results and Discussion

*5.2.3.1 SV**O** versus VO**S*** Figure 5.3 shows the grand average ERPs in the third phrase of the SVO and VOS conditions (i.e., the O of SVO and the S of VOS). Note that negativity is plotted upward, following the convention in this field. A visual inspection suggested that the ERPs of SV**O** showed a greater positivity than those of VO**S**. This was confirmed by statistical analyses. SV**O** elicited a significantly greater positivity compared to the syntactically basic word order, VO**S**, reflecting the increased syntactic processing cost at the third region. This result is consistent with the (5a) prediction of the IGV. Furthermore, it supports the syntactic analysis shown in (3), according to which there is a gap associated with the subject after the object in SVO: [S_i [VO gap$_i$]].

One may suggest that these positivities appeared so early in the third phrase that they did not reflect filler-gap integration processes, which have been assumed to be

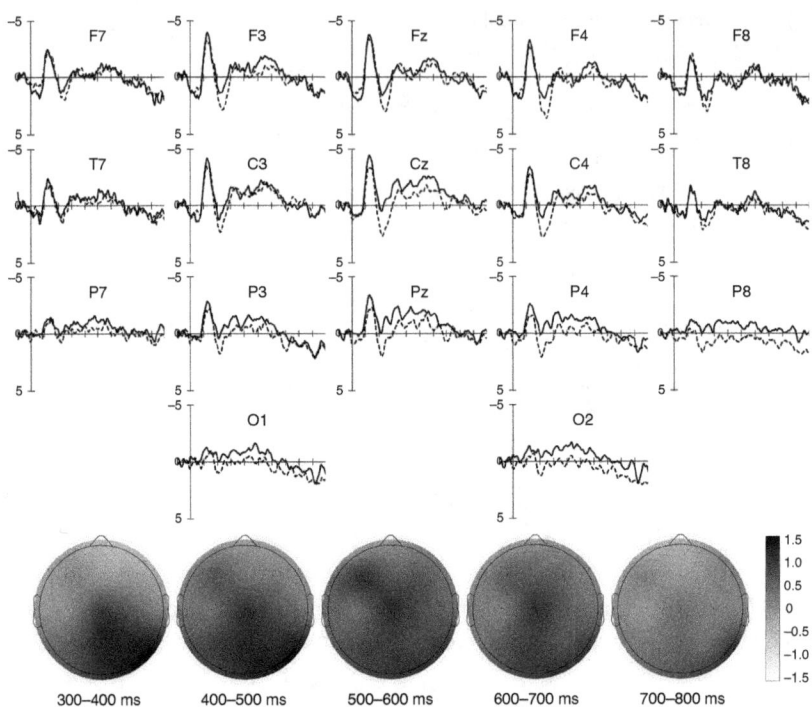

Figure 5.3 The grand average ERPs for the third phrase of SVO and VOS (i.e., the O of SVO and the S of VOS). The dotted line indicates the SVO condition, and the solid line indicates the VOS condition. The X-axis represents time, with marks representing 100 ms. The Y-axis represents voltage, ranging from –5 to 5 μV. Negativity is plotted upward. The topographical voltage maps represent the mean of the difference calculated as SVO minus VOS for every 100 ms from 300 to 800 ms.
(Adapted from Yano, Yasunaga, and Koizumi 2017 with permission.)

performed in the P600 time window (500–1,000 ms). Accordingly, we also analyzed ERPs time-locked to the onset of the first phrase to assess the ERP difference in the second phrase of VOS and SVO even though these words were categorically different (i.e., the O of VOS and the V of SVO). Statistical analyses revealed a significant main effect of word order due to a greater positivity for the V of SVO than the O of VOS. This suggests that the late posterior positivity for SVO appeared at the second phrase, which increased in amplitude at the third phrase, which in turn is why the positivities appeared so early at the third phrase. In other words, the parser was already aware of the presence of a filler-gap dependency at the second phrase of SVO, which is reasonable given that the syntactically

5.2 Identifying Gap Positions

basic word order of Kaqchikel is VOS and that agreement morphemes cross-referencing S and O are included in V.

5.2.3.2 VSO versus VOS In the comparison of VSO and VOS, the effects of interest were not observed in the second phrase in any array. Figure 5.4 shows the grand average ERPs in the third phrase of the VSO and VOS conditions (i.e., the O of VSO and the S of VOS). VSO elicited a greater posterior positivity than VOS, which shows that VSO sentences were harder to process than VOS sentences. This result is consistent with the IGV because in VSO sentences, the parser encountered at the third region a filler that had to be associated with the gap position (i.e., [[V gap$_i$ S] O$_i$]), and gap-filling processing incurred higher cognitive load per the prediction in (5b).

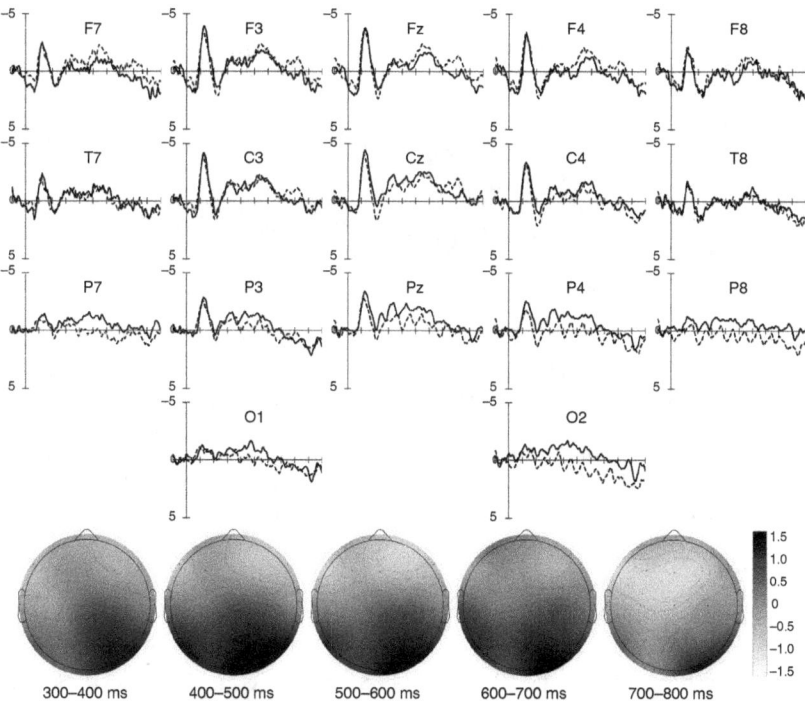

Figure 5.4 The grand average ERPs for the third phrase of VSO and VOS. The dotted line indicates the VSO condition, and the solid line indicates the VOS condition. The X-axis represents time, with marks representing 100 ms. The Y-axis represents voltage, ranging from −5 to 5 µV. Negativity is plotted upward. The topographical voltage maps represent the mean of the difference calculated as VSO minus VOS for every 100 ms from 300 to 800 ms. (Adapted from Yano, Yasunaga, and Koizumi 2017 with permission.)

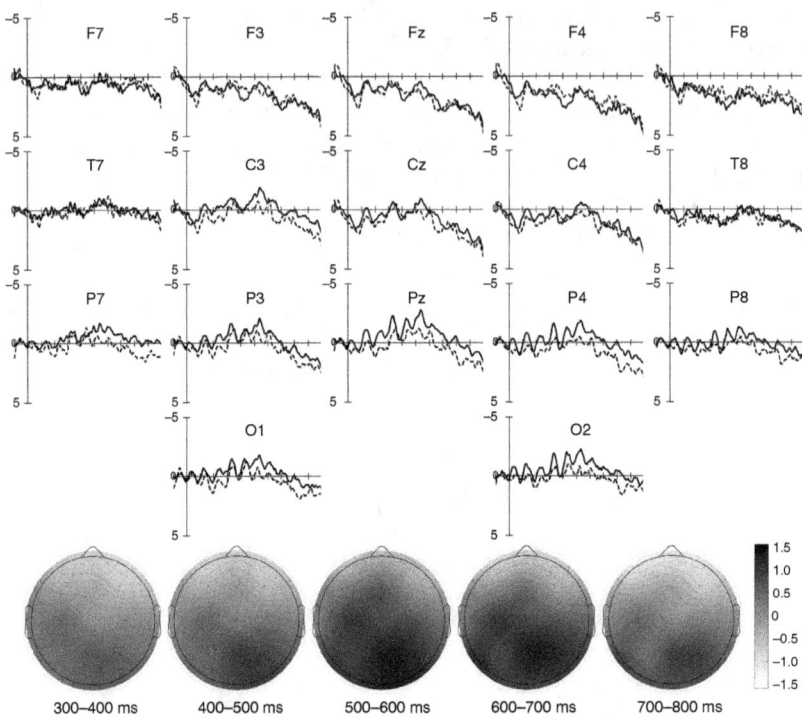

Figure 5.5 The grand average ERPs for the second phrase of OVS and SVO. The solid line indicates the SVO condition, and the dotted line indicates the OVS condition. The X-axis represents time, with marks representing 100 ms. The Y-axis represents voltage, ranging from −5 to 5 μV. Negativity is plotted upward. The topographical voltage maps represent the mean of the difference calculated as OVS minus SVO for every 100 ms from 300 to 800 ms.
(Adapted from Yano, Yasunaga, and Koizumi 2017 with permission.)

5.2.3.3 *SVO versus OVS*

Figures 5.5 and 5.6 show the grand average ERPs in the second and third phrase, respectively, of the SVO and OVS conditions. In the second phrase, OVS elicited a higher posterior positivity than SVO, probably reflecting the cost of the processes that associate O with its gap after V per the prediction in (5c): [O_i [V gap_i S]]. In the third phrase, in contrast, SVO elicited a greater frontal positivity than OVS. This is most likely due to the gap-filling processing necessary for the subject, per the prediction in (5d): [S_i [VO gap_i]].

5.3 Conclusion

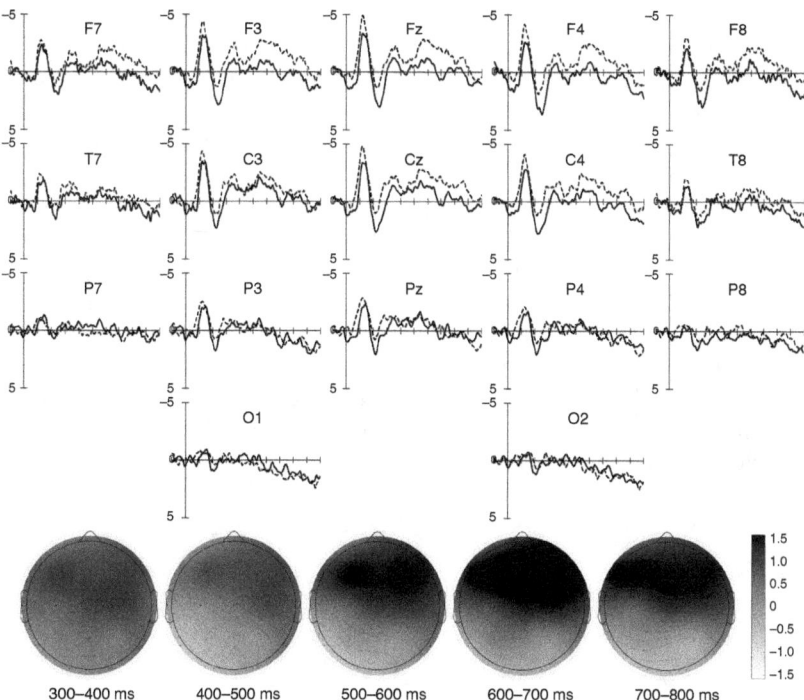

Figure 5.6 The grand average ERPs for the third phrase of SVO and OVS. The solid line indicates the SVO condition, and the dotted line indicates the OVS condition. The X-axis represents time, with marks representing 100 ms. The Y-axis represents voltage, ranging from −5 to 5 μV. Negativity is plotted upward. The topographical voltage maps represent the mean of the difference calculated as SVO minus OVS for every 100 ms from 300 to 800 ms. (Adapted from Yano, Yasunaga, and Koizumi 2017 with permission.)

5.3 Conclusion

To recapitulate, through the investigation of whether the syntactically canonical VOS word order in Kaqchikel is preferred to other grammatically available word orders during sentence comprehension, the present experiment explored the relation between syntactic complexity and processing load. Our predictions were borne out by the results of the ERP experiment. First, SVO was found to elicit a greater positivity than VOS in the second and third phrases. VSO elicited a similar posterior positivity relative to VOS in the third phrase. OVS showed a greater positive shift than SVO in the second phrase, whereas the opposite pattern was observed in the third phrase, as expected. This range of properties follows naturally from the combination of (i) what we have called the Individual Grammar View and (ii) the syntactic structures of Kaqchikel transitive sentences given in (3) above. Most importantly, they clearly indicate that VOS is the easiest word order to process among the grammatically possible word orders, which is in line with our previous findings, presented in Chapters 3 and 4. In other words, a VOS preference was observed in Kaqchikel during sentence comprehension, which provides empirical support for the IGV. If the SO preference that has been observed in the sentence comprehension of many languages is attributable to universal aspects of human cognition independent of particular grammars, as posited by the UCV, a P600 effect would have appeared in the VOS sentences, which was not the case. Therefore, the often observed SO preference in the comprehension of sentences in SO languages cannot be fully grounded in the universal properties of human cognition; rather, processing loads are closely tied to syntactic complexities, reflecting filler-gap integration processes as indexed by P600 effects.

NOTE

1. This section is based on Yano, Yasunaga, and Koizumi (2017).

6 Word Order Preference in Sentence Comprehension IV: ERP Studies with Context

A weakness of the Kaqchikel studies reported in the previous chapters concerns contextual effects. As mentioned in Chapter 2, in Kaqchikel, the VOS order can be felicitously used in a wide range of contexts, including the absence of any substantial context, whereas SVO is frequently used in contexts where the subject is a topic (Ajsivinac Sian et al. 2004: 178–180; García Matzar and Rodríguez Guaján 1997: 334; Tichoc Cumes et al. 2000: 219–223). It is therefore likely that the higher processing load of the SVO word order observed in the studies reported in Chapters 3, 4, and 5 is at least partially attributable to the lack of felicitous contexts; SVO sentences might be easier to process in the appropriate context. In other words, it is not yet clear to what extent the OS preference in Kaqchikel found in the previous studies is due to syntactic rather than contextual factors. We addressed this question using a picture–sentence matching task rather than a sentence–picture matching task. There is good reason to believe that the presentation of a picture before the corresponding sentence provided an appropriate non-verbal context not only for the VOS but also for the SVO word order, as we will see in Chapter 9 through Chapter 11.

6.1 Sentence Comprehension within Context

In this experiment, we examined the time course of Kaqchikel sentence processing with appropriate non-verbal context in the form of a picture describing an event pertaining to the content of an aurally presented sentence.[1]

6.1.1 Methods

Sixteen native speakers of Kaqchikel participated in the experiment. All participants had normal or corrected-to-normal vision and self-reported as being right-handed.

An EEG was recorded while participants engaged in the picture–sentence matching task. In this task, a picture was presented in the center of a computer screen for three seconds and, after the picture disappeared, a Kaqchikel sentence was aurally presented through a headset. After the sentence ended, a question mark appeared in the center of the screen. The participant was instructed to answer, upon seeing the question mark, whether the content of the picture was congruent with the meaning of the sentence by clicking a mouse button to indicate either YES or NO.

The stimulus sentences and pictures used in this experiment were basically the same as those used in Yano, Yasunaga, and Koizumi (2017).

6.1.2 Results

6.1.2.1 SVO versus VOS
Figure 6.1 shows the grand average ERPs in the third phrase of the SVO and VOS conditions. A visual inspection of the ERPs

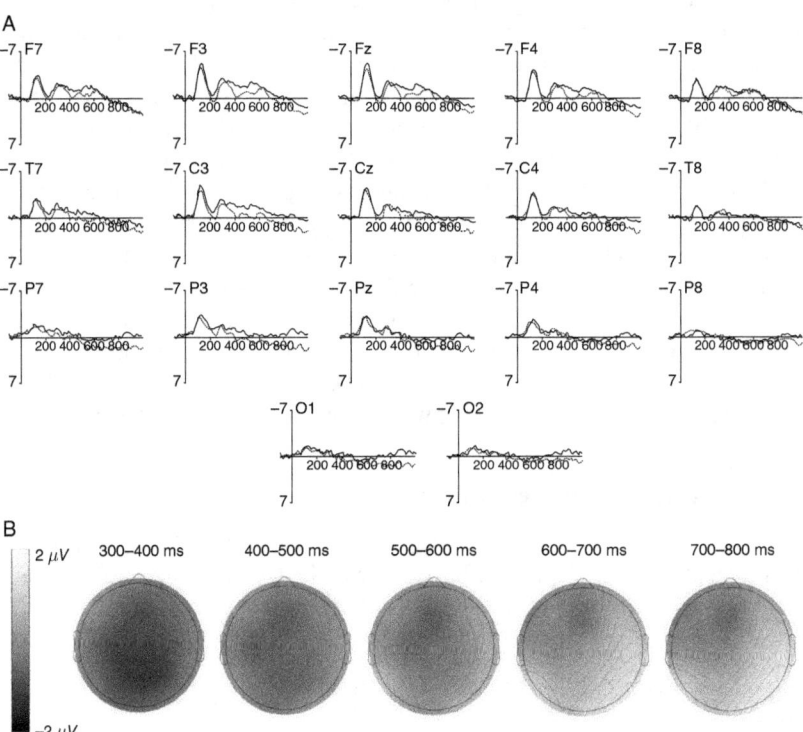

Figure 6.1 Panel A: The grand averaged ERP waveforms for the third region in the SVO (O, dotted lines) and VOS (S, solid lines) word order conditions for all seventeen electrode sites. Negativity is plotted upward. Panel B: Voltage maps for the difference ERPs (SVO – VOS) for every 100 ms between 300 and 800 ms.
(Adapted from Yasunaga et al. 2015.)

6.1 Sentence Comprehension within Context 63

indicated that the O of SVO, as compared to the S of VOS, shifted positively in the time window of 300–800 ms, being distributed mainly in the left parietal domain. This distribution was confirmed by statistical analyses. The results suggest that the O of SVO elicited a long-lasting positivity relative to the S of VOS, even when an appropriate non-verbal context was given for SVO.

6.1.2.2 VSO versus VOS Figure 6.2 shows the results of the comparison of the S of VSO and the O of VOS. The S of VSO elicited positivity at the parietal domain relative to the O of VOS. This is consistent with the prediction that more complex constructions with a filler-gap dependency would elicit a late positive component. Statistical analyses were also conducted for the O of VSO and the S of VOS. The effect of word order was not significant for any of the time windows. We will come back to this in Section 6.2.

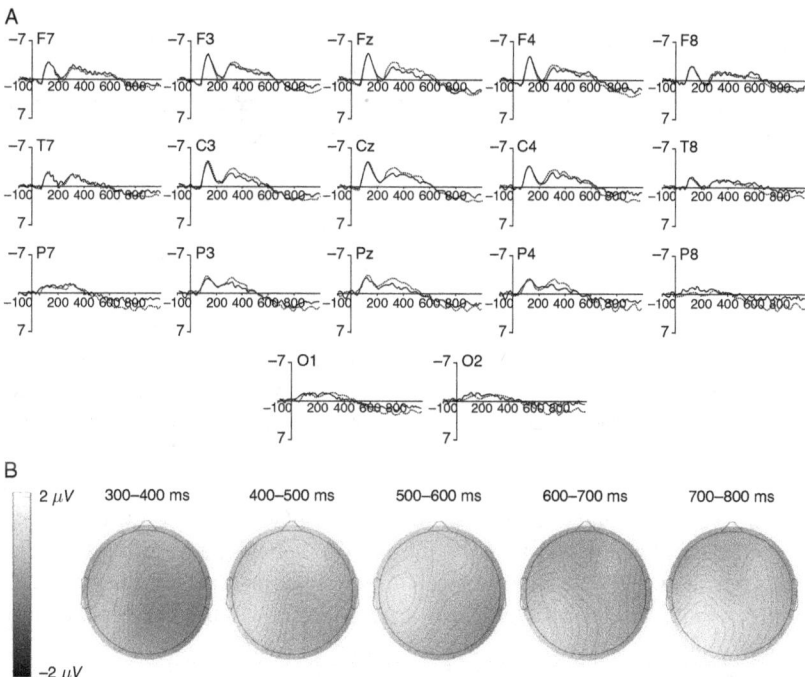

Figure 6.2 Panel A: The grand averaged ERP waveforms for the second region in the VSO (S, dotted lines) and VOS (O, solid lines) word order conditions for all seventeen electrode sites. Negativity is plotted upward. Panel B: The voltage maps of the difference ERPs (VSO – VOS) for every 100 ms between 300 and 800 ms.
(Adapted from Yasunaga et al. 2015.)

6.1.2.3 SVO versus OVS In the second region, the V of OVS elicited a late positivity relative to the V of SVO, consistent with our expectation that the O would be associated with a gap upon encountering the V in the processing of OVS sentences. Finally, a visual inspection indicated that the O of SVO, as compared to the S of OVS, shifted positively in the time window of 500–900 ms, as expected. This contrast (i.e., the main effect of word order), however, did not reach statistical significance, which might be due to a spillover effect from the second region, where the V of OVS elicited a long-lasting positivity still observable at the onset of the third region.

6.2 Discussion

In the two ERP experiments, Yano, Yasunaga, and Koizumi (2017) (reported in Chapter 5) and Yasunaga et al. (2015) (reported in this chapter), we obtained parallel results: the syntactically canonical VOS word order in Kaqchikel incurred the lowest processing cost. In contrast, the SVO word order, even with an appropriate non-verbal context in the form of a picture describing the event, requires additional resources in order to process the dependency between the initial S in the sentence and the corresponding gap after the O.

Notably, however, there are some important differences between the results of Yano, Yasunaga, and Koizumi (2017) and those of Yasunaga et al. (2015) with respect to the timing of P600 in the comparison of VOS and VSO. Yano, Yasunaga, and Koizumi (2017) reported a P600 effect for VSO in the third phrase (i.e., the O), where the parser encountered a filler that had to be associated with the gap position (according to the structure [[V gap$_i$ S] O$_i$]). Yasunaga et al. (2015), in contrast, observed a P600 effect for VSO in the second phrase. Because the picture and auditory stimuli used in these two experiments were the same, this difference pertains to the relative order of the picture and sentence presentation, namely, the availability of context prior to the sentence. In Yano, Yasunaga, and Koizumi (2017), without useful explicit context while listening to a sentence, the participants could not know the lexical item of the filler upon encountering the S of VSO, having to wait for the filler (the O) to associate it with the gap location and confirm semantic compatibility between the filler and the verb. Therefore, the P600 was observed in the third phrase, reflecting the increased gap-filling cost. In a similar vein, the preceding visual context in Yasunaga et al.'s experiment may have encouraged their participants to predict the O of VSO because the picture depicted a transitive event with an agent (S) and a patient (O), allowing the participants to predictively build the syntactic structure of [[V gap$_i$ S] O$_i$] and check semantic compatibility between the filler and the verb to facilitate efficient sentence processing. Accordingly, P600 was elicited in the second phrase, reflecting the predictive gap-filler association process. If this is the case, it suggests that the parser can predictively associate a filler that is unseen but highly predictable with a gap site in the gap-filler dependency as long as there is a non-linguistic context that is useful for identifying the lexical item of the filler (see also Yano, Tateyama, and Sakamoto 2014 for a similar discussion). Alternatively, it is plausible that the picture presentation could trigger an expectation for VOS sentences, although there is no specific prediction for a sentence form without contextual information. If VOS is predicted before encountering S, the second phrase in this case (the S of VSO) would lead to an expectation mismatch, inducing a tentative conflict between the picture and the sentence. To reconcile this conflict, syntactic reanalysis was required, and P600 was elicited in the second phrase in Yasunaga et al.'s experiment. This view may be supported by their observation that the P600 effect for VSO was preceded by an N400 effect enhanced by lexico-semantic surprise.

6.3 Conclusion

Through examinations of ERP effects in the processing of Kaqchikel sentences with various word orders, we have seen that the syntactically canonical VOS word order incurs the lowest processing cost. The other word orders require additional resources in order to process the dependency between the shifted argument and the corresponding gap in the sentence. This supports the suggestion that the preference for SO in sentence comprehension may not be universal; rather, the syntactic features of individual languages significantly influence the sentence processing load.[2]

NOTES

1. This section is based on Yasunaga et al. (2015), which is licensed under a Creative Commons Attribution 4.0 International License.
2. Admittedly, a single picture might not be sufficient to provide a suitable context for non-canonical word orders. We will come back to this issue in Chapter 14. See Imamura, Sato, and Koizumi (2016), Koizumi and Imamura (2016), and Yano and Koizumi (2018, 2021) for relevant discussion.

7 Basic Word Order in Language and Natural Order of Thought

We have seen in the previous chapters that the word order preference in sentence comprehension is largely attributable to the grammatical factors of individual languages, reflecting the flexible nature of the human mind that allows us to acquire languages regardless of their basic word order. Once a person is exposed to a language with a particular basic word order and internalizes it, that word order becomes easiest to process for him/her. For example, for a person who has mastered a VOS language, VOS sentences are easiest to understand. One might infer from this that there is no hard-wired disposition in the human mind toward a specific word order. However, such a conjecture clashes with the fact that a vast majority of the world's languages have one of the SO word orders as their basic word order, rather than the logically possible six word orders being evenly distributed (Dryer 2013; Gell-Mann and Ruhlen 2011; Greenberg 1966; Tomlin 1986). In this and the next chapters, we will address the question of where this preference comes from.

7.1 SO Preference in Basic Word Order

In his seminal work, Greenberg (1966: 77) observed that, "[i]n declarative sentences with nominal subject and object, the dominant order is almost always one in which the subject precedes the object," a generalization known as Greenberg's Universal 1. Parallel to the SO Preference in Sentence Comprehension, we may refer to it as the SO Preference in Basic Word Order.

(1)   SO Preference in Basic Word Order
        A vast majority of the world's languages have one of the SO word orders as their basic word order.

Although the database used as the basis for this proposal only included thirty languages, empirical coverage has been significantly expanded by subsequent studies (e.g., Dryer 2013; Gell-Mann and Ruhlen 2011; Tomlin 1986). Constructing an extensive sample of 1,377 languages, Dryer (2013) observed the distribution shown in Table 7.1, in which the frequencies of each word order are calculated after excluding 189 languages that apparently lacked a dominant

7.1 SO Preference in Basic Word Order

Table 7.1 *Order of subject, object, and verb I*

SO languages		OS languages	
SOV	47.6%	OSV	0.3%
SVO	41.1%	OVS	0.9%
VSO	8.0%	VOS	2.1%
SO total	**96.7%**	**OS total**	**3.3%**

Note: Based on Dryer (2013).

Table 7.2 *Order of subject, object, and verb II*

SO languages		OS languages	
SOV	50.1%	OSV	0.6%
SVO	38.3%	OVS	0.8%
VSO	8.2%	VOS	2.0%
SO total	**96.6%**	**OS total**	**3.4%**

Note: Based on Gell-Mann and Ruhlen (2011).

order. Gell-Mann and Ruhlen (2011), analyzing the distribution of word orders in a sample of 2,135 languages extracted based on a different sampling method, reported a similar pattern (Table 7.2), excluding 125 languages with two competing word orders. Given these data, it is beyond doubt that SO word orders are strongly preferred over OS word orders as a basic word order in human languages.

Kimmelman (2012) further observed that the SO preference in Basic Word Order holds not only in spoken languages, as studied by the researchers above, but also in sign languages. In his sample of twenty-four sign languages, eleven were SVO and eight were SOV. Two had both SVO and SOV as dominant orders, one had SOV and OSV, and the last two had a preference for the Topic-Comment order (see Napoli and Sutton-Spence 2014 for a related review).

It is interesting to note at this point that the distribution of word orders across languages is not uniform even among the SO orders. In both Table 7.1 and Table 7.2, SOV has the highest ratio, followed by SVO, with VSO in a distant third place. This seems to indicate that SOV has some special status, a conjecture that receives support from three different directions. First, as pointed out by Dryer (2013), SOV is not only the most frequent order, but also the most widely distributed across the globe (Figure 7.1). In contrast, the second most frequent order, SVO, predominates in certain areas but is

A. SOV

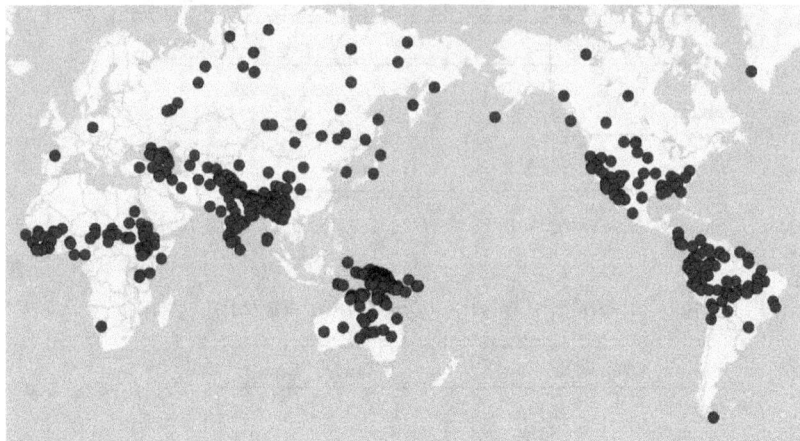

B. SVO

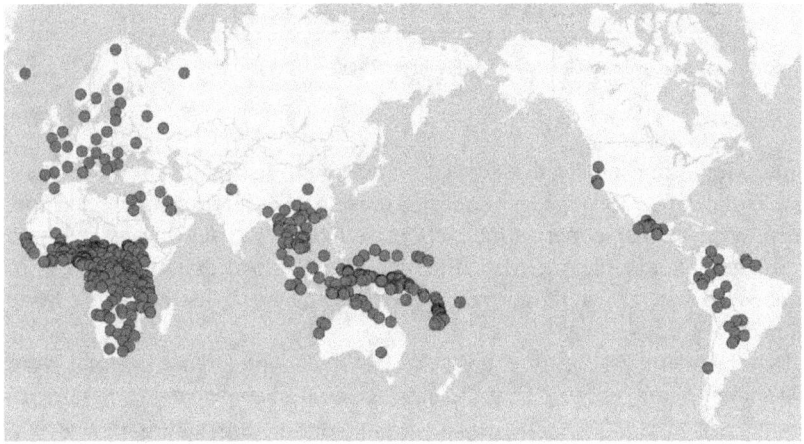

Figure 7.1 The distribution of word order types in the world. Each circle represents a SOV language in (A) and a SVO language in (B).
(Adapted from Dryer 2013. Available online at: http://wals.info/chapter/81 [last accessed August 23, 2022].)

absent in others, notably a part of Eurasia and North America. The other four word orders have an even more limited geographical distribution.

Second, by comparing the distribution of the existing structural types with the putative phylogenetic tree of human languages, Gell-Mann and Ruhlen (2011) concluded that the direction of diachronic word order change has been mostly from SOV to SVO to VSO or VOS, with occasional reversion to SVO,

7.1 SO Preference in Basic Word Order

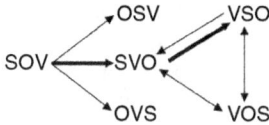

Figure 7.2 Evolution of word order. The bold lines indicate the most frequent changes caused by natural drift without diffusion, and the other lines indicate other possible changes.
(Adapted from Gell-Mann and Ruhlen 2011: 17291 with permission.)

but not to SOV (Figure 7.2). A shift toward SOV does not occur except through language contact. A similar trend in word order change has been observed in sign languages as well. For example, Fischer (1975) points out that American Sign Language has undergone a shift from SOV to SVO.

Gell-Mann and Ruhlen (2011) further note that most of the 125 languages with two common word orders in their database can be considered to be in the process of transitioning from one basic order to another, based on the arrows in Figure 7.2, as shown in (3). The most common combinations are SOV/SVO and SVO/VSO, consistent with the bold arrows in Figure 7.2. The other four combinations in (3) correspond to the thin arrows in Figure 7.2.

(3) Languages with mixed word order (Gell-Mann and Ruhlen 2011: 17292)

SOV/SVO	46
SVO/VSO	24
VSO/VOS	17
SVO/VOS	11
SOV/OVS	9
SOV/OSV	6

This indicates that the ratio of SOV was even higher in the past than it is now. In other words, SOV seems to predominate in the early stages of spoken and signed languages. Indeed, some researchers have argued that the human protolanguage was SOV (Fischer 1975; Gell-Mann and Ruhlen 2011; Givón 1979; Newmeyer 2000).

Finally, the word orders of emerging languages also point to the default status of SOV. In some cases, sign languages emerge in communities to fulfill necessary communicative purposes, such as Nicaraguan Sign Language (Senghas, Coppola, Newport, and Supalla 1997) and "Tzotzil" Sign Language (Haviland 2011). In other cases, deaf children who receive no linguistic input create their own manual communication systems, known in general as home sign (Coppola and Newport 2005; Goldin-Meadow and Mylander 1998; see Goldin-Meadow 2003 for a review). In either case, the signs are consistently aligned in the SOV order (agent–patient–action), even when the surrounding language uses the SVO order (Goldin-Meadow and Feldman 1977; Napoli and Sutton-Spence 2014; Sandler et al. 2005; Senghas et al. 1997). A particularly striking case is Al-Sayyid Bedouin Sign Language, which arose within the last one hundred years in an isolated community with a high incidence of profound prelingual deafness. Within one generation, it assumed a grammatical structure characterized by the SOV order (Sandler et al. 2005). Given that none of its neighboring languages are SOV, the SOV order seems to have emerged spontaneously without any apparent external influence. The emergence of dominant SOV sign languages cross-culturally with minimal or no spoken language contact or exposure indicates that a preference for the SOV order is the most natural and the most basic for human cognitive systems.[1]

Taken together, the above considerations suggest the following scenario of the evolution of word order in human language. The agent–patient–action order is most compatible with the way that human cognitive systems tend to organize event knowledge. For this reason, emerging languages initially have the SOV word order. Some languages subsequently shift to SVO, and possibly further to VSO/VOS. The shifts occur in some areas and/or language families but not in others, accounting for the non-uniform geographic/phylogenetic distribution.

7.2 Natural Order of Thought

As we have seen above, SO orders are strongly preferred to OS orders as the basic word order of each language; furthermore, SOV appears to be the default word order in human language. The question then naturally arises of why this should be the case. In order to address this, Goldin-Meadow et al. (2008) conducted an elicited pantomime (or gesture production) study. They showed short animations depicting transitive events (e.g., a girl twisting a knob, a boy opening a box) to speakers of four languages (Chinese, English, Spanish [all SVO], Turkish [SOV]). The participants were then asked to describe the depicted events using only their hands. In doing so, the speakers of all four languages dominantly used the agent–patient–action order regardless of the basic word order of their language. Goldin-Meadow et al. (2008) interpret this result as suggesting that the agent–patient–action order may reflect a natural sequence for representing events, and that a developing language would initially use this order as a default pattern, yielding SOV.

Goldin-Meadow et al.'s (2008) findings have been replicated and extended in a number of subsequent studies (Futrell et al. 2015; Gibson et al. 2013; Langus and Nespor 2010). Langus and Nespor (2010), for instance, found a preference for the agent–patient–action order in both gesture production and gesture comprehension. Reaction times were shorter for the agent–patient–action order than the agent–action–patient order in their gesture comprehension experiment, in which participants were instructed to watch

7.2 Natural Order of Thought

a gesture clip and decide which of the two drawn vignettes shown matched the clip. These results support the notion that human beings tend to think about transitive events such that they are more efficiently linearized in the agent–patient–action order.[2]

If the agent–patient–action order reflects the most natural order of thought, and if emerging languages use this order as the default pattern, yielding the SOV word order, as suggested by Goldin-Meadow et al. (2008), any subsequent word order change from the initial SOV must be caused by other factors. What these factors are and why SVO is such a common shift are key questions that have two major proposed explanations: (i) the noisy channel hypothesis by Gibson et al. (2013), and (ii) the role conflict hypothesis by Hall, Mayberry, and Ferreira (2013).

Gibson et al. (2013) propose that the shift from SOV to SVO occurs in order to maximize meaning recoverability in a noisy communicative situation, which is known as the noisy channel hypothesis. Consider the SOV sentence in (3a), *the girl the boy kicks*. If either noun in (3a) is lost because of noise as shown in (3b)/(3c), the thematic role of the remaining noun phrase is ambiguous: the single NP could be either an agent or a patient. However, if the SVO word order is used instead, as in (4a), a deletion will not change the interpretation of the remaining NP. *The girl kicks* will be understood by the listener to convey an event of "the girl kicking someone or something," and *kicks the boy* will be interpreted as "someone kicking the boy."

(3) SOV
   a. the girl the boy kicks
   b. the girl kicks
   c. the boy kicks

(4) SVO
   a. the girl kicks the boy
   b. the girl kicks
   c. kicks the boy

Thus, if SVO is employed rather than SOV, the positions of the NPs with respect to the verb can provide a clue about whether a given noun is the subject or the object. In other words, SVO is more robust than SOV in a noisy circumstance. According to Gibson et al. (2013), this is the reason for the shift from SOV to SVO.

To support this proposal, Gibson et al. (2013) present the results of their gesture production experiment, in which participants were asked to gesture events presented as animations. In half of the crucial vignettes, as in Goldin-Meadow et al.'s (2008) experiment, the patient was an inanimate entity, i.e., the events were semantically non-reversible, such as "the girl kicking the ball." In this condition, the word order should have little effect on how easily the meaning can be recovered in the presence of noise; in this example, a ball cannot kick a girl. In the other half of the vignettes, which is the crucial condition added by Gibson et al., the patient was a human. With semantically reversible events, the word order matters, according to the noisy channel hypothesis. The results show that most produced gestures had the agent–patient–action order in the inanimate patient condition, parallel to what had been reported in Goldin-Meadow et al. (2008) and others. Critically, however, in the human patient condition, a majority of vignettes were described by gestures consistent with the agent–action–patient order (e.g., "the girl kicks the boy"). In other words, the agent–patient–action order decreased in frequency and the agent–action–patient order increased when describing events where the agent and patient were both animate (e.g., a *girl* pushes a *boy*) and could be reversed to create another semantically valid event (e.g., a *boy* pushes a *girl*). Note that, according to Gibson et al., the noisy channel hypothesis applies even if there is only one individual involved, encoding an event meaning for himself/herself. That is, the individual will choose a representation that maximizes meaning recoverability regardless of whether the information needs to be transmitted to another person.

In addition to providing gesture production data, Gibson et al. (2013) mention four cross-linguistic typological tendencies that can be explained by their noisy channel hypothesis. (1) Case marking is more frequently used in SOV languages than SVO languages. According to Dryer (2002), for example, 72 percent of SOV languages (181 of 253) are case-marked, whereas only 14 percent of SVO languages are (26 of 190). This is expected from the noisy channel hypothesis because case marking can mitigate the confusability of utterances like (3b)/(3c) in SOV languages, thereby reducing the motivation to shift to SVO. (2) In many languages with so-called differential object marking, only animate objects are case-marked. Again, case marking may contribute to disambiguating reversible sentences. (3) In many flexible word order languages, SVO is preferred in reversible constructions when case marking does not disambiguate semantic roles. (4) Non-SVO languages (e.g., SOV, VSO) tend to have greater word order flexibility because they must have means other than word order to unambiguously convey the meaning of reversible sentences.

Another account of the relative prevalence of SVO is the role conflict hypothesis, proposed in Hall, Mayberry, and Ferreira (2013), according to which using the agent–patient–action order for reversible events is likely to entail a role conflict between patient and action. Suppose, for example, that a participant is describing via gestures a reversible event (e.g., a man lifting a woman) using the agent–patient–action order. He or she would first adopt the role of the agent (e.g., flexing muscles), and then the patient (e.g., indicating long hair). The participant is now ready to produce the action, which requires him or her to be in the agent role. "If the participant were to produce an action gesture without first doing something to switch back into the agent role, it may 'feel' to him or her as if it is the patient and not the agent that is carrying out the action" (Hall, Mayberry, and Ferreira 2013: 7). That is, when a human patient is followed by an action, there is a risk of the patient being misinterpreted as an agent. The role conflict hypothesis suggests that patient–action order is avoided for this reason for reversible events.

As empirical evidence in support of the role conflict hypothesis and against the noisy channel hypothesis, Hall, Mayberry, and Ferreira (2013) present the results of their gesture production experiment with English speakers, in which the frequency of both the agent–action–patient order and the patient–agent–action order were higher in the reversible condition than in the non-reversible condition. The increased use of the patient–agent–action order for reversible events is compatible with the role conflict hypothesis because this order helps avoid a possible confusion that would arise from putting the patient immediately before the action. The noisy channel hypothesis, in contrast, would wrongly predict that the patient–agent–action order should be avoided in the reversible condition because, with both the agent and patient on the same side of the action, this order should be as susceptible to noise as the agent–patient–action order (see also Hall et al. 2015).

7.3   Conclusion

To summarize, gesture production studies such as those conducted by Goldin-Meadow et al. (2008), Gibson et al. (2013), and Hall, Mayberry, and Ferreira (2013), have demonstrated that agent-before-patient orders are preferred to patient-before-agent orders in event representations. In particular, the agent–patient–action order seems to be most compatible with human thought, accounting for the default status of the SOV word order in languages. However, when representing a reversible event, the agent–action–patient order is more likely to be employed, thereby changing the word order from SOV to SVO (Figure 7.3). This is consistent with both the noisy channel hypothesis and the role conflict hypothesis. Of the other two attested historical

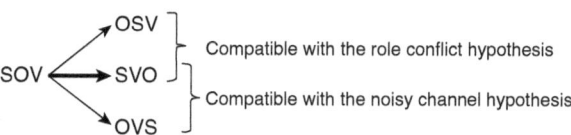

Figure 7.3 Historical word order changes from SOV and the two competing hypotheses.

word order changes from SOV, the shift to OSV is compatible with the role conflict hypothesis, but not with the noisy channel hypothesis, while the shift to OVS is congruent with the noisy channel hypothesis, but not with the role conflict hypothesis. This may be because these three orders are common shifts from the initial SOV, of which SVO is most preferred.

NOTES

1. Primarily based on a consideration of creole languages, such as the rapid convergence on SVO when a pidgin (a contact language that results when speakers of different languages are forced to communicate) becomes a creole (a stable natural language developed from a pidgin through acquisition by children as a native language), Bickerton (1981) argues that the original word order of human language must be SVO. However, the predominance of SVO among creole languages may be attributed partly to the fact that most creole languages are derived from SVO languages (Gell-Mann and Ruhlen 2011), and partly to the strong tendency of diachronic word order shift from SOV to SVO in the process of creolization from pidgin (Hall, Mayberry, and Ferreira 2013).
2. Although it is possible that a mental event representation is static and does not have precedence relations between its components, it is certain that the processes of creating or accessing the representation proceed incrementally, spanning a certain period of time. Thus, we assume, in accordance with Slobin (1996), that the relations of thinking, if not thought, have internal precedence. See also Note 2 of Chapter 1.

8 Constituent Order Preference in Event Representation

As we have seen in Chapter 7, previous studies on gesture production have claimed that the agent-before-patient order is universally preferred when humans apprehend the world and describe it non-linguistically, although the position of the action may be affected by factors such as the animacy of the patient. Let us call this generalization the Agent–Patient Preference in Thought.

(1) Agent–Patient Preference in Thought:
In non-verbal event representation, agent–patient orders are more frequently employed than patient–agent orders.

In this chapter, we will consider possible origins of this preference.

8.1 Competing Hypotheses

Previous studies on gesture production only assessed speakers of languages in which the subject precedes the object in the basic word order (SVO in English, Chinese, and Spanish and SOV in Turkish in Goldin-Meadow et al. 2008, SVO in Italian in Langus and Nespor 2010, SOV in Japanese and Korean in Gibson et al. 2013, VSO in Irish and Tagalog in Futrell et al. 2015). Evidence from speakers of SO languages alone is not sufficient to conclude that humans universally perceive the world in the agent–patient order.

We can think of two possible sources of the Agent–Patient Preference in Thought observed in the previous studies, given in (2) and (3).

(2) Universal Cognition View [Order of Thought]
Constituent order preference in non-verbal event representation is largely attributable to grammar-independent human cognitive features that are universal.

(3) Individual Grammar View [Order of Thought]
Constituent order preference in non-verbal event representation is largely attributable to the grammatical factors of one's language.

The basic idea behind the Universal Cognition View [Order of Thought] (hereafter, UCV) is that, because all human beings share similar physiological or anatomical characteristics, they perceive the surrounding information in similar ways, primarily through the five senses of vision, hearing, smell, taste, and touch. This is what is presupposed in most previous studies, including Goldin-Meadow et al. (2008), Gibson et al. (2013), and Hall, Mayberry, and Ferreira (2013).

The basic argument for the Individual Grammar View [Order of Thought] (hereafter, IGV) is that the language people use plays an influential role in their cognitive systems, working below the level of conscious thought to modulate or shape how they perceive the world. Because both producing and comprehending language involve the linearization of words associated with specific meanings or thoughts (Bock and Loebell 1990; Bock, Loebell, and Morey 1992, Levelt 1989), it seems reasonable to assume that constant exposure to a particular word order would influence and establish a pattern of thinking or interpreting the world. A well-known version of this idea is Slobin's (1991, 1996, 2003, 2006) "thinking for speaking" hypothesis, which claims that "[i]n the evanescent time frames of constructing utterances in discourse one fits one's thoughts into available linguistic frames. 'Thinking for speaking' involves picking those characteristics of objects and events that (a) fit some conceptualization of the event, and (b) are readily encodable in the language" (Slobin 1996: 76). Similarly, Pederson et al. (1998: 586) state as follows:

Any particular experience might need to be later described, and many are. Accordingly, many experiences must be remembered in such a way as to facilitate this. . . . . That is, the linguistic system is far more than just an AVAILABLE pattern for creating internal representations: to learn to speak a language successfully REQUIRES speakers to develop an appropriate mental representation which is then available for nonlinguistic purposes.

Studies performed only with speakers of SO languages cannot help us disentangle whether the apparent preference for agent–patient sequences is the result of universal cognitive factors (UCV) or the influence of the word order of SO languages (IGV). To achieve this, it is crucial to also examine OS languages, for which the two views have divergent predictions. The UCV predicts that, in non-verbal event representations, agent–patient orders should be more frequently used than patient–agent orders by speakers of OS languages. In contrast, the IGV predicts that patient–agent orders should be more frequently used in the same condition. We tested these predictions with native speakers of Kaqchikel, a VOS language.

8.2   Order of Thought in Kaqchikel

The purpose of this gesture production study with Kaqchikel speakers was threefold. First, we intended to test the predictions of the UCV and the IGV

8.2 Order of Thought in Kaqchikel

regarding the relative order of agent and patient by examining if the agent–patient order is preferred over the patient–agent order even by Kaqchikel speakers, which would be consistent with the suggestion that the SO Preference in Basic Word Order originates from the preferred order of thought.[1] Another purpose was to investigate to what extent the preferred constituent orders of non-verbal event description are affected by the word order of one's native language. To do so, we compared Kaqchikel (VOS) and Japanese (SOV) speakers. Finally, we intended to examine the effects of event reversibility on preferred constituent orders.

8.2.1 Methods

Thirty-one native speakers of Kaqchikel and ten native speakers of Japanese participated in this experiment. A picture description task by gesture production was employed. In this task, participants described simple transitive events using only gestures. To motivate them to describe both the agent and the patient of the event, a collaborator pretended not to have seen the pictures before and wrote down the participants' gestures.

Eighteen line-drawn pictures depicting simple transitive events were used (Figure 8.1). The agent was always human, and the patient was presented in three conditions of animacy (human, animal, or object) to see if Gibson et al.'s (2013) noisy channel hypothesis or Hall, Mayberry, and Ferreira's (2013) role conflict hypothesis also applied to speakers of an OS language such as Kaqchikel. Six pictures showed the Human–Human condition, where the patient was also a human, six showed the Human–Animal condition, where the patient was a non-human animal, and a final six showed the Human–Object condition, where the patient was an inanimate object. Because humans tend to land their initial look at a scene on the left side and then shift to the right, the

Human–Human　　　**Human–Animal**　　　**Human–Object**

Figure 8.1 Pictures with different patient animacy conditions.
(Adapted from Kubo et al. 2015 with permission.)

78   Constituent Order Preference in Event Representation

materials counterbalance the left–right positions in which the agent and patient appear in the picture.

8.2.2   Results and Discussion

8.2.2.1   Agent–Patient versus Patient–Agent   Figure 8.2 presents the distribution of the agent-before-patient and patient-before-agent orders, abstracting away the positions of action, in Kaqchikel and Japanese speakers' gestures describing transitive events. Overall, speakers of both languages produced gestures with an agent–patient order (Kaqchikel 86.2 percent, Japanese 82.8 percent) significantly more frequently than a patient–agent order (Kaqchikel 13.8 percent, Japanese 17.2 percent). The difference between the two languages was not significant. This result demonstrates that the Agent–Patient Preference in Thought given in (1) above holds true even for speakers of Kaqchikel, an OS language, which supports the UCV and not the IGV. This finding is in striking contrast with the conclusion we obtained for Kaqchikel sentence comprehension that, for Kaqchikel speakers, the easiest word order to process is VOS, an OS order, which thematically corresponds to the (action–) patient–agent order.

As for the effects of the animacy of the patient, speakers of both languages used the patient–agent order more frequently in the Human–Human condition than in the others (Figure 8.3). The differences between the two languages were not significant. This result is consistent with previous studies reporting that conceptually more accessible entities such as humans tend to occur earlier in sentences (Bock and Warren 1985; Bornkessel-Schlesewsky and Schlesewsky

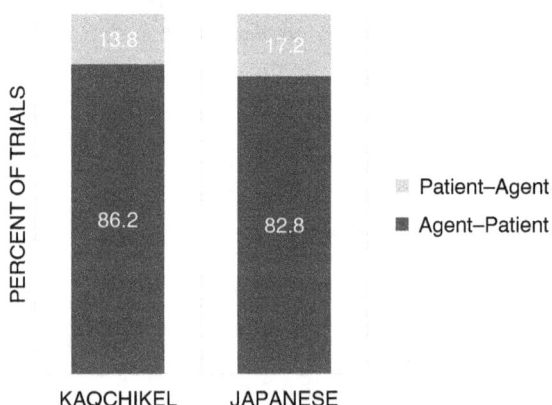

Figure 8.2   Frequencies of gestures with agent–patient and patient–agent orders.

8.2 Order of Thought in Kaqchikel

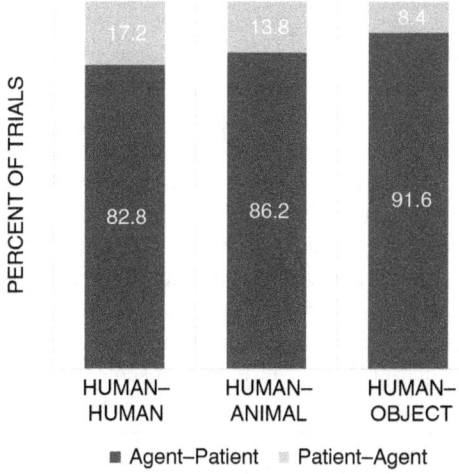

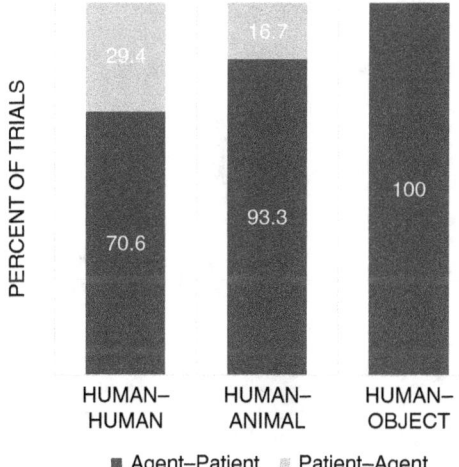

Figure 8.3 Effects of the animacy of the patient on the relative order of agent and patient.

2009a; Branigan, Pickering, and Tanaka 2008; Hirsh-Pasek and Golinkoff 1996; Primus, 1999; Slobin and Bever 1982), although the present study concerns gesture rather than language production.

8.2.2.2 Individual Constituent Orders The distribution of the six possible constituent orders is summarized in Figure 8.4. Kaqchikel speakers produced gestures with the agent–action–patient order more often than the agent–patient–action order, while Japanese speakers produced agent–patient–action gestures more than agent–action–patient gestures. The differences between the two languages were significant. Kaqchikel speakers used the agent–action–patient order more frequently than Japanese speakers, and Japanese speakers used the agent–patient–action order more frequently than Kaqchikel speakers. This shows that natural orders in non-verbal event descriptions are influenced to a certain extent by one's native language. However, it is also evident that the word order of one's native language does not directly predict how a language's speakers depict events in a non-verbal way, as (i) the action–patient–agent order, which corresponds to VOS, the basic word order of Kaqchikel, was virtually absent from Kaqchikel speakers' gestures, and (ii) the agent–patient–action order, which corresponds to the rarely used SOV word order in Kaqchikel, constituted nearly 40 percent of the gestures. We suggest that the frequent use of agent–action–patient gestures by Kaqchikel speakers can be ascribed to the routine use of the VOS language with its highly salient and morphologically complex verbs, which would facilitate the speakers' cognitive attention to action

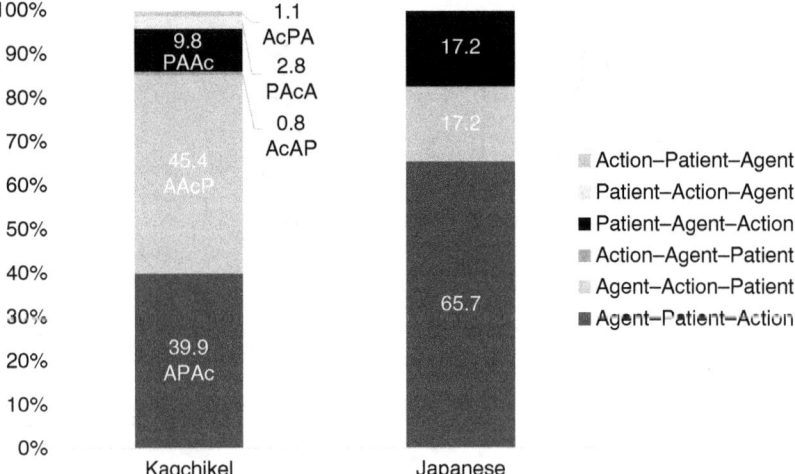

Figure 8.4 Distribution of constituent orders.
Abbreviations: AAcP = Agent–Action–Patient; AcAP = Action–Agent–Patient; APAc = Agent–Patient–Action; PAAc = Patient–Agent–Action; PAcA = Patient–Action–Agent; AcPA = Action–Patient–Agent.

entities. In a verb-initial head-marking language such as Kaqchikel, speakers must always pay attention to action and its linguistic realization (i.e., an inflected verb). Thus, action may be more salient in the mind of Kaqchikel speakers than the mind of speakers of languages such as Japanese, which is a dependent-marking verb-final language. Based on the assumption that gesture reflects how we generate non-verbal messages, the saliency of action in Kaqchikel can be accounted for by theories such as Slobin's (1996) "thinking for speaking" hypothesis. That is, VOS speakers accommodate their thoughts to the demands of linguistic encoding. As such, we observed some effects of grammatical factors as well, partially supporting the IGV. The saliency of action, however, does not seem to be strong enough to overcome the agent-first preference even for speakers of verb-initial languages (see also Futrell et al. 2015).

8.2.2.3 Event Reversibility and the Position of Action Let us now consider the effects of patient animacy on the order of constituents in gesture production. According to Gibson et al. (2013), the noisy channel hypothesis predicts a shift from the default agent–patient–action order to the agent–action–patient order for semantically reversible events, where ambiguity could arise in the former because two plausible agents appear on the same side of the action. Consistent with this prediction, as shown in Figure 8.5, Japanese speakers produced gestures with the agent–patient–action order most frequently when the patient was an inanimate object and least frequently when the patient was a human. The frequency of the agent–action–patient order was in the reverse order, being most frequent for human patients and least frequent for objects. However, one aspect of the results is not expected from the noisy channel hypothesis. The patient–agent–action order was most frequently employed for human patients and was not used at all for object patients, which is exactly the opposite of what is predicted by the noisy channel hypothesis. In the patient–agent–action order, the agent and the patient are on the same side of the action, so this order should be as vulnerable to noise as the agent–patient–action order and should hence be avoided for semantically reversible events according to the noisy channel hypothesis. A conceivable factor that might be responsible for this discrepancy is conceptual accessibility. As mentioned previously, it has been demonstrated that entities with a higher conceptual accessibility, such as a human, tend to occur earlier in sentences than those with a lower conceptual accessibility, such as inanimate objects. In the present experiment, the conceptual accessibility of the patient in the three conditions follows the order of Human–Human > Human–Animal > Human–Object, which corresponds to the relative frequencies of the patient–agent–action order.

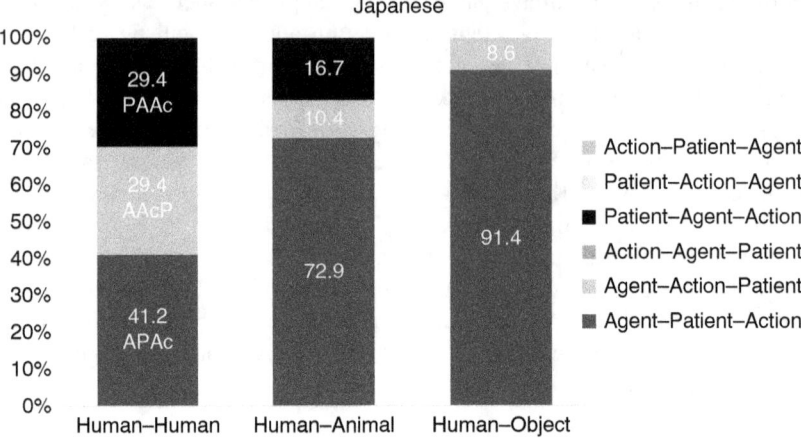

Figure 8.5 Effects of patient animacy on the distribution of gesture orders (Japanese speakers).
Abbreviations: AAcP = Agent–Action–Patient; APAc = Agent–Patient–Action; PAAc = Patient–Agent–Action.

Thus, the overall distribution of constituent orders in the gestures produced by the Japanese speakers may be accounted for by a combination of the noisy channel hypothesis and conceptual accessibility, if we assume their effects are additive. However, the role conflict hypothesis by Hall, Mayberry, and Ferreira (2013) provides a straightforward explanation for the Japanese data shown in Figure 8.5 without invoking the notion of conceptual accessibility.

In the gesture production of Kaqchikel speakers (Figure 8.6), the agent–patient–action order was most frequently used when the patient was an inanimate object and least frequently when the patient was an animal. This shows that Kaqchikel speakers had a tendency to avoid the agent–patient–action order when describing semantically reversible events, as expected from both the noisy channel hypothesis and the role conflict hypothesis. This finding confirms the conclusion drawn from previous studies with speakers of SO languages that the agent–patient–action order might be suboptimal for describing events in which both the agent and patient are plausible agents.

As for the other constituent orders, at least three aspects of the results seem to be difficult to reconcile with the noisy channel hypothesis. First, although the frequency of the agent–action–patient order should be highest in the Human–Human condition according to the noisy channel hypothesis, it was in fact lower than in the Human–Animal condition and comparable to the Human–Object condition. Second, the frequency of the patient–agent–action order

8.2 Order of Thought in Kaqchikel

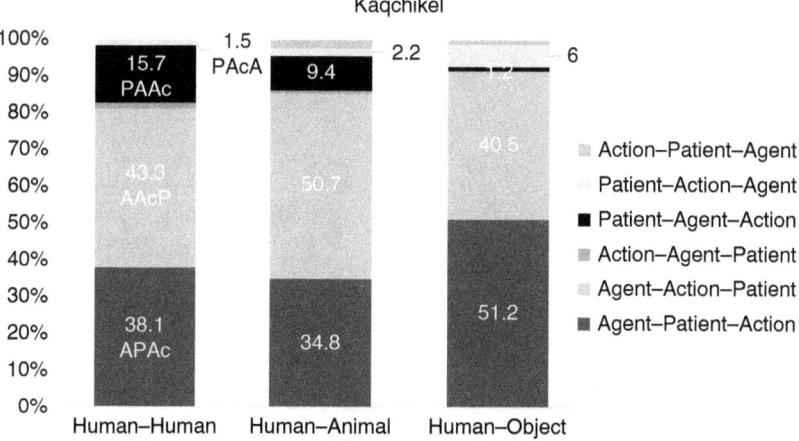

Figure 8.6 Effects of patient animacy on the distribution of gesture orders (Kaqchikel speakers).
Abbreviations: AAcP = Agent–Action–Patient; APAc = Agent–Patient–Action; PAAc = Patient–Agent–Action; PAcA = Patient–Action–Agent.

increased with the animacy of the patient. As two plausible agents are on the same side of the action in this order, as in the agent–patient–action order, this order's frequency should decrease in the case of reversible events according to the noisy channel hypothesis. Third, the frequency of the patient–action–agent order was highest when the patient was an object, and lowest when the patient was a human, the opposite of what is expected from the noisy channel hypothesis, according to which patient–action–agent should be favored in semantically reversible conditions because it should be robust against noise, with the agent and the patient on opposite sides of the action.

One might say that the second problem, i.e., the fact that the patient–agent–action order was favored when the animacy of the patient was higher, might be due to the higher conceptual accessibility of humans and animals. This account appears to be plausible considering that, as mentioned previously, it has been demonstrated that entities with a higher conceptual accessibility tend to occur earlier in sentences. This explanation, however, cannot be extended to the third problem's trend, i.e., the higher the animacy of the patient, the lower the frequency of the patient–action–agent order. The noisy channel hypothesis makes the specific prediction that utterances with agent and patient on the same side of action should be less common for reversible events than for non-reversible events. If we combine the agent–action–patient order and the patient–action–agent order to examine the effect of the position of action (Figure 8.7), it is clear that action-medial orders are not particularly favored

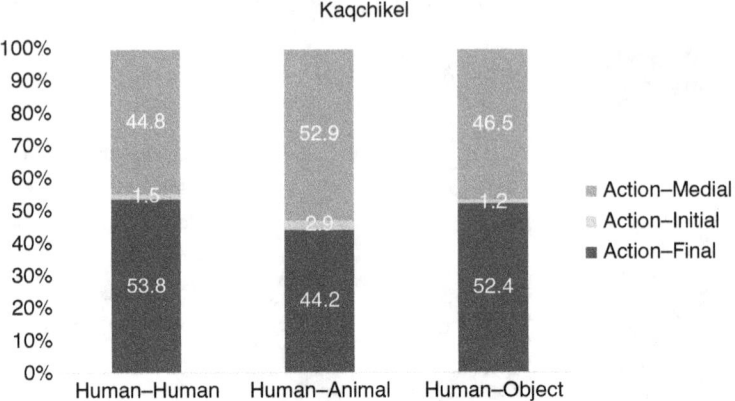

Figure 8.7 Effects of patient animacy on the distribution of gesture orders II (Kaqchikel speakers).

in the Human–Human condition, contrary to the prediction of the noisy channel hypothesis. Taken together, therefore, the three problems mentioned above seem to constitute a substantial challenge to the noisy channel hypothesis.

The data summarized in Figure 8.6 above show that, in semantically reversible events, patient–agent–action gestures were more frequent, and agent–patient–action and patient–action–agent gestures were less frequent. Common among these trends is the avoidance of animate patients being followed by an action gesture in semantically reversible contexts (Figure 8.8). To put it differently, in semantically reversible contexts, there is a strong preference for agents being immediately followed by actions (Figure 8.8). Similar findings were also reported in Hall, Mayberry, and Ferreira's (2013) study with English speakers, as well as Meir et al.'s (2010) study with speakers of Hebrew and Turkish, as cited in Hall, Mayberry, and Ferreira (2013), who observed a marked increase in patient–agent–action for reversible events. These results are problematic for the noisy channel hypothesis but consistent with the role conflict hypothesis.

8.3 Conclusion

In conclusion, our investigation of Kaqchikel speakers confirms that agent–patient is the natural order of non-verbal event description possibly universally across speakers of typologically different languages. This suggests that the prevalence of SO word orders in the world's languages may arise in part because SO orders are most compatible with how we conceptually represent

8.3 Conclusion

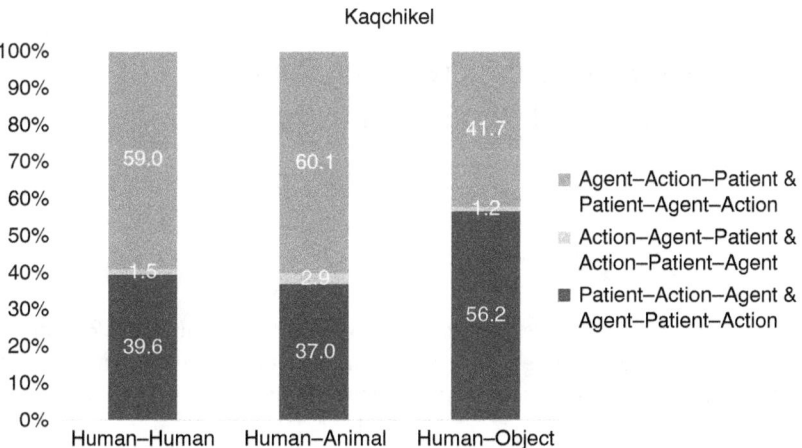

Figure 8.8 Effects of patient animacy on the distribution of gesture orders III (Kaqchikel speakers).

transitive events, although speakers partially accommodate their thought to the demands of linguistic encoding with respect to properties such as head-marking and verb-initiality.

NOTE

1. This section is based on a reanalysis of the data reported in Sakai et al. (2012).

9 Word Order Preference in Sentence Production I: Production Frequency

In this chapter, we will investigate whether SO word orders are more frequently used than OS word orders in Kaqchikel and consider the underlying factors determining word order selection in sentence production.

9.1 Previous Studies

It is well known in the literature that sentences with SO word orders are far more frequently used than those with OS word orders in many of the world's languages with a flexible word order. In Japanese, for example, in the corpus of novels Imamura and Koizumi (2011) studied, of all the transitive sentences with a nominal subject and a nominal object, SO sentences constituted more than 97 percent (Table 9.1). Similarly, it has been reported that the frequency of SO sentences is 79 percent in Turkish (Slobin and Bever 1982; Table 9.2), 87 percent in Serbo-Croatian (Slobin and Bever 1982; Table 9.3), 75 percent in Finnish (Hakulinen and Karlsson 1980; Table 9.4), 95 percent in Italian (Bates 1976; Table 9.5), 83.7 percent in Greek (Lascaratou 1989; Table 9.6), and 81.4 percent in Polish (Siewierska 1993; Table 9.7), among many others.

While the exact ratio of SO sentences may vary to some extent depending on the types of texts examined and the sampling methods used, it is unlikely that the overwhelming trend observed in each of the languages above will be overturned. Let us refer to this disposition as the SO Preference in Sentence Production.

(1) SO Preference in Sentence Production
In individual languages with flexible word order, SO word orders are more frequently used than OS word orders.

Why should this be the case? Does it hold universally in all languages with flexible word order?

9.2 Competing Hypotheses

Parallel to the case of the SO Preference in Sentence Comprehension, we can think of two general competing hypotheses pertaining to the SO Preference in

9.2 Competing Hypotheses

Table 9.1 *Distribution of word orders in Japanese (based on data published in Imamura and Koizumi 2011)*

SOV	97.3%	OSV	2.8%
SO Total	**97.3%**	**OS Total**	**2.8%**

Table 9.2 *Distribution of word orders in Turkish (based on data published in Slobin and Bever 1982)*

SOV	48%	OSV	8%
SVO	25%	OVS	13%
VSO	6%	VOS	0%
SO Total	**79%**	**OS Total**	**21%**

Table 9.3 *Distribution of word orders in Serbo-Croatian (based on data published in Slobin and Bever 1982)*

SOV	16%	OSV	8%
SVO	55%	OVS	2%
VSO	16%	VOS	3%
SO Total	**87%**	**OS Total**	**13%**

Table 9.4 *Distribution of word orders in Finnish (based on data published in Hakulinen and Karlsson 1980)*

SOV	0.9%	OSV	5.1%
SVO	71.6%	OVS	16.5%
VSO	2.6%	VOS	3.4%
SO Total	**75.0%**	**OS Total**	**25.0%**

Sentence Production: the Individual Grammar View (IGV) and the Universal Cognition View (UCV).

(2) Individual Grammar View [Word Order Selection]
Word order selection in sentence production is largely attributable to grammatical factors of individual languages, such as syntactic complexities.

Table 9.5 *Distribution of word orders in Italian (based on data published in Bates 1976)*

SOV	2%	OSV	0%
SVO	82%	OVS	5%
VSO	11%	VOS	0%
SO Total	**95%**	**OS Total**	**5%**

Table 9.6 *Distribution of word orders in Greek (based on data published in Lascaratou 1989)*

SOV	1.2%	OSV	0.7%
SVO	80.7%	OVS	14.4%
VSO	1.8%	VOS	1.2%
SO Total	**83.7%**	**OS Total**	**16.3%**

Table 9.7 *Distribution of word orders in Polish (based on data published in Siewierska 1993)*

SOV	2.4%	OSV	1.5%
SVO	72.5%	OVS	7.4%
VSO	6.5%	VOS	9.5%
SO Total	**81.4%**	**OS Total**	**18.4%**

(3) Universal Cognition View [Word Order Selection]
Word order selection in sentence production is largely attributable to grammar-independent human cognitive features that are universal, such as conceptual accessibility.

Both views correctly account for the SO word order preference in sentence production in SO languages. In Japanese, for example, SOV is more frequently used than OSV, which may be because SOV is (i) the syntactically basic word order (IGV) and/or (ii) an SO order (UCV). However, previous sentence production studies have mostly targeted SO languages, so it remains unclear whether this preference reflects the basic word orders in individual languages or more universal human cognitive features. In order to investigate this, it is necessary to examine OS languages, for which the two views offer different predictions. The IGV would predict that OS word orders should be more frequently used than SO word orders in OS languages such as Kaqchikel. In contrast, the UCV leads us to expect that SO word orders should be more frequently used than OS word orders even in OS languages. To investigate, we conducted sentence production experiments with a picture description task to clarify word order selection in Kaqchikel, a VOS language.

9.3 Word Order Frequency in Kaqchikel

The primary purpose of this experiment was to test the divergent predictions by the IGV and the UCV mentioned in the previous section.[1] In addition, we also aimed to elucidate the effects of patient animacy on the distribution of generated word orders in Kaqchikel, in relation to the noisy channel hypothesis of Gibson et al. (2013) and the role conflict hypothesis of Hall, Mayberry, and Ferreira (2013).

9.3.1 Methods

Fifty-nine native speakers of Kaqchikel participated in this experiment. The target stimuli consisted of twenty-four black-and-white line drawings depicting transitive events (Figure 9.1). In all twenty-four pictured events, the agent was a human character. The patient was a human in eight events (the Human–Human condition), an animal in eight events (the Human–Animal condition), and an inanimate object in eight events (the Human–Object condition). As filler stimuli, we included eighteen line drawings depicting intransitive events. Similar to the target stimuli, the filler stimuli comprised six events featuring a human, six featuring an animal, and six featuring an object. We also included six practice pictures featuring similar kinds of events, which we did not include among the target and filler stimuli. The assignment of left–right position of the agent and patient was counterbalanced across all the stimulus pictures.

Human–Human   Human–Animal   Human–Object   Filler

Figure 9.1 Pictures of different patient animacy conditions.
(Adapted from Kubo et al. 2015 with permission.)

The participants' responses were recorded and transcribed by two Kaqchikel-speaking experimenters. The utterances were divided into VOS active sentences, SVO active sentences, and passive sentences.[2] The subject of passive sentences in Kaqchikel may either precede or follow the verb, but all the passive sentences obtained in this experiment had a preverbal subject, as exemplified in (4c).

(4) a. VOS active
     X-Ø-u-ch' äy   ri ak'wal   ri xtän
     CP-ABS3sg-ERG3sg-slap   DET boy   DET girl
     "The girl slapped the boy."

   b. SVO active
     Ri xtän   x-Ø-u-ch' äy   ri ak'wal
     DET girl   CP-ABS3sg-ERG3sg-slap   DET boy
     "The girl slapped the boy."

   c. Passive
     Ri ak'wal   x-Ø-ch'ay   r-oma'   ri xtän
     DET boy   CP-ABS3sg-slap:PASS   GEN3sg-by   DET girl
     "The boy was slapped by the girl."

9.3.2 Results and Discussion

Figure 9.2 shows the distribution of the three categories of sentences in each experimental condition. Speakers of Kaqchikel had a general preference for producing the SVO order in active sentences, which is consistent with the prediction of the UCV, but not the IGV.

The rate of VOS sentence production was inversely correlated with patient animacy (28.5 percent Human–Object, 12.8 percent Human–Animal, 8.3 percent Human–Human). SVO sentences were produced at a significantly lower rate in the Human–Object condition (70.7 percent) than in either the Human–Animal (85.6 percent) or Human–Human (86.3 percent) condition. There was no significant difference in production frequency between the Human–Animal and Human–Human conditions. This finding shows that SVO sentences generally occur more frequently in semantically reversible sentences than in non-reversible ones. The rate of passive SVX sentences was correlated with patient animacy (0.8 percent Human–Object, 1.6 percent Human–Animal, 5.4 percent Human–Human).

As we have alluded to above, previous studies on SO languages have amply demonstrated that conceptually more accessible entities such as humans tend to occur earlier in sentences. The rate of Kaqchikel passive sentences across the three conditions is compatible with this trend: The higher the animacy of the patient, the more it occurs as the preverbal subject. Other than that, however, the overall result of the present experiment reveals that a reverse animacy effect occurs in Kaqchikel: SVO is preferred to VOS when the animacy of the object

9.3 Word Order Frequency in Kaqchikel

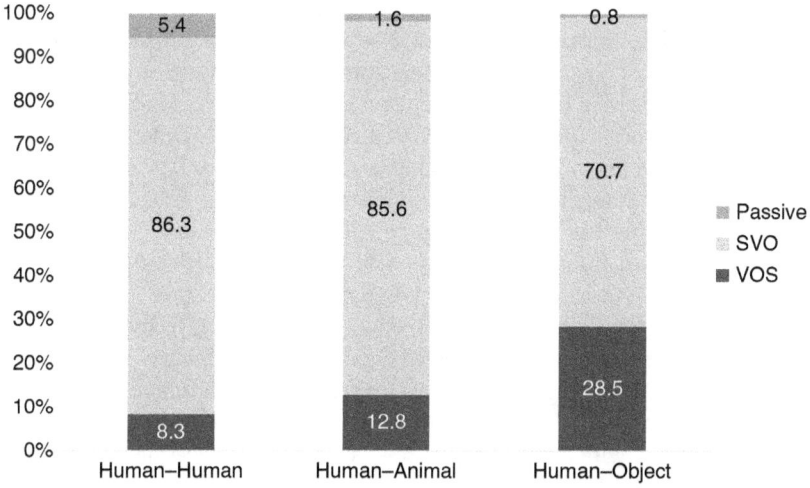

Figure 9.2 Word order preference in Kaqchikel in the picture description task.

is greater and its conceptual accessibility therefore higher. Why should this be the case? In other words, why is SVO, which is generally preferred over VOS in Kaqchikel sentence production, even more preferred when the patient is human, compared to when the patient is inanimate? One possibility is that the VOS word order is potentially syntactically ambiguous between agent and patient when both the subject and the object are animate. In Kaqchikel, VSO is also a grammatically possible word order (Ajsivinac Sian et al. 2004). Furthermore, as Kaqchikel is a head-marking language, it does not use case-marking particles or other markers of grammatical relations in noun phrases. Accordingly, as shown in example (5) below, in sentences featuring subject and object nouns in the third person singular, the sequence V-NP-NP could be grammatically construed as either VOS or VSO. On a related note, England (1991) observed that Mayan speakers may utilize SVO sentences as a strategy to eliminate the ambiguity that may arise in verb-initial sentences (i.e., VOS or VSO).

(5) X-Ø-u-ch'äy   ri ak'wal   ri xtän.
    CP-ABS3sg-ERG3sg-slap   DET boy   DET girl
    "The girl slapped the boy." / "The boy slapped the girl."

To reiterate the conditions in our experiment, the agent was always a human character, while the patient's animacy varied. As such, in the VOS sentences produced in the Human–Human condition (and probably the Human–Animal condition as well), either of the two noun phrases could be construed as the agent, potentially creating the ambiguity described above. In the Human–Object condition, however, there would be very little room for ambiguity in VOS sentences, as it is unlikely that an inanimate entity would be construed as the agent. Thus, in the Human–Human and Human–Animal conditions in this experiment, the participants might have opted against VOS sentences to avoid the syntactic ambiguity between VOS and VSO.

The syntactic ambiguity illustrated in example (5) arises because the agent and patient are both in the third person singular, and because it is not clear which of the two nouns is agreeing with the ergative affix that indicates agreement with the subject. While it is uncertain how much it shaped the results, this syntactic ambiguity is probably a confounding factor. Therefore, in the next experiment, we investigated once again how animacy affects word order selection, this time eliminating the source of the above ambiguity. That is, we presented pictures of events featuring multiple patients to elicit the production of sentences with a plural object (and a singular subject) such as the one in (6).

(6)   X-e-ru-ch'äy   ri ak'wal-**a'**   ri xtän.
        CP-ABS3**pl**-ERG3sg-slap   DET boy-**pl**   DET girl
        "The girl slapped the boys."

As the above example features a plural patient, the absolutive (Set B) appears as an affix agreeing with the third-person plural element, and the object NP appears with a suffix or quantifier indicating the object's plurality, which removes any syntactic ambiguity between VOS and VSO.

9.4   Effects of Animacy on Word Order in Syntactically Unambiguous Sentences

In this experiment, we investigated the effects of patient animacy on word order selection in syntactically unambiguous sentences.[3]

9.4.1   Methods

Thirty-one native speakers of Kaqchikel participated in this experiment. The target stimuli consisted of twenty-two black-and-white line drawings depicting transitive events. In all events, the agent was a human character. The patient, however, was human in eleven of the events (the Human–Human condition) and an inanimate entity in eleven events (the Human–Object condition) (see Figure 9.3). In this experiment, all the depicted events featured multiple patients. We used twenty-two pictures as filler stimuli, comprising twelve intransitive events and ten transitive events featuring multiple agents. We depicted multiple agents in the fillers to ensure that, when viewing the target

Human–Human   **Human–Object**   **Filler**

Figure 9.3 Pictures used in the second experiment. (Adapted from Kubo et al. 2015 with permission.)

stimulus pictures, the participants would not focus on the patients any more than normal.

The experimental procedure was generally the same as in the experiment reported above.

9.4.2 Results and Discussion

Figure 9.4 shows the distribution of the three categories of sentences in each experimental condition. As in the previous experiment, the SVO word order was employed far more frequently than the VOS word order, congruent with the UCV.

As for the animacy effect, active VOS sentences were produced more frequently when the patient was inanimate (24.8 percent) than when it was human (7.2 percent). Conversely, passive SVX sentences and active SVO sentences were produced more frequently when the patient was human (passive 4.8 percent, SVO 87.9 percent) than when it was inanimate (passive 0 percent, SVO 75.2 percent). Having pre-empted the syntactic ambiguity of verb-initial sentences by featuring multiple patients, this result demonstrates that the patient's animacy affects word order choice in Kaqchikel. This experiment yielded the same general finding as the previous one: when the patient is human, speakers are less likely to produce VOS sentences and more likely to produce SVO sentences.

9.5 General Discussion

The data presented above have shown that (i) SVO is more frequently used than VOS in Kaqchikel and (ii) SVO is even more preferred when the object is human than when it is inanimate. Below, we consider these two findings in turn.

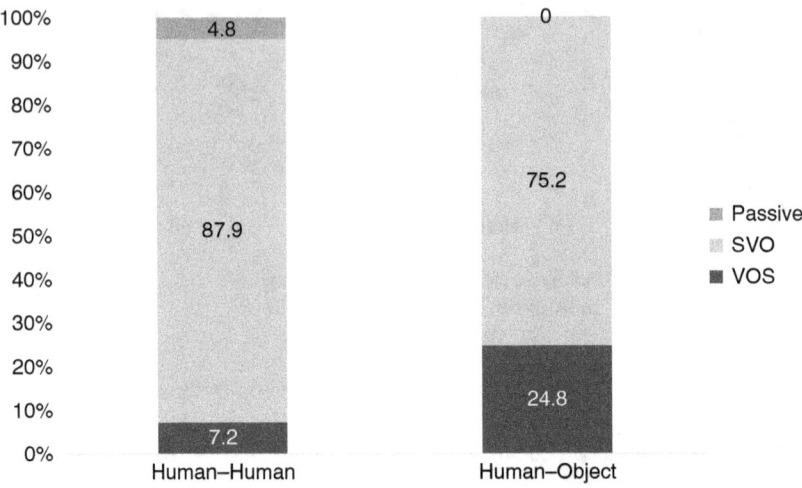

Figure 9.4 Effects of animacy in the picture description task.

9.5.1 General Preference of SVO over VOS

Language production is the process of converting one's intended message into speech (or letters or signs) based on the vocabulary and grammar of an individual language. It is generally assumed to involve three main stages: conceptual processing, grammatical processing, and articulation (e.g., Levelt 1989; Figure 9.5). During conceptual processing, the message to be expressed is determined; grammatical processing concerns translating the message into linguistic form; and articulation realizes the ensuing linguistic structure as a series of motor movements. At a certain level of abstraction, language comprehension proceeds in the opposite direction, from perception to grammatical processing to conceptual processing. It is generally agreed that both sentence production and comprehension proceed incrementally. As a unit of information becomes available at one stage of processing, it triggers processing at the next stage in the system.

We have seen in the previous sections that SVO is more frequently used than VOS in Kaqchikel, despite the fact that SVO is not the syntactically basic word order and is more difficult to process than VOS. Why should this be the case? We suggest three possible reasons in relation to the language production model sketched above (Koizumi et al. 2014).

9.5.1.1 Direct Influence of Conceptual Saliency First, universal cognitive features in the sense of the UCV primarily concern the relative saliency of and

9.5 General Discussion

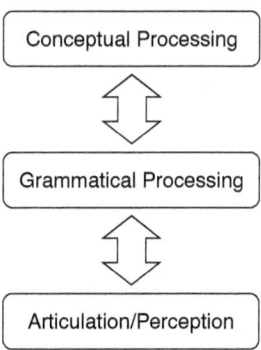

Figure 9.5 A schematic model of language processing.

the relation between concepts, such as entities (e.g., books, girls), states (happy), and actions (hitting), at the level of conceptual processing. We have seen in the previous chapter that the most preferred constituent order at the conceptual level for Kaqchikel speakers is agent–action–patient (see Figure 8.4 in Chapter 8), showing that agent is conceptually more salient than the others.

There are two interrelated but different ways in which relative conceptual saliencies affect word order selection in sentence production. First, conceptual factors may directly affect word order selection (e.g., Branigan and Feleki 1999; De Smedt 1990; Kempen and Hoenkamp 1987; Myachykov and Tomlin 2008; Tanaka et al. 2011). The order of word retrieval from the mental lexicon at the stage of grammatical processing may be determined by the availability of individual concepts at the stage of conceptual processing, and the structure of the sentence being generated is accordingly constrained by whichever word is retrieved first, a strategy MacDonald (2013) has referred to as "Easy First." In other words, conceptually more accessible entities may claim early word order positions irrespective of grammatical function. In this respect, SVO is preferred over VOS in Kaqchikel partly because of the preferred order in thought (i.e., the relative conceptual saliency of agent > action > patient) directly influencing the word order of utterances in the Kaqchikel language.

9.5.1.2 Indirect Influence of Conceptual Saliency Second, conceptual factors may influence the way in which grammatical functions are assigned, which in turn indirectly affects word order choice through the mediation of the grammar of a particular language (e.g., Bock and Warren 1985; Christianson and Ferreira 2005; Lee, Brown-Schmidt, and Watson 2013; McDonald et al. 1993). It is generally assumed that grammatical functions are assigned according to a noun phrase accessibility hierarchy (Keenan and Comrie 1977) such that the subject function is assigned first, followed by the direct object, and so on, as shown in (7) (Bock and Warren 1985). A conceptually more accessible entity is assigned to a higher grammatical function; hence, agent tends to align with the subject and patient with the direct object.

(7) Grammatical function hierarchy relevant to functional assignment according to conceptual accessibility:
subject > direct object > indirect object > ...

The second reason why SVO is more frequently used than VOS in Kaqchikel has to do with this indirect impact. It is known that agent, being highly salient, tends not only to be a subject, as mentioned above, but also a topic. Thus, in languages that morpho-syntactically distinguish between a topicalized subject and a non-topicalized one, agent is more likely to realize as a topicalized subject. In fact, it has been observed in many languages that subjects tend to become topics of conversation more easily than other immediate sentence constituents, and topics tend to appear at the beginning of sentences. Take Japanese, for example, in which the subject is marked with the nominative case marker *ga* and the object with the accusative case marker *o* in pragmatically neutral contexts. When the referent of the subject is discourse-given, and hence more salient, the subject is preposed and marked with the topic marker *wa* (Kishimoto 2009; Kitagawa 1982; Kuroda 1988; Saito 1985; Shibatani 1990; Tateishi 1990; among many others). The object may be either scrambled or topicalized when salient. The four basic types of Japanese sentences that follow from this are shown in (8). The schematic syntactic structures of (8a) and (8b) are shown in (9a) and (9b), respectively (Kishimoto 2009: 481; Shibatani 1990: 274).

(8) a. Naomi ga meron o kitta. [SOV]
Naomi NOM melon ACC cut
"Naomi cut the melon."

b. Naomi wa meron o kitta. [SOV]
Naomi TOP melon ACC cut

c. Meron o Naomi ga kitta. [OSV]
melon ACC Naomi NOM cut

d. Meron wa Naomi ga kitta. [OSV]
melon TOP Naomi NOM cut

(9) a. [S-NOM O-ACC V]
b. [S-TOP [__ O-ACC V]]

Importantly, sentences with a topicalized subject such as (8b) are far more frequently used than sentences with a non-topicalized subject such as (8a) in Japanese, as shown in Table 9.8 (Imamura and Koizumi 2011).

9.5 General Discussion

Table 9.8 *Distribution of four transitive constructions in Japanese (based on data published in Imamura and Koizumi 2011)*

S-NOM O-ACC V	14.7%	O-ACC S-NOM V	1.0%
S-TOP O-ACC V	82.5%	O-TOP S-NOM V	1.8%
SO Total	**97.3%**	**OS Total**	**2.8%**

In Kaqchikel, and in Mayan languages more generally, the default status of transitive subject is as topic, and the default status of object is as part of the comment (Aissen 2017: 295). Thus, the VOS vs. SVO relation in Kaqchikel seems to parallel [S-NOM O-ACC V] vs. [S-TOP O-ACC V] in Japanese. VOS in Kaqchikel and [S-NOM O-ACC V] in Japanese are syntactically simple and typically used in pragmatically neutral contexts; SVO and [S-TOP O-ACC V] are syntactically more complex and used in contexts where the subject is a topic. Furthermore, the production frequencies of SVO and [S-TOP O-ACC V] are several times higher than those of VOS and [S-NOM O-ACC V], respectively. Indeed, in Mayan languages, constituents that appear before verbs are often interpreted as the topic of the utterance, and the observation that there is a syntactically designated position for the topic before verbs is widely supported (Aissen 1992; England 1991; García Matzar and Rodríguez Guaján 1997: 334). This means that, although VOS is syntactically the basic word order used in pragmatically neutral contexts and therefore induces a lower processing load, SVO is used more frequently in conversation because subjects are often preposed as the topic (Ajsivinac Sian et al. 2004: 178–180; Tichoc Cumes et al. 2000: 219–223). In fact, word orders with preposed subjects appear more frequently than the syntactically determined basic word order in many other Mayan languages as well (but see Norcliffe et al. 2015; Robinson 2002). Therefore, it has been suggested that, when examining the "basic word order" of Mayan languages, the "syntactically determined word order" from the standpoint of syntactic complexity needs to be distinguished from the "pragmatically determined word order" commonly used for pragmatic purposes (Brody 1984; England 1991). It may, therefore, be the norm rather than an exception that sentences with a topicalized subject (presumably associated with the most commonly used information structure) are more frequently produced than corresponding sentences with a non-topicalized subject in languages that morpho-syntactically distinguish between the two. In light of this, there is nothing surprising about the fact that SVO with a topicalized subject is used more frequently than VOS with a non-topicalized subject in Kaqchikel. This reasoning is consistent with the notion that conceptual saliency affects word order indirectly by interacting with the grammar of a language. Japanese grammar morpho-syntactically differentiates a topicalized subject and a non-topicalized one, but it places both in a sentence-initial position. Kaqchikel grammar differentiates the two kinds of subject syntactically by placing the topicalized subject in the preverbal position and the non-topicalized subject postverbally at the end of the sentence. An indirect version of the UCV would predict in this case that, in a language whose grammar detects topicalized subjects at the end of a sentence, for example, that may be the most frequently used word order in that language (cf. Herring 2012; Tomlin and Rhodes 1992).

9.5.1.3 Influence of Head-Marking A third and final reason considered here for the prevalence of SVO in Kaqchikel sentence production has to do with the head-marking nature of the language. As mentioned earlier, Kaqchikel features subject and object agreement markers on the verb. The verbal complex of a transitive sentence, [Aspect-ABS-ERG-Verb stem], contains information about the person and number of the subject and object. It has been shown in other languages (e.g., English) that information about the verb (e.g., selectional restrictions) can immediately be used to facilitate the processing of the subsequent region (Altmann and Kamide 1999; Trueswell, Tanenhaus, and Kello 1993). Nichols (1986) argues that, if the verb comes first in a head-marking language, then the grammatical relations are established at the beginning, which may be communicatively efficacious in that it streamlines the hearer's processing. If so, in Kaqchikel, having a verbal complex in the sentence-initial position may be advantageous in sentence comprehension in that it helps develop predictions about the upcoming subject and object, rendering the processing of the subsequent portions of the sentence easier. From the perspective of production, in contrast, verb-initial word orders may be more disadvantageous than nominal-initial orders such as SVO in Kaqchikel because, in order to initiate a sentence with a verbal complex, conceptual and grammatical information about the subject and object must have been activated and processed to a certain degree prior to the beginning of the utterance. Again, it has been shown in other languages that the complexity of the sentence-initial phrase correlates with the time required to initiate the utterance (e.g., Smith and Wheeldon 1999), and that latencies are shorter for subject-verb utterances than for verb-only utterances (Lindsley 1975). For this reason, therefore, SVO may be less demanding to initiate than verb-initial orders for Kaqchikel speakers, and hence it is produced more frequently than VOS. It is thus important to test whether production latencies are indeed shorter for SVO than VOS. We will come back to this issue in Chapter 10.

9.5.2   Effects of Animacy on Word Order Selection

Recall that, in the two experiments on sentence production in Kaqchikel reported above, the rate of VOS sentence production was lower and that of

SVO production higher when the patient was human than when it was inanimate. In other words, VOS was less preferred and SVO was more preferred in describing reversible events. This finding is consistent with Gibson et al.'s (2013) noisy channel hypothesis, according to which verb-medial word orders are more robust than verb-initial or verb-final word orders in a noisy communicative situation, especially when the message to be transmitted is a reversible event. The results are also congruent with Hall, Mayberry, and Ferreira's (2013) role conflict hypothesis, which claims that the OV order tends to be avoided when O is higher animate because of the danger of O (patient) being misinterpreted as S (agent).

Still another factor potentially shaping the observed distribution of utterance word orders is a similarity-based competition. Gennari, Mirković, and MacDonald (2012) argue that, when there is a temporal overlap in the planning of two conceptually similar nouns, the similarity leads to interference between the semantic information of the nouns. As a result, when the concept of one noun is activated, the concept of the other noun is inhibited, and the latter noun is either mentioned away from the initially activated noun or simply omitted. Moreover, the effect of conceptual similarity interacts with language-specific grammatical constraints, and the actual instantiation may vary across languages. The production of VOS sentences in Kaqchikel is interesting because the most accessible element, an animate agent noun usually realized as the subject, must be retained in memory until the end of the sentence, and hence it potentially competes with other elements. If similarity-based competition arises between the subject and object in Kaqchikel, it should be preferred for one of them to be realized away from the other rather than for them to occur adjacent to each other. As the object usually follows the verb in Kaqchikel, this increase in competition would lead to a lower rate of the VOS word order. The results of the two experiments above can be taken to indicate that native Kaqchikel speakers are sensitive to the competition caused by the similarity of noun concepts involved in an event described in a sentence, and they select the sentence pattern that best resolves the competition between nouns with similar concepts (Kubo et al. 2015). This point will also be addressed in the next chapter.

9.6 Conclusion

Kaqchikel speakers have a general preference for producing the SVO order over the VOS order. This is consistent with the prediction of the UCV, according to which conceptual saliency both directly and indirectly affects speakers' word order selection, and hence the agent tends to occupy the designated topic position rather than the canonical subject position in languages whose grammar makes this distinction.

NOTES

1. This section is based on Kubo et al.'s (2015) experiment 1.
2. Other types of sentences were excluded from the analysis, either because they are irrelevant (e.g., intransitive sentences) or because their number was too small for statistically meaningful analysis (e.g., VSO active, antipassive). The rate of VSO sentences was 0.7 percent, and no OVS sentence was produced.
3. This section is based on Kubo et al.'s (2015) experiment 2.

10 Word Order Preference in Sentence Production II: Time Course and Cognitive Load

Building on the sentence production studies discussed in Chapter 9, in this chapter we will further consider the roles of conceptual and grammatical processing in the course of utterance generation. In particular, we will test four predictions derived from the discussions in the previous chapters.

10.1 Introduction

The experimental studies of Kaqchikel reviewed so far suggest that the cognitive load during sentence comprehension is primarily determined by grammatical processes operating on linguistic representations, whereas word order selection in sentence production more faithfully reflects event apprehension and preverbal message construction at the stage of conceptual processing (Figure 10.1). In particular, agent-first orders are likely to be selected over others in Kaqchikel because of its complex verbal morphology, the conceptual accessibility of agents, perspective-taking, and so on. This hypothesis leads us to the following three expectations. First, if subject-initial sentences are easier to initiate than verb-initial sentences in Kaqchikel because of its head-marking nature and the conceptual saliency of the agent, then utterance latency should be shorter for SVO than for VOS in Kaqchikel. Second, if the agent is conceptually more salient than other entities even for speakers of VOS languages, Kaqchikel speakers should pay more attention to agents than to other elements during sentence production. Third, despite these, the cognitive load during sentence production should be higher for SVO sentences than for VOS sentences because the production of a sentence surely includes, as its central part, the construction of linguistic representations, and the grammatical processes involved in this are presumably similar to those involved in the comprehension of a parallel sentence, although there may be some differences (Kempen, Olsthoorn, and Sprenger 2012; MacWhinney, Malchukov, and Moravcsik (eds.) 2014; Momma 2016; Momma and Phillips 2018). Additionally, it is interesting to observe how the animacy of the patient may or may not influence

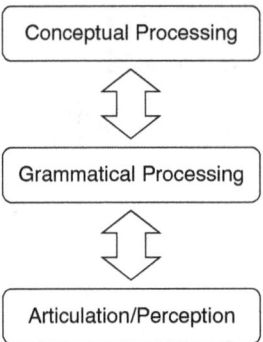

Figure 10.1 A schematic model of language processing.

time course and cognitive load in Kaqchikel sentence production. In particular, the similarity-based competition in the sense of Gennari, Mirković, and MacDonald (2012) would incur some cognitive load in VOS sentences compared to SVO sentences. This factor should impede the production processes of VOS compared to SVO especially when the subject and object are similar to each other (e.g., both are human). If this is so, we would expect the interaction of the effect of syntactic complexity and that of similarity-based competition: the difference between SVO and VOS, in cognitive load, should be smaller when the event is reversible (i.e., the human agent is acting on the human patient) than when the event is non-reversible (i.e., the human agent acting on the inanimate patient).

In this chapter, we report a sentence production experiment with a picture description task conducted to test these predictions by measuring the utterance latencies, eye movements, and cortical activations of Kaqchikel speakers. The results confirmed all but the last expectation, as reported in detail below. To provide a basis for comparison, in the next section we will discuss a parallel study we had previously conducted with Japanese speakers.

10.2 Time Course and Cognitive Load of Japanese Sentence Production

This section reports on a Japanese sentence production experiment.[1]

10.2.1 Methods

Twenty native speakers of Japanese participated in this experiment. All participants were classified as right-handed based on the Edinburgh Handedness Inventory (Oldfield 1971), and all of them had normal or corrected-to-normal vision.

In this experiment, the participants described pictures of simple transitive events involving familiar characters and actions while their gaze, speech, and brain activation were recorded. We used a voice recorder, an eye tracker (Tobii TX300), and a multi-channel near-infrared spectroscopy (NIRS) system (Shimadzu FOIRE-3000) to record the participants' utterances, eye movements, and the relative concentration changes in oxygenated, deoxygenated, and total hemoglobin (Coxy-Hb, Cdeoxy-Hb, and Ctotal-Hb). A whole-head probe cap was used. The probes were placed over the prefrontal cortex of each hemisphere, each consisting of a 4×3 array with six emitters and six detectors, constituting seventeen channels per hemisphere (see Figure 10.2a). We arranged these probes with reference to the International 10–20 system (see Figure 5.2 in Chapter 5).

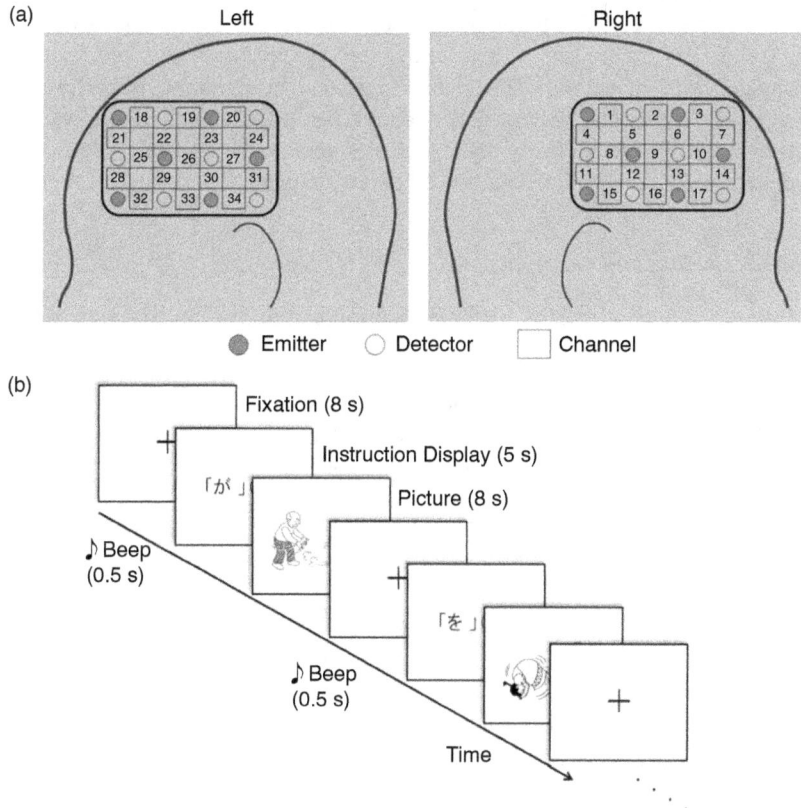

Figure 10.2 (a) Locations of the probes used in NIRS measurements. (b) Schematic representation of the procedure in the present experiment. (Adapted from Takeshima et al. 2015 with permission.)

We prepared twenty pictures depicting a two-character transitive event. Half the pictures showed human agents acting on human patients, and the other half showed human agents acting on inanimate patients. The agent was depicted on the left side and the patient on the right side. In order to counterbalance the locations, we also prepared twenty pictures that were mirror images of the originals. The sizes of the agent and patient were nearly identical.

Each trial started with the presentation of a fixation cross for 8 seconds (s), followed by an instructional display for word order for 5 s (Figure 10.2b). The nominative case marker *ga* or the accusative case marker *o* was shown in the instructional display using Japanese cursive syllabary. After the instructional display, a picture was presented for 8 s. The participants were instructed to describe the event in the picture using Japanese as concisely as possible, starting with the subject after the *ga* display and the object after the *o* display. Thus, it was expected that participants would produce Japanese sentences in the SOV and OSV orders after the *ga* and *o* displays, respectively. The fixation cross appeared again after the picture display. The participants performed a total of forty trials, with twenty pictures per word order. Of the twenty pictures each participant saw, the agent was depicted on the left side in ten pictures, and on the right side in the other ten pictures.

10.2.2 Results and Discussion

10.2.2.1 Utterance Latency Utterance latency was defined as the interval between the onset of the picture presentation and the starting point of the participant's utterance. The results of utterance latency analyses revealed that the latency was significantly shorter in the SOV condition than in the OSV condition (Table 10.1). This is consistent with our expectation that the subject (agent) is conceptually more salient than the object (patient) for Japanese speakers.

Table 10.1 *The means and standard deviations of utterance latency for word order conditions (M = mean, SD = standard deviation)*

Word order	Utterance latency (ms)	
	M	SD
SOV	1,592	216
OSV	1,771	321

10.2 Time Course and Cognitive Load of Japanese Sentence Production

10.2.2.2 Eye Movement We calculated the mean fixation time on the agent and patient during the period of each picture presentation (8 s) using area of interest (AOI) analysis. We used two AOIs of comparable size (but not necessarily the same shape) to properly cover the agent and patient (Figure 10.3). As people tend to look at the things they are thinking about and will talk about (Gleitman et al. 2007; Griffin and Bock 2000), the timing of gaze shifts between characters in an event is a sensitive index of when the various units involved in the event are conceptually and linguistically processed during the course of sentence production.

Figures 10.4a and 10.4b show the time course of the formulation of SOV and OSV sentences. We compared fixation times between the agent and patient in the two word order conditions for every 100 milliseconds (ms).

The formulation of Japanese SOV sentences (Figure 10.4a) was similar to earlier results obtained with English SVO sentences (e.g., Griffin and Bock 2000). When producing SOV sentences, Japanese speakers quickly directed their gaze to the agent character (subject) and continued fixating on it preferentially until speech onset. Shifts of gaze to the patient character (object) occurred only after speech onset. Statistical analyses revealed a significant difference in

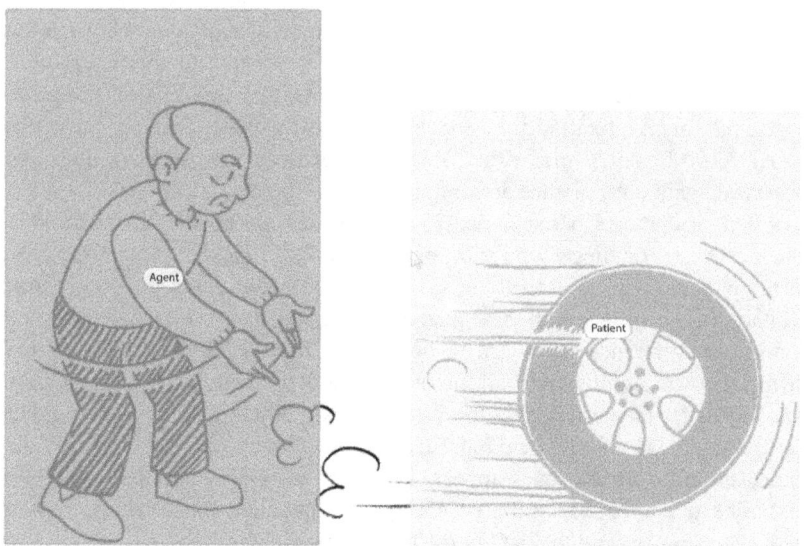

Figure 10.3 An example of area of interest (AOI) setting. The left AOI covers the agent area, and the right AOI covers the patient area, with the sizes of the two AOIs being comparable.
(Adapted from Takeshima et al. 2015 with permission.)

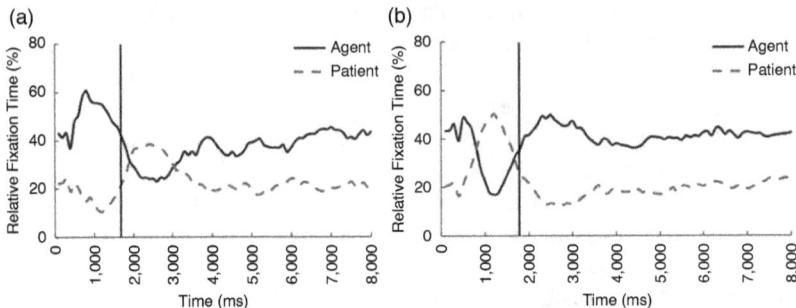

Figure 10.4 Relative fixation time during the picture presentation for (a) canonical SOV utterances and (b) scrambled OSV utterances. The black vertical lines represent speech onset.
(Adapted from Takeshima et al. 2015 with permission.)

all time periods except from 1,800 to 2,100 ms and from 2,900 to 3,400 ms. The relative fixation time was higher for the agent than for the patient in all periods except from 2,100 to 2,900 ms. In other words, the participants initially fixated on the agent more than the patient, with agent-directed fixation bias peaking 700–800 ms after picture presentation. Then, during the 1,800–1,900 ms period, the relative fixation times were approximately equivalent between the agent and the patient. The utterance was initiated between this agent-peak period and the equivalent fixation time period (at 1,592 ms). After utterance onset, the relative fixation time for the patient was higher than for the agent (from 2,100 to 2,900 ms), after which the agent-directed fixation bias was observed again until picture presentation offset.

When producing OSV sentences, Japanese speakers initially fixated on the agent character (subject) for a short period, and then quickly shifted their gaze to the patient (object). Reversion of gaze to the agent character occurred at around speech onset. Statistical analyses revealed that, while there was no significant difference from 700 to 800 ms or from 1,500 to 1,800 ms, the difference was significant in all the other time periods. Relative fixation time was higher for the patient than for the agent from 800 to 1,500 ms, and higher for the agent in all other periods. Compared with the SOV condition, the patient-directed fixation bias appeared faster in the OSV condition (800–900 ms). The utterance was initiated during an equivalent fixation time period between the agent and the patient (at 1,771 ms).

In both the SOV and OSV conditions, the relative fixation times were higher for the agent than for the patient during the first 700 ms after the onset of the picture presentation. This means that Japanese speakers initially paid attention to the agent in the picture even when the first constituent of the utterance they needed to produce was a patient (object). The period of the first several hundred milliseconds (until around 400 to 600 ms) after picture onset arguably corresponds to event apprehension at the stage of conceptual processing (Griffin and Bock 2000; Norcliffe et al. 2015). Therefore, this pattern of eye movement, together with the shorter utterance latency for SOV than OSV, confirms the saliency and early processing of agent at the stage of conceptual processing in Japanese sentence production.

The subsequent period between 600 ms and 3,000 ms is normally associated with linguistic encoding at the stage of grammatical processing. The data above are compatible with the view that the period between 600 ms and speech onset is primarily devoted to the grammatical processing of the first constituent of the utterance (e.g., the S of SOV), and the grammatical processing of the second constituent (e.g., the O of SOV) commences around the time of speech onset.

10.2.2.3 Brain Activity We used the relative concentration changes in oxygenated hemoglobin values during the picture presentation period (8 s) as an index of neural activation during sentence production. We analyzed the data from channels 29, 30, 32, and 33, which were placed over regions centered on the left inferior frontal gyrus (IFG). As shown in Figure 10.5, the participants showed significantly higher peak values in the OSV condition than in the SOV condition on channel 32. Significant differences were not observed between word order conditions on the other analyzed channels. This shows that OSV sentences require more cognitive resources than SOV sentences not only in comprehension, as has been observed, but also in production, which is congruent with the generally held view that a derived word order is associated with more complex syntactic structures and hence more difficult to process than the canonical word order in each individual language.

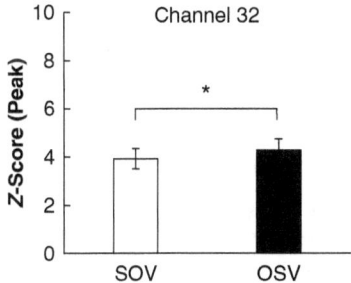

Figure 10.5 Average peak concentration changes of oxyhemoglobin under the two word order conditions on channel 32, which is estimated to be in the left IFG. The error bars represent the standard errors of the means. (Adapted from Takeshima et al. 2015 with permission.)

10.3 Time Course and Cognitive Load of Kaqchikel Sentence Production

This section reports on a Kaqchikel sentence production experiment.[2]

10.3.1 Methods

Eighteen native speakers of Kaqchikel participated in this experiment. All participants were classified as right-handed based on the Edinburgh Handedness Inventory (Oldfield 1971), and all of them had normal or corrected-to-normal vision.

The experimental methods used were basically the same as those in the Japanese experiment reported in the previous section, except for the following. Rather than a Japanese case marker, the Kaqchikel word *B'anöl* "subject" or *B'anoj* "verb" was shown in the instructional display. The participants were instructed to describe the event in the picture using Kaqchikel as concisely as possible, starting with the subject after the *B'anöl* display or the verb after the *B'anoj* display. Thus, it was expected that the participants would produce Kaqchikel sentences in the SVO and VOS orders after the *B'anöl* and *B'anoj* displays, respectively.

10.3.2 Results and Discussion

10.3.2.1 Utterance Latency The utterance latency results are shown in Table 10.2. Utterance latency was significantly shorter in the SVO condition than in the VOS condition. On the other hand, the main effect of patient animacy and the interaction were not significant. In other words, utterance latency was not modulated by patient animacy. The result is consistent with our first expectation that utterance latency should be shorter for subject-initial utterances than for the other types.

10.3.2.2 Eye Movement We analyzed the data for 6,000 ms from picture onset because the mean utterance offsets were less than 6,000 ms. The gaze

Table 10.2 *The means and standard deviations of utterance latency (ms) for word order and patient animacy conditions*

	Patient animacy	
	Animate	Inanimate
SVO	1,921 (265)	1,919 (219)
VOS	2,246 (411)	2,230 (404)

Note: n = 13. The values in parentheses indicate the standard deviation.

data were aggregated into 50 ms time bins. For each bin, we then calculated the probability of looks at the agent and patient. For the statistical analysis, we used the target advantage score (Kronmüller and Barr 2015), which is typically defined as the probability of looks at the target object minus the probability of looks at the non-target object (see, for instance, Symeonidou et al. 2016). Here, we designated the agent entity in a picture as the "target" and the patient entity as the "non-target," so that a higher score indicated that the participant looked more at the agent entity than the patient. The time courses of the target advantage score for each experimental condition are shown in Figure 10.6.

We divided the data into six 1,000-ms time windows and conducted statistical analyses to see how the mean target advantage score for the corresponding 1,000-ms time window was affected by word order (VOS, SVO), patient animacy (human, inanimate), and time window (0–1,000 ms, 1,000–2,000 ms, 2,000–3,000 ms, 3,000–4,000 ms, 4,000–5,000 ms, 5,000–6,000 ms). The analyses demonstrated a significant main effect of word order, a significant main effect of time window, and a significant interaction between word order and time window; the other main effects and interactions were not found to be significant. Since the interaction between word order and time window was significant, we conducted follow-up analyses to test the simple main effects of word order for each time window. The analyses revealed that the simple main effect of word order was significant for the 1,000–2,000 ms time window. This indicated that, for this time window, the target advantage score was higher in the SVO word order condition than in the VOS condition. The simple main effect was also significant for the 3,000–4,000 ms window and approached significance for the 4,000–5,000 ms

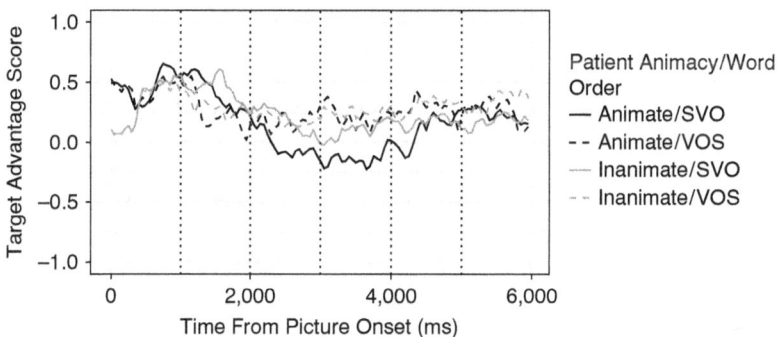

Figure 10.6 Mean target advantage scores (proportion of looks to the agent minus proportion of looks to the patient) for each experimental condition. The vertical dotted lines represent the boundaries of the time windows used for statistical analyses.
(Adapted from Koizumi et al. 2019.)

window. Contrary to the case of the 1,000–2,000 ms window, the target advantage score was higher in the VOS condition than in the SVO condition for 3,000–4,000 ms and 4,000–5,000 ms windows. This shows that the participants looked at the agent more in the SVO condition than in the VOS condition during the 1,000–2,000 ms time window, whereas they looked at the agent more in the VOS condition than in the SVO condition during the 3,000–4,000 ms and 4,000–5,000 ms windows.

We also tested the simple main effects of time window for each word order condition. The analyses found a significant simple main effect of time window in the SVO condition, revealing (i) that the target advantage score of the 0–1,000 ms window was significantly higher than that of the 2,000–3,000 ms, 3,000–4,000 ms, and 4,000–5,000 ms windows, and (ii) that the target advantage score of the 1,000–2,000 ms window was significantly higher than that of the 2,000–3,000 ms, 3,000–4,000 ms, and 4,000–5,000 ms windows. That is, in the SVO condition, participants fixated on the agent more during the first 2,000 ms than the later time periods. In the VOS condition, no significant simple main effect of time window was found. This is because the formulation of VOS sentences shows a different pattern from that of SVO sentences, with the participants' gaze more evenly distributed between the agent and patient over the entire time window, with an advantage for the agent (Figure 10.7b).

Thus, the eye tracking data shown above support our second prediction that Kaqchikel speakers would pay more attention to agents than to other elements during sentence production because of the saliency of agents.

10.3.2.3 Brain Activity We analyzed the same channels as in the Japanese study, i.e., channels 29, 30, 32, and 33, which were placed over regions centered on the left IFG. As shown in Figure 10.8, the participants showed significantly lower peak values in the VOS condition than in the SVO condition on channel 29. Significant differences were not observed between the two word order conditions on the other channels. Both the main effect of patient animacy and the two-way interaction were not significant in any of the four channels. This suggests that the overall processing load during Kaqchikel sentence production is higher for SVO sentences than for comparable VOS sentences, just like the overall processing load during Kaqchikel sentence comprehension. Our third prediction, that the cognitive load during sentence production should be higher for SVO sentences than for VOS sentences, was thus borne out.

10.4 General Discussion

We began this chapter by stating the following four predictions (or expectations) that we drew based on the findings of the previous chapters. If subject-initial sentences are easier to initiate than verb-initial sentences

10.4 General Discussion

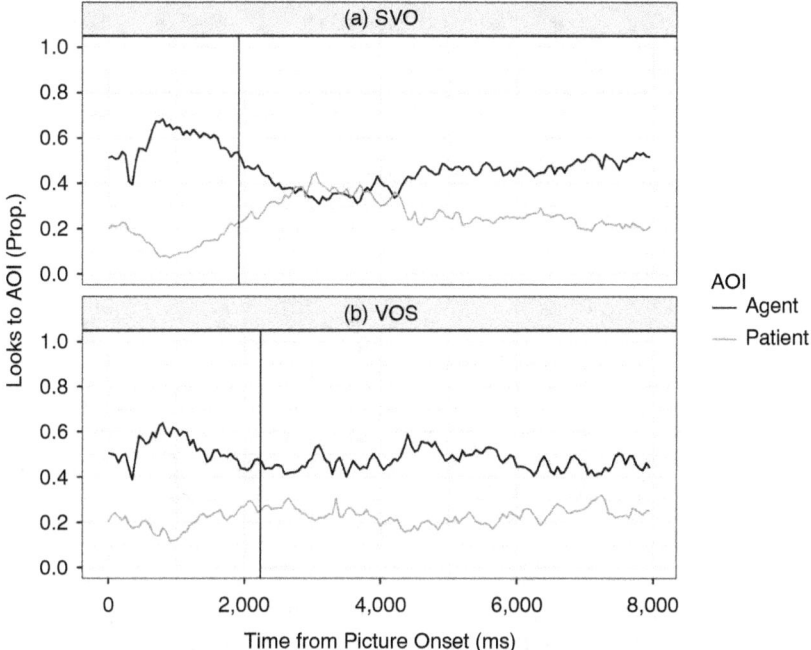

Figure 10.7 Proportion of looks to the agent/patient AOI during the picture presentation for (a) SVO and (b) VOS utterances. The black vertical lines represent speech onset.
(Adapted from Koizumi et al. 2019.)

because of the head-marking nature of Kaqchikel and the conceptual saliency of the agent among speakers of Kaqchikel, then (i) utterance latency should be shorter for SVO than VOS sentences. If the agent is conceptually more salient than the patient for speakers of Kaqchikel, (ii) they should pay more attention to the agent than to the patient during sentence production. (iii) Despite (i) and (ii), the cognitive load during sentence production should be higher for SVO sentences than for the corresponding VOS sentences, because the former are syntactically more complex than the latter. Furthermore, if there occurs larger similarity-based competition between the subject and the object in VOS than in SVO, (iv) the difference between SVO and VOS in cognitive load should be smaller in the human patient condition than in the inanimate patient condition. The results of the Kaqchikel experiment reported in the previous section confirmed all these predictions except the last. This constitutes empirical support for the conclusion that Kaqchikel speakers preferentially employ the SVO word order at

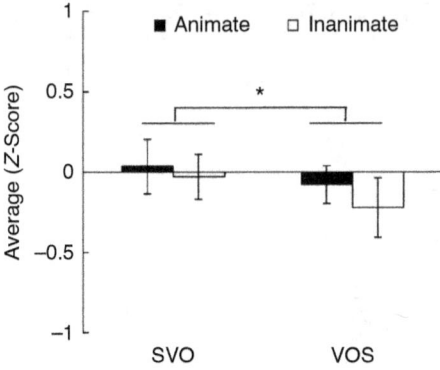

Figure 10.8 Average peak concentration changes of oxyhemoglobin under the four conditions in channel 29, which is estimated to be in the left IFG. The error bars represent the standard errors of the means.
(Adapted from Koizumi et al. 2019.)

least partly because of the conceptual saliency of the agent. However, SVO incurs a greater cognitive load than the syntactically basic VOS word order primarily due to its syntactic complexity during both sentence production and sentence comprehension.

The utterance latencies were shorter for SOV than OSV in Japanese (Takeshima et al. 2014), and shorter for SVO than VOS in Kaqchikel. What is common between these results is that the subject-initial word orders had shorter utterance latencies, meaning that utterance latency is not correlated with the syntactic complexity of the entire utterance, as SOV is syntactically simpler than OSV in Japanese and SVO is syntactically more complex than VOS in Kaqchikel. The results are in line with the view that the conceptual saliency of the initial constituent has a relatively large effect on how early the utterance starts. Another possible factor in the longer latency of VOS utterances in Kaqchikel, as mentioned in Section 10.1, is its conceptually and morphologically complex verb, with two agreement markers, one each for the subject and object, that must be determined by the speaker before initiating such an utterance. This may also be a reason that the difference in utterance latency between the two word orders is larger in Kaqchikel (SVO vs. VOS) than in Japanese (SOV vs. OSV).

The conceptual saliency of the agent receives further support from the eye tracking data. Both Japanese and Kaqchikel speakers initially fixated preferentially on the agent and continued to do so for most of the subsequent time periods. An initial fixation on the agent was observed even when OSV

10.4 General Discussion

sentences were being produced in Japanese, which shows that speakers initially pay more attention to the agent (subject) than the patient (object), regardless of the word order of the utterance to be generated. While producing SVO sentences, Kaqchikel speakers looked quickly at the agent, continued fixating on this character until the onset of speech, and finally shifted their gaze to the patient (Figure 10.7a). Kaqchikel VOS sentences exhibited a different fixation pattern than either SVO sentences in Kaqchikel or SOV and OSV sentences in Japanese. During the production of the latter three types, speakers initially fixated on the agent, shifted their attention to the patient to some extent, and then reverted to the agent. During the production of VOS sentences in Kaqchikel, however, such a triphasic pattern was not observed. The relative ratios of agent and patient fixations were fairly uniform across the entire time span (Figure 10.7b). This result is similar to Norcliffe et al.'s (2015) observation that the patterns of eye fixation during the conceptual encoding and linguistic encoding periods differ between VOS and SVO sentence production in Tzeltal. This suggests that during the production of VOS sentences, Kaqchikel (and Tzeltal) speakers process agent, patient, and action, as well as their corresponding linguistic representations, more in parallel (or less linearly) than when producing SVO sentences. This may be because initiating an utterance with a verb in a head-marking language such as Kaqchikel requires both agent and patient, as well as action, to have been processed to a certain degree in order to determine the form of the verb before its onset.

The brain activation data obtained using NIRS revealed that the production of OSV utterances yielded a higher left IFG activation than did the production of SOV utterances in Japanese, and the production of SVO utterances did the same with respect to VOS utterances in Kaqchikel. This clearly shows that sentences with a syntactically derived word order require more cognitive resources to represent than comparable sentences with the syntactically basic word order in a given language, not only in sentence comprehension but also in sentence production, whether it is an SO or an OS language.

Finally, we could not find evidence for larger similarity-based competition effects in VOS sentences than SVO sentences. The NIRS data show that the differences in the cognitive loads between SVO and VOS sentences are comparable in the human patient and inanimate patient conditions. This is in line with the results of Kiyama et al.'s (2013) Kaqchikel sentence comprehension experiment, reported in Chapter 3, that VOS was processed faster than SVO, regardless of the animacy of the object, and that the effect of object animacy and the interaction between word order and object animacy were not significant. This indicates that similarity-based competition, if present, may not be the primary factor for the higher production ratio of SVO in the reversible event condition than in the non-reversible event condition. Communicative approaches such as the noisy channel hypothesis of Gibson et al. (2013) and the role conflict hypothesis of Hall, Mayberry, and Ferreira (2013) seem to be promising avenues to pursue, as discussed in Chapters 8 and 9.

10.5   Conclusion

The results of the eye-tracked picture description experiment reported in this chapter support the conclusion that, although Kaqchikel speakers preferentially use the SVO word order because of the saliency of the agent, SVO sentences require more processing resources than VOS sentences both in comprehension and in production.

NOTES

1. This section is based on Takeshima et al. (2015).
2. This section is based on Koizumi et al. (2019), which is licensed under a Creative Commons Attribution 4.0 International License.

11 Grammatical Processing and Event Apprehension

In this chapter, we will examine the interaction between grammatical processing and event apprehension as observed in a sentence–picture matching task with Kaqchikel speakers. In due course, we will also attempt to clarify how bilingualism with Spanish would affect Kaqchikel sentence processing.

11.1 Introduction

In the event-related potential (ERP) experiment of Yano, Yasunaga, and Koizumi (2017) discussed in Chapter 5, a Kaqchikel sentence was first presented aurally through a headset. Afterwards, a picture was presented in the center of a screen, either matching the event described by the preceding sentence or not. The time between the offset of the sentence and the onset of the picture was 500 milliseconds (ms). Upon seeing the picture, the participants were asked to judge whether the picture was congruent with the sentence by pressing a YES button or a NO button (Figure 11.1).

Consistent with the results of the behavioral and fMRI experiments reported in Chapter 3 and Chapter 4, Yano, Yasunaga, and Koizumi (2017), as well as Yasunaga et al. (2015), found a P600 effect for the SVO, VSO, and OVS word orders, relative to VOS, the basic word order in Kaqchikel. In Chapter 5, we took these results to support the Individual Grammar View (IGV), which claims that it is the grammatical factors of individual languages, such as syntactic complexity, that primarily determine the word order preference in sentence comprehension in each language.

In addition to ERPs, Yano, Yasunaga, and Koizumi (2017) also measured the response times in the sentence–picture matching task. In cases where the participants gave correct responses to congruent sentence–picture pairs, the response times for SVO were significantly faster than those for VOS and OVS. Furthermore, participants responded significantly faster to VSO than to OVS. The response times for VSO were shorter than those for VOS, but the difference was not significant. This pattern, i.e., the longer reaction times after VOS sentences than SVO sentences in deciding whether the picture is congruent with the preceding sentence, is somewhat surprising, given that the processing

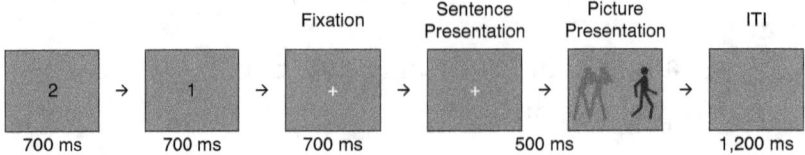

Figure 11.1 Design of the sentence–picture matching experiment.
(Adapted from Yano, Yasunaga, and Koizumi 2017 with permission.)

costs associated with sentence comprehension are lower in VOS sentences than in SVO sentences. What could have caused such a pattern? Note that this pattern is reminiscent of the results of the gesture and sentence production experiments reported in Chapters 8 and 9, in that they all featured an SVO (or agent–action–patient) preference. Recall that, in the experiments in these chapters, native speakers of Kaqchikel were asked to describe an event depicted in a picture using either gesture (Chapter 8) or speech (Chapter 9). The most frequently employed orders in these studies were agent–action–patient and SVO, respectively, which we interpreted as showing that, in the apprehension of an event depicted in a picture, agent, being more salient, tends to be activated and processed earlier than other concepts or entities, frequently giving rise to a nonverbal event representation with the agent–action–patient order, which in turn likely leads to the production of an SVO sentence, a conclusion that received further support in Chapter 10. If this construal is correct, the same should hold of the event apprehension in the sentence–picture matching task. That is, upon encountering a picture after a sentence, participants try to capture the event described in the picture. When the event is a transitive one, as in the crucial trials of Yano, Yasunaga, and Koizumi (2017), a nonverbal event representation with the agent–action–patient order may be preferentially constructed. In addition, a corresponding SVO sentence might be internally generated. In making the judgment of whether the picture is congruent with the preceding sentence, participants attempt to compare the nonverbal event representation (and/or internally generated sentence) evoked by the picture with the previously presented sentence. As the internally generated event representation and/or sentence are most likely in the agent–action–patient/SVO order, the picture-matching task may be easier when the preceding sentence is also in the SVO order. That may explain why the response times were shorter for the SVO condition than the VOS condition.

If the above conjecture is on the right track, the advantage of VOS over SVO in sentence comprehension and the advantage of SVO over VOS in the sentence–picture matching task should also work in the opposite direction. In Yano, Yasunaga, and Koizumi (2017), there was a 500-millisecond interstimulus interval between the offset of a sentence and the onset of the associated picture. We could therefore separately measure the effects of grammatical processing during sentence comprehension on the one hand, and the effects of the matching task on the other hand. If participants were required to carry out both tasks simultaneously, the advantage of VOS in grammatical processing and the advantage of SVO in the matching task would cancel each other out. If the effect of the VOS preference in grammatical processing were greater than that of the SVO preference in the matching task, VOS would be preferred to SVO overall, although the difference in preference between the two word orders should be smaller than when only the sentence comprehension task is carried out. In contrast, if the effect of the matching task were larger than that of the grammatical processing, SVO would be more preferred overall. Finally, if the magnitudes of the two effects were comparable, neither order would be preferred. To address this issue, we conducted two picture–sentence matching experiments in which the picture and the sentence were presented at the same time. We observed a higher cognitive load for VOS than for SVO, consistent with the above conjecture in general and the second scenario in particular, suggesting that the effect of the matching task is larger than that of grammatical processing. In the following sections, we will discuss these two studies, the first of which also investigated the relationship between bilingualism and word order preference in Kaqchikel.

11.2 A Picture–Sentence Matching Behavioral Study

In this study, we investigated the effects of grammatical processing, event apprehension, and bilingualism on word order preference in Kaqchikel.[1]

11.2.1 Method

Sixty healthy native Kaqchikel speakers participated in this experiment. In order to assess individual degree of Kaqchikel–Spanish bilingualism, the participants completed a questionnaire (originally created for this study) concerning their use of the two languages in daily life.

The materials for our picture–sentence matching task consisted of pictures depicting a transitive action with agent(s) and patient(s) (Figure 11.2), and the corresponding auditorily presented Kaqchikel transitive sentences, all of which were identical with the stimuli used by Yasunaga et al. (2015).

Target sentences corresponding to the stimulus pictures were arranged into the four word orders of VOS, VSO, SVO, and OVS, as exemplified in (1).

Figure 11.2 Examples of the stimulus pictures depicting a transitive action with agent(s) and patient(s) used in the picture–sentence matching task. (Adapted from Kiyama et al. 2017 with permission.)

(1) "The reds called the blue."
    a. X-Ø-k-oyoj / ri xar / ri taq käq.   [VOS]
       CP-ABS3sg-ERG3pl-call / DET blue / DET PM red
    b. X-Ø-k-oyoj / ri taq käq / ri xar.   [VSO]
       CP-ABS3sg-ERG3pl-call / DET PM red / DET blue
    c. Ri taq käq / x-Ø-k-oyoj / ri xar.   [SVO]
       DET PM red / CP-ABS3sg-ERG3pl-call / DET blue
    d. Ri xar / x-Ø-k-oyoj / ri taq käq.   [OVS]
       DET blue / CP-ABS3sg-ERG3pl-call / DET PM red

All the target sentences included a definite animate subject, a definite animate object, and an action verb in the past tense. In order to morpho-syntactically differentiate the agent–patient relationship, half of the sentences contained a singular subject and a plural object, and the other half contained a plural subject and a singular object. In addition, filler sentences were prepared to allow participants to make judgments of a mismatch with given pictures. Mismatch trials were created by reversing the agent–patient relationship, changing the color assignment, or indicating an incorrect action. The sentences were recorded by a male native Kaqchikel speaker.

The participants were seated in front of a monitor and asked to look at a fixation mark at the center of the monitor for 1,000 ms before simultaneously being presented with an auditory transitive sentence through headphones and a picture on the monitor. They were instructed to indicate via button press

11.2 A Picture–Sentence Matching Behavioral Study

whether the picture was congruent with the content of the given sentence as quickly and accurately as possible.

11.2.2 Results

On average, the participants' accuracy in the picture–sentence matching task (Figure 11.3) was the highest for SVO and the lowest for OVS. The mean reaction times were 3,270 ms for SVO, 3,334 ms for VOS, 3,371 ms for VSO, and 3,590 ms for OVS (Figure 11.4). OVS was by far the most inaccurate and slowest, and

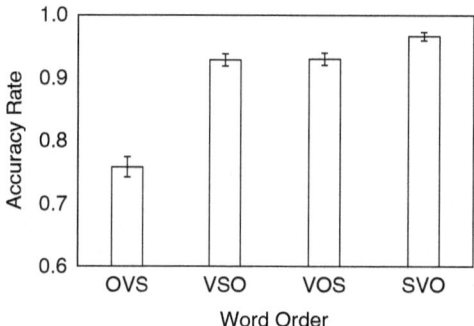

Figure 11.3 Accuracy rate of the picture–sentence matching task of Kaqchikel reversible sentences. Error bars indicate 95 percent confidence intervals.
(Adapted from Kiyama et al. 2017 with permission.)

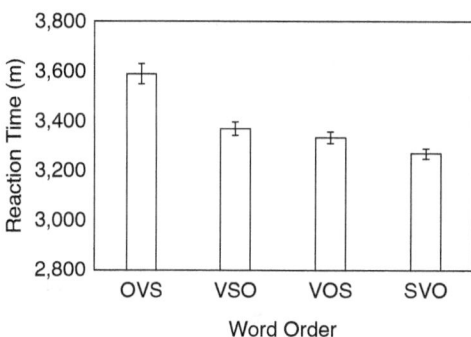

Figure 11.4 Reaction time of the picture–sentence matching task of Kaqchikel reversible sentences. Error bars indicate 95 percent confidence intervals.
(Adapted from Kiyama et al. 2017 with permission.)

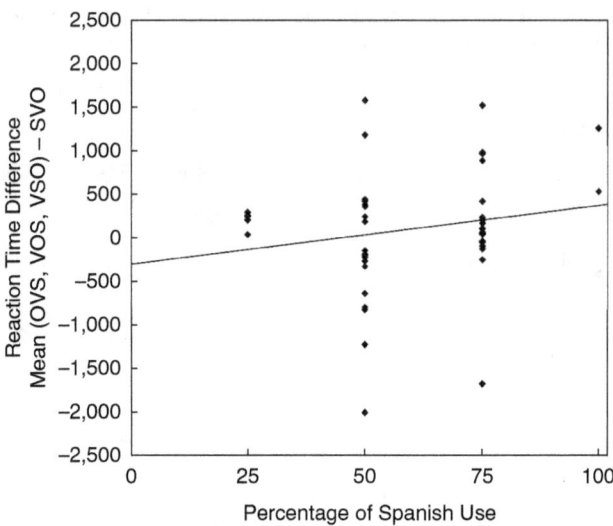

Figure 11.5 Plot of percentage of Spanish use in daily life and SVO preference in terms of reaction time in a picture-matching task of Kaqchikel sentences with animate objects (average of OVS, VOS, and VSO minus SVO).
(Adapted from Kiyama et al. 2017 with permission.)

the other three word orders were processed more accurately and quickly. The differences in reaction time between SVO and VOS and between SVO and VSO were significant, while the difference between VSO and VOS was not.

Statistical analysis revealed a significant interaction between word order and rate of Spanish use in the reaction time data. Participants with a higher ratio of Spanish use in daily life processed SVO and VSO faster, but no significance was found for VOS. The facilitation effect for SVO processing by Spanish-dominant participants is as plotted in Figure 11.5.

11.2.3 Discussion

Our previous studies have produced some inconsistent findings for word order preference in Kaqchikel, such as that, while the syntactically determined canonical order of VOS is the most efficient in sentence comprehension, SVO has the fastest response time in the sentence–picture matching task. To investigate the nature of this discrepancy, the present study re-examined word order preference in Kaqchikel reversible sentences with multiple animate entities, utilizing a picture–sentence matching task wherein participants simultaneously listened to a sentence and saw a picture depicting a scene. The

11.2 A Picture–Sentence Matching Behavioral Study

findings obtained from the present study elucidate how native Kaqchikel speakers comprehend reversible sentences when they are given a picture–sentence matching task, and to what extent those speakers' bilingualism in Spanish correlates with the word order preference in their native language.

The results revealed that, when the sentence comprehension and picture–sentence matching processes had to be carried out simultaneously, SVO was the most accurately and quickly processed order in Kaqchikel. This finding differs from the previous findings of sentence comprehension tasks without accompanying simultaneous picture-matching tasks, where VOS was preferred to SVO both in terms of behavior (Chapter 3) and neural activity (Chapters 4, 5, and 6), but it is consistent with the results of picture description experiments (Chapters 8 and 9), which found that SVO was the most frequently used order. This suggests that the advantage of VOS in grammatical processing and the advantage of SVO in the matching task cancel each other out, and that the effect of the matching task is larger than that of grammatical processing.

The preference for a subject denoting an animate agent to precede an object denoting an animate patient in Kaqchikel sentence processing seems to interfere with individual native speakers' bilingualism in Spanish. The reaction time for word orders in which the subject precedes the object (i.e., SVO and VSO) was shorter for participants with a higher ratio of daily Spanish use. No such effect was found for VOS and OVS, in which the object precedes the subject. Given that prolonged exposure to a second language has influences on information processing in the first language (e.g., Marian and Spivey 2003), our Kaqchikel-speaking participants' familiarity with the canonical order of SVO in Spanish may partially underlie their processing of subject-before-object orders in the picture–sentence matching task. The finding that individual native Kaqchikel speakers' bilingualism in Spanish enhances their SVO preference even in sentence comprehension in a picture-matching task (rather than just in picture description production) might indicate that the syntactically assumed VOS canonicity could be diachronically replaced by the frequently used SVO, as Spanish is widespread in the current Kaqchikel-speaking population. It should be noted, however, that this does not mean that the grammatical system of Kaqchikel has already shifted in this direction. As convincingly demonstrated in Yano, Yasunaga, and Koizumi (2017) and Yasunaga et al. (2015), reviewed in Chapters 5 and 6, the word order associated with the simplest syntactic structure in Kaqchikel is still VOS, with the other word orders being syntactically more complex and involving a filler-gap dependency, as schematically shown in (2). Thus, the results of the experiment reported here should be interpreted as indicating that the effects of the task and of bilingualism on sentence processing load were larger than the effect of syntactic factors.

(2)	Order	Schematic syntactic structure
	VOS	[VOS]
	VSO	[[V gap$_i$ S] O$_i$]
	SVO	[S$_i$ [VO gap$_i$]]
	OVS	[O$_i$ [V gap$_i$ S]]

To summarize, this study utilized a picture–sentence matching task to demonstrate that such a task facilitates Kaqchikel native speakers' processing of SVO sentences, and that this facilitation effect is enhanced in those with a higher ratio of daily Spanish use. As such, the prolonged exposure to the canonical order of SVO in Spanish may interfere with the syntactic canonicity of VOS in native Kaqchikel speakers.

11.3 A Picture–Sentence Matching fMRI Study

The purpose of this study was two-fold. One was to test whether the advantage of VOS over SVO observed in Koizumi and Kim's (2016) fMRI sentence comprehension study would be overridden if a picture–sentence matching task were employed instead of a sentence plausibility judgment task, as may be expected given the results of Kiyama et al. (2017) reviewed in the previous section.[2] The second purpose of the study was to extend Koizumi and Kim's (2016) study by examining the VSO and OVS orders on top of their VOS and SVO, thereby further elucidating the effects of word order alteration on cortical activations in areas associated with language processing.

11.3.1 Methods

Data from seventeen right-handed, healthy Kaqchikel native speakers with normal hearing were analyzed. The task, procedure, and stimuli were all similar to those in Kiyama et al. (2017). For each trial of the picture–sentence matching task, auditory and visual stimuli were simultaneously presented. One important difference in the experimental design was the inclusion of a color-picture matching condition as a baseline, in addition to the four crucial picture–sentence matching conditions with four different word orders (VOS, SVO, VSO, OVS). In the color-picture matching condition, the participants judged whether the colors in a picture matched the color words in the auditory stimuli.

The MRI scans were conducted on a 3.0 T MRI system while the matching tasks were conducted. Readers are referred to Ohta et al. (2017) for a detailed explanation of the image acquisition and data analyses.

11.3 A Picture–Sentence Matching fMRI Study

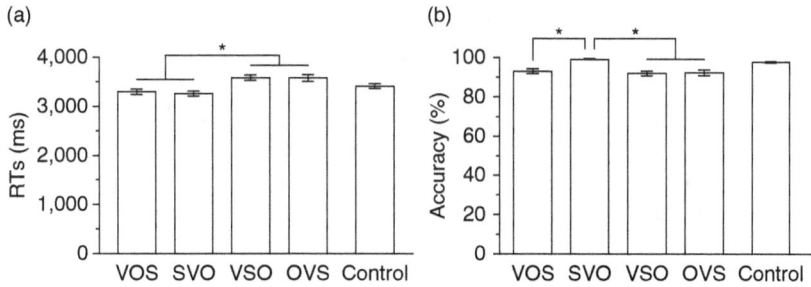

Figure 11.6 (a) Reaction times (RTs) from the onset of the picture in the picture–sentence matching and control tasks. (b) Accuracy in the picture–sentence matching and control tasks.
(Adapted from Ohta et al. 2017.)

11.3.2 Results and Discussion

The behavioral data for the picture–sentence matching task are shown in Figure 11.6. Reaction times were longer in the VSO and OVS conditions than in the VOS and SVO conditions. Accuracy was significantly higher in the SVO condition than in the other three. Taken together, these data show that SVO was the easiest order to process for Kaqchikel speakers in the picture–sentence matching task, which conforms with Kiyama et al.'s (2017) conclusion that the advantage of VOS over SVO in grammatical processing and the advantage of SVO over VOS in the picture–sentence matching task cancel out, and the effect of the latter tends to be larger.

In order to identify the brain activity associated with accuracy, we compared the SVO condition as the most accurate with the other three conditions. The contrast of (VOS + VSO + OVS) − SVO showed increased activation in the left superior and middle temporal gyri (L. STG/MTG) (Figure 11.7). In the literature, the L. STG/MTG have been implicated in lexical access (lexical semantics and phonology) (Boatman et al. 2000; Lau, Phillips, and Poeppel 2008; Pylkkänen and Marantz 2003). Crucially, the activated region found here is different from the one found in Koizumi and Kim (2016) in the comparison of SVO − VOS, the left inferior frontal gyrus (L. IFG), which subserves syntactic processing. The present result therefore confirmed our interpretation of the advantage of SVO in the picture–sentence matching task as deriving from the saliency of the agent facilitating the retrieval of information relevant to the agentive subject, rather than from the putative lower grammatical processing load of SVO.

In order to clarify the effects of grammatical processing on word order preference, we directly compared the cortical activation in VSO − VOS, observing

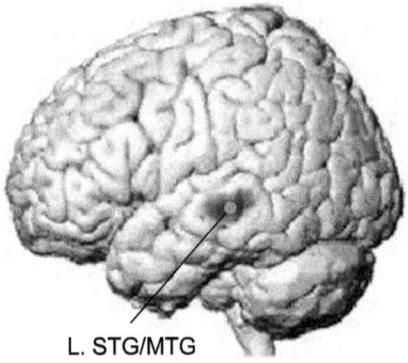

Figure 11.7 Regions identified by the contrast of (VOS + VSO + OVS) − SVO.
(Adapted from Ohta et al. 2017.)

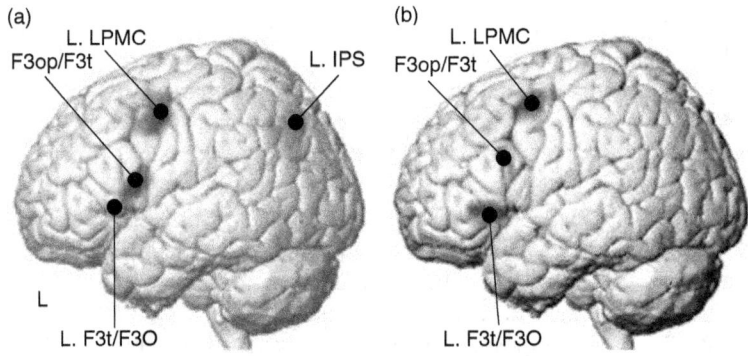

Figure 11.8 (a) Regions identified by the contrast of VSO − VOS. (b) Regions identified by the contrast of OVS − SVO.
(Adapted from Ohta et al. 2017.)

localized activation in the L. IFG (Figure 11.8a). More precisely, elevated activation was found in the opercular and triangular parts (L. F3op/F3t) and the triangular and orbital parts (L. F3t/F3O) of the L. IFG, as well as the left lateral premotor cortex (L. LPMC) and the left intraparietal sulcus (L. IPS). The comparison of the activation in OVS − SVO identified similar brain regions, except for the L. IPS (Figure 11.8b). These results further support the conclusion from the previous chapters that VSO and OVS are syntactically more complex and hence more difficult to process than VOS and SVO in Kaqchikel.

11.4 Conclusion

Different tasks activate different aspects of cognitive processes in the brain. In this chapter, we have shown that the picture–sentence matching task facilitates the processing of SVO in comparison with the other orders in Kaqchikel, at least partially because of the saliency of agentive concepts accelerating memory retrieval. We have also seen that Kaqchikel speakers who use more Spanish in daily life tend to process Kaqchikel sentences in the SVO and VSO orders more quickly.

NOTES

1. This section is based on a reanalysis of the data reported in Kiyama et al. (2017).
2. This section draws on material in Ohta et al. (2017).

12 Syntactic Structure of Kaqchikel Revisited

There are two major proposals regarding how to derive the VOS word order in the Mayan family. One is a right-specifier analysis, according to which specifiers of lexical categories are located to the right of the heads and the subject occupies a right-specifier. The other is a predicate fronting analysis, in which vP is preposed across the subject. Comparing two Mayan languages, Chol and Kaqchikel, we argue that Kaqchikel reaches VOS via a right-specifier route rather than a predicate fronting route, and then suggest a possibility that the right-specifier analysis can also be extended to Chol VOS sentences with a few parametric differences between these languages.[1]

12.1 Agreement and Hierarchical Structure in Kaqchikel

As the starting point of our discussion of Kaqchikel syntax, we adopt Imanishi's (2014) proposal about agreement and hierarchical structure in the language, which is schematically shown in (1) and (2) below.[2] (In the discussion in this section, constituent orders are irrelevant and arbitrarily represented in syntactic diagrams. We discuss linear ordering in the next section.) At the point of a derivation in (1), Voice undergoes agreement with the subject (SUB), which will eventually be reflected as an ergative agreement morpheme in the verbal complex.[3]

(1)   Ergative agreement

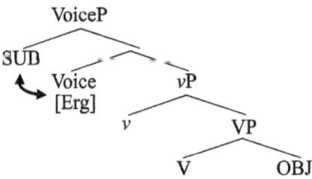

The subject then raises to Spec,TP to satisfy an EPP feature on T. This movement makes it possible for T to agree with the object, resulting in the absolutive agreement morpheme. Thus, the subject movement feeds the absolutive agreement between T and the object (Imanishi 2014: 60).

12.1 Agreement and Hierarchical Structure in Kaqchikel

(2) Absolutive agreement

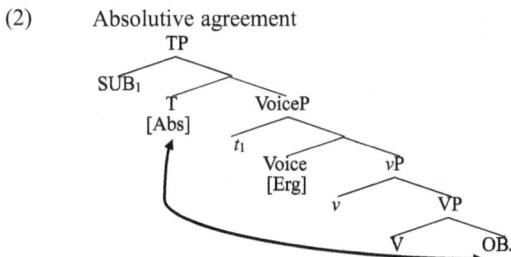

The structure in (2) captures the following two basic characteristics of Kaqchikel transitive sentences. First, the absolutive agreement morpheme occurs outside the ergative agreement morpheme in the verbal complex ([Aspect-ABS-ERG-Verb stem]). The Mirror Principle proposed by Baker (1985) (i.e., morpheme order should mirror syntactic structure) suggests that the functional head responsible for the absolutive agreement should be structurally higher than the functional head implicated in the ergative agreement, as is the case in (2).

Second, the subject is structurally higher than the object in the sense that the former asymmetrically c-commands the latter. This point can be shown by well-known syntactic diagnostics. For example, anaphors (e.g., *herself, himself, themselves, each other*) must be c-commanded by their antecedents in a local domain (i.e., anaphors must be locally bound), a condition known as Binding Condition A (cf. Chomsky 1981). Thus, (3a), in which the anaphor *each other* in a verb phrase (VP) is bound by *Mary and John*, is grammatical, whereas (3b) is ungrammatical, because *each other* is not c-commanded by its potential antecedent *Mary and John*.

(3) a. [Mary and John [$_{VP}$ saw each other]].
    b. * [Each other [$_{VP}$ saw Mary and John]].

Now consider the following Kaqchikel sentence:

(4) X-Ø-ki-tz'ët   (jub'ey chik)   k-i'   a Lolmay   chuqa'
    CP-ABS3sg-ERG3pl-see (once again)   each.other   CL Lolmay and
    a Xwan.
    CL Juan
    "Lolmay and Juan saw each other (again)."

In this sentence, the subject is *a Lolmay chuqa' a Xwan* "Lolmay and Juan," which is cross-referenced with the third-person plural ergative agreement morpheme, *ki*, prefixed to the verb. The object is the anaphor *k-i'* "*each other*," associated with the third-person singular absolutive agreement morpheme, Ø, which is phonetically null. As this sentence is grammatical, the ergative subject *a Lolmay chuqa' a Xwan* "Lolmay and Juan" c-commands the absolute object *k-i'* "*each other.*"

Another syntactic test that can be used to detect a c-command relation between nominal arguments is Binding Condition C, which states that R-expressions (e.g., *Mary, the book that John wrote*) must be free (i.e., R-expressions must not be c-commanded by noun phrases coreferential with them) (cf. Chomsky 1981). The first three examples in (5) are grammatical under the interpretations in which *John* is coreferential with *his* or *him*. In contrast, (5d) is ungrammatical if *John* and *He* are coreferential. This is because only in (5d) is *John* c-commanded by the pronoun coreferential with it.

(5) a. John$_1$ is looking for his$_1$ wife.
     b. His$_1$ wife is looking for John$_1$.
     c. John$_1$'s wife is looking for him$_1$.
     d. *He$_1$ is looking for John$_1$'s wife

Turning back to Kaqchikel, consider the sentences in (6), which are parallel to the English counterparts in (5). In (6c) and (6d), *pro* indicates a phonetically null pronoun in the object and subject position, respectively.

(6) a. N-Ø-u-kanoj   [ri r$_1$-ixjayil]   a Xwan$_1$.
       IC-ABS3sg-ERG3sg-seek DET GEN3sg-wife   CL Juan
       "Juan$_1$ is looking for his$_1$ wife."

    b. N-Ø-u-kanoj   a Xwan$_1$ [ri r$_1$-ixjayil].
       IC-ABS3sg-ERG3sg-seek CL Juan   DET GEN3sg-wife
       "His$_1$ wife is looking for Juan$_1$."

    c. N-Ø-u-kanoj   pro$_1$ [ri r-ixjayil   a Xwan$_1$].
       IC-ABS3sg-ERG3sg-seek   DET GEN3sg-wife   CL Juan
       "Juan$_1$'s wife is looking for him$_1$."

    d. *N-Ø-u-kanoj   [ri r-ixjayil   a Xwan$_1$]   pro$_1$.
       IC-ABS3sg-ERG3sg-seek DET GEN3sg-wife   CL Juan
       Lit. "He$_1$ is looking for Juan$_1$'s wife."

The grammaticality of (6c) suggests that the object does not c-command the subject; the ungrammaticality of (6d) indicates that the subject c-commands the object. Taken together, the paradigm in (6) shows again that in Kaqchikel transitive sentences, the thematic position of the ergative subject c-commands that of the absolutive object, but not vice versa.[4]

12.2 A Right-Specifier Analysis

In this section, we show that a right-specifier analysis such as that by Aissen (1992) is readily applicable to Kaqchikel with minimal modification.

12.2.1 Right-Specifier Analysis of Tzotzil (Aissen 1992, 1996)

To account for VOS word orders in Mayan languages in general and those in Tzotzil (Tseltalan branch) in particular, Aissen (1992) proposes parameterizing the order of specifiers with respect to their heads as follows: The specifier of a functional category X' precedes X', whereas the specifier of a lexical category X' follows X'. Assuming that the base-position of the external argument (subject) is Spec,VP, the VOS order is obtained when both the subject and object remain *in situ*, as shown in (7). If the subject undergoes movement to the specifier of a functional category outside VP, the SVO order is obtained, because the specifiers of functional categories are all located to the left, according to Aissen (1992, 1996).

(7)   [$_{CP}$ [$_{IP}$ [$_{VP}$ [$_{v'}$ V OBJ] SUB]]]

12.2.2 Extension to Kaqchikel

We now consider how various word orders can be derived in Kaqchikel if we apply to this language a right-specifier analysis similar to that by Aissen (1992, 1996). Following Imanishi (2014), we have assumed a slightly elaborated hierarchical structure than does Aissen (1992). Specifically, the subject overtly raises to Spec,TP in our analysis. To make this analysis compatible with Aissen's right-specifier analysis, we propose that in Kaqchikel, in addition to lexical categories, all categories up to TP have specifiers to the right, correctly resulting in the VOS order, as shown in (8).[5] Following Imanishi (2014), we also assume that V raises to C via *v*, Voice, and T.[6]

(8)   Kaqchikel VOS

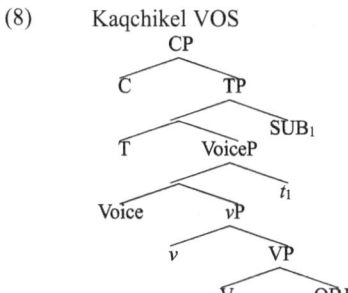

If the object undergoes a right-ward scrambling to TP across the subject, the VSO order is obtained, as shown in (9).

(9)   Kaqchikel VSO

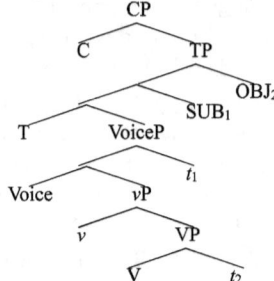

The SVO word order is derived from a structure similar to (8) by moving the subject to Spec,CP, which we assume, following Aissen (1992), is located to the left, as shown in (10).[7]

(10)   Kaqchikel SVO

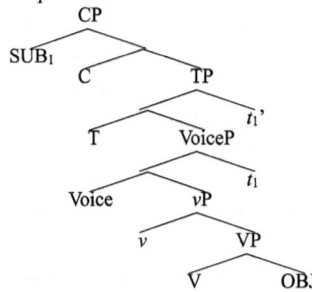

Similarly, we can get the OVS order by topicalizing the object to Spec,CP, as shown in (11).

(11)   Kaqchikel OVS

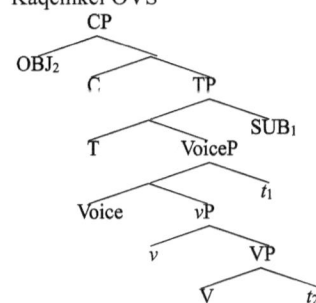

12.3 A Predicate Fronting Analysis

The right-ward scrambling in (9), subject topicalization in (10), and object topicalization in (11) are all A-bar movements.[8] Thus, they do not alter A-binding relations between the subject and the object, as is detected in the anaphor binding test, for example.

12.3 A Predicate Fronting Analysis

In this section, we argue that Coon's (2010) predicate fronting analysis of Chol cannot easily be extended to Kaqchikel, because of crucial grammatical differences between the two languages.

12.3.1 Predicate Fronting Analysis of Chol (Coon 2010)

Coon (2010) proposes an alternative account of the VOS order in Chol (Cholan branch) called a predicate fronting analysis. According to this analysis, all specifiers precede their heads *a la* Kayne's (1994) Linear Correspondence Axiom (LCA), and the subject remains *in situ* in Spec, VoiceP. The maximal predicate projection, *v*P, fronts to Spec,TP, giving rise to the VOS order, as schematically shown in (12). Coon (2010) argues that T in Chol has strong agreement features requiring the verb to move overtly to T; V cannot move to T, because head movement is generally absent in this language. Therefore, the entire predicate phrase *v*P must front as a last resort.

(12) Chol VOS

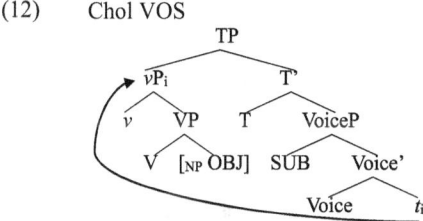

Evidence for this analysis stems from different restrictions on objects in VOS and VSO sentences. In Chol, the object must be a bare (determiner-less) noun phrase (NP) in VOS sentences, and full determiner phrases (DPs) with an overt determiner (D) are prohibited from occupying the VOS object position, as shown in (13).

(13)　　VOS
　　　　a. Tyi　　i-kuch-u　　[NP si'　] aj-Maria
　　　　　　PRFV　A3-carry-TV　　wood　DET-Maria
　　　　　　"Maria carried wood."

b. *Tyi   i-kuch-u   [DP jiñi   si']   aj-Maria
   PRFV A3-carry-TV   DET   wood   DET-Maria
   "Maria carried the wood."

(Coon 2010: 355)

In contrast, the object must be a DP in VSO sentences, as shown in (14).

(14) VSO
  a. Tyi   i-kuch-u   aj-Maria   [DP jiñi   si']
      RFV   A3-carry-TV   DET-Maria   DET   wood
      "Maria carried the wood."

  b. *Tyi   i-kuch-u   aj-Maria   [NP si']
      RFV   A3-carry-TV   DET-Maria   wood
      "Maria carried the wood."

(Coon 2010: 355)

These restrictions on objects are readily accounted for by assuming that a bare NP object must remain *in situ* within VP, as in (12), whereas a full DP object must undergo an object shift to Spec,AbsP before the remnant *v*P preposing, as shown in (15), yielding the VSO order.

(15) Chol VSO

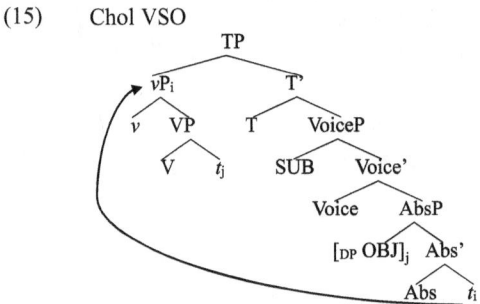

Further empirical support for Coon's analysis pertains to adjunct positions. The predicate fronting analysis makes two predictions. First, the verb and a bare NP object are adjacent to each other within VP: nothing can intervene between them. Second, the verb and a full DP object are separated by several functional projections so that some adverbial expressions may intervene between them. These predictions are well borne out, as illustrated in (16), in which the subjects are all phonetically empty (i.e., *pro*).[9]

(16) a. Tyi   k-wuts'-u   **abi**   [DP ili   pisil].
          PRFV A1-wash-TV   yesterday   DET   clothes

      b. *Tyi   k-wuts'-u   **abi**   [NP pisil].
          PRFV A1-wash-TV   yesterday   clothes

12.3 A Predicate Fronting Analysis

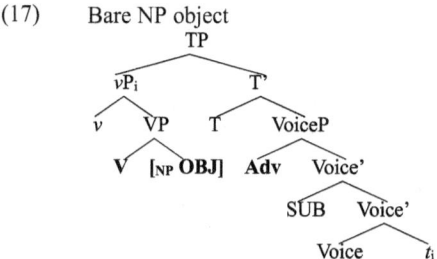

c. Tyi   k-wuts'-u   [NP pisil]   **abi**.
   PRFV A1-wash-TV   clothes   yesterday

(Coon 2010: 367)

More concretely, if the adverb *abi* "yesterday" is left-adjoined to VoiceP, the pattern in (16) is as expected, as shown in (17) and (18).[10]

(17) Bare NP object

(18) Full DP object

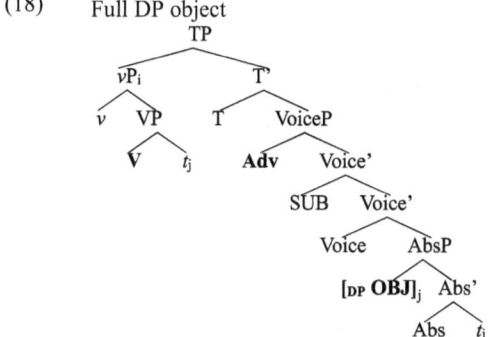

12.3.2 Extension to Kaqchikel

In attempting to extend Coon's predicate fronting analysis of Chol to Kaqchikel, however, we face at least three problems. First, if *v*P raises to Spec,TP in Kaqchikel parallel to the structure of Chol in (17), and the object in the fronted VP must be a bare NP, we expect that the VOS object in Kaqchikel must be a bare NP as well. However, this expectation does not materialize. As shown in (19), in Kaqchikel, unlike in Chol, both a bare NP object and a full DP object (either definite or indefinite) are acceptable in the VOS order. The object must be definite in VSO, as shown in (20).

(19) a. X-Ø-u-qüm raxya' ri ajanel.
CP-ABS3sg-ERG3sg-sip cold.water DET carpenter
"The carpenter sipped cold water."

b. X-Ø-u-ch'äj ri ch'ich' ri a Xwan.
CP-ABS3sg-ERG3sg-wash DET car DET CL Juan
'Juan washed the car.'

c. X-Ø-u-ch'äj jun ch'ich' ri a Xwan.
CP-ABS3Sg-ERG3sg-wash a car DET CL Juan
"Juan washed a car."

(20) a. X-Ø-u-ch'äj ri a Xwan ri ch'ich'.
CP-ABS3sg-ERG3sg-wash DET CL Juan DET car
"Juan washed the car."

b. *X-Ø-u-ch'äj ri a Xwan jun ch'ich'.
CP-ABS3sg-ERG3sg-wash DET CL Juan a car
"Juan washed a car."

Second, the predicate fronting analysis accounts well for the fact that adjuncts cannot intervene between the verb and the object in the VOS order in Chol. If Kaqchikel had the same structure as Chol, adverbs could not occur between the verb and its object in the VOS order in Kaqchikel, either, contrary to the fact. In Kaqchikel, unlike in Chol, a time adverb such as *iwir* "yesterday" may freely occur between the verb and the object, as shown in (21).

(21) a. V **Adv** OS
X-Ø-u-ch'äj **iwir** ri ch'ich' ri a Xwan.
CP-ABS3sg-ERG3sg-wash yesterday DET car DET CL Juan

b. VO **Adv** S
X-Ø-u-ch'äj ri ch'ich' **iwir** ri a Xwan.
CP-ABS3sg-ERG3sg-wash the car yesterday DET CL Juan

c. VOS **Adv**
X-Ø-u-ch'äj ri ch'ich' ri a Xwan **iwir**.
CP-ABS3sg-ERG3sg-wash the car DET CL Juan yesterday

The final problem with the application of the predicate fronting analysis of Chol to Kaqchikel is that it cannot account for the absolutive agreement. Chol is a so-called low absolutive language, in which absolutive agreement of a transitive object is licensed within a predicate phrase. The morpheme order in the verbal complex is [Aspect-ABS-Verb stem-ERG] in this language. We might assume that *v* enters into an absolutive agreement relation with the object. In contrast, Kaqchikel is a high absolutive language, in which the functional head responsible for the absolutive agreement with the object is structurally higher than the base position of the transitive subject, as reflected in the morpheme order [Aspect-ABS-ERG-Verb stem]. As mentioned in Section 12.1, following Imanishi (2014), we assume that

12.3 A Predicate Fronting Analysis

T enters into an absolutive agreement relation with the object. If the subject stays in situ, and the object together with the verb raises to Spec,TP parallel to (17) in Kaqchikel, then the object should not be able to agree with T even before the predicate fronting, because of a defective intervener, i.e., the subject.

To summarize, it is unreasonable and unsubstantiated to posit a predicate fronting to account for the VOS word order in Kaqchikel, because of the three empirical differences between Chol and Kaqchikel as described.

On the other hand, the right-specifier analysis of Kaqchikel outlined in the previous section can readily account for the cases problematic for the predicate fronting analysis. First, the fact that the VOS object may be either definite or indefinite follows if we assume that a subject obligatorily moves to Spec,TP, resulting in the VOS order even if a definite object undergoes object shift to Spec,VoiceP.[11] Second, if an adverb such as *iwir* "yesterday" is adjoined to TP/ T', as schematically shown in (22), then its distribution shown in (20) is as expected. The [V Complex] in (22) stands for the verbal complex resulting from V raising to C through v to T.

(22)   Kaqchikel VOS

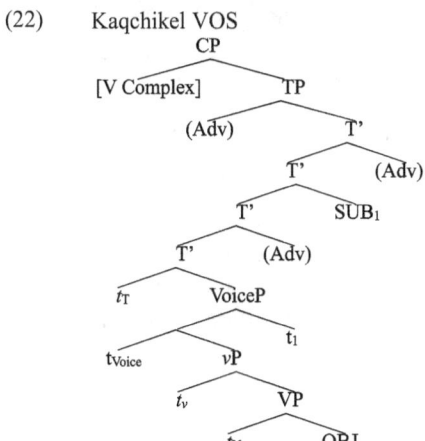

Finally, T can agree with the object before it raises to C, because the subject does not intervene between them on this account.[12]

12.3.3 Right-Specifier Analysis of Chol

To derive the VOS in Chol, Coon (2010) posits that (i) specifiers uniformly occur to the left, (ii) *v*P is obligatorily fronted to Spec,TP, (iii) V does not move (no head movement in Chol), and (iv) the external argument stays in situ in Spec,VoiceP (T does not have an EPP feature). On the other hand, on our account of Kaqchikel, (i) specifiers occur to the right except for CP, (ii) there is no *v*P fronting, (iii) V raises to C, and (iv) the external argument moves to Spec, TP. These differences between the two languages are summarized in (23).

(23) Parametric differences between Chol and Kaqchikel (to be revised)

	Chol (Coon 2010)	Kaqchikel
Directionality of specifiers	left	right (except for CP)
vP fronting to Spec,TP	present	absent
V raising to C	absent	present
Subject raising to Spec,TP	absent	present

We will show below that we can dispense with some of the parametric differences given in (23), and that it is possible to reduce the parametric differences between Chol and Kaqchikel into two.

Exploring the possibility that there is no predicate fronting even in the derivation of Chol VOS sentences, we suggest that VOS sentences in Chol and Kaqchikel have the structures represented in (24a) and (24b), respectively.

(24) a. Chol VOS   b. Kaqchikel VOS

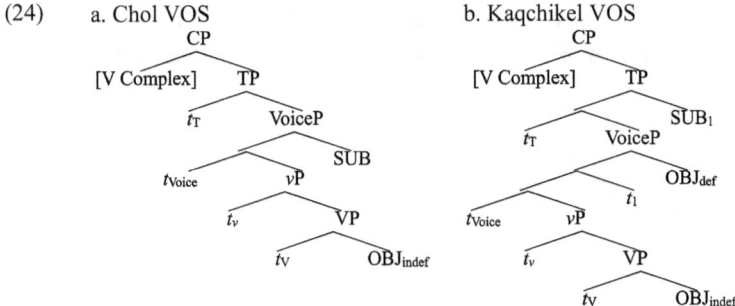

The only difference between (24a) and (24b) is that the subject moves to Spec, TP in Kaqchikel, but not in Chol (the subject remains in Spec,VoiceP). This difference is necessary to explain the fact that definite objects invariably result in the VSO order in Chol: a full definite DP undergoes object shift to the periphery of the phase (i.e., VoiceP), skipping over a subject, as shown in (25). A comparable object shift in Kaqchikel, on the other hand, does not alter word order because the subject is located in Spec,TP.

(25) Chol VSO

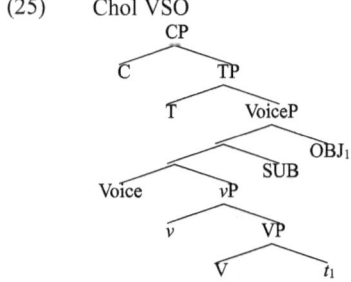

Given the structure in (24a), an immediate question arises as to why nothing can intervene between V and bare NPs in Chol. We assume that bare NPs in Chol must undergo (pseudo-)incorporation to be licensed. This means that (pseudo-)incorporation is prohibited in cases where some element (such as a subject and adverb) intervenes between V and NPs. Therefore, we can explain the fact that V and bare NPs must be adjacent in Chol, without invoking vP-fronting.[13] In contrast, such (pseudo-)incorporation is not necessary for indefinite objects to be licensed in Kaqchikel, presumably because it has the indefinite article *jun*. The table in (26) summarizes the parametric differences between Chol and Kaqchikel.[14]

(26) Parametric differences between Chol and Kaqchikel (revised)

	Chol	Kaqchikel
Subject raising to Spec,TP	absent	present[15]
(Peudo-)incorporation of bare NP objects	present	absent

12.4 Conclusion

There are multiple syntactic routes to the VOS order (Chung 2017). Different VOS languages may have different syntactic structures. There are two major proposals regarding how Mayan VOS word order is grammatically obtained. We proposed in this chapter that Kaqchikel, and possibly Chol as well, derive the VOS order through a right-specifier route, rather than a predicate fronting route.

Before concluding the chapter, we would like to briefly comment on the linearization of specifiers. What is clear from the discussion above is that we need to depart from Kayne's (1994) LCA-based approach to word order, which assumes that precedence relations are determined by dominance relations: since subjects in the VOS order in Kaqchikel are structurally higher than objects, the LCA predicts that subjects precede objects, contrary to the fact. This conclusion is not incompatible with either the view that the word order is determined in narrow syntax or that precedence is not represented in syntax and linear orders are determined post-syntactically. Choosing between the two will be an issue for future research.

NOTES

1. This chapter is a partial reproduction of Otaki et al. (2019) with some modification. I am grateful to the Linguistic Society of Japan for permission to use it in this book.
2. Imanishi (2014) assumes that vP dominates VoiceP, whereas Coon (2010) assumes that VoiceP dominates vP. This difference does not have crucial bearing on the main points of this chapter, and we remain agnostic between the two possibilities. For the

sake of exposition, we assume that VoiceP dominates vP (for arguments for this structure, see Pylkkänen 2002 and Harley 2013, among others).
3. More specifically, Imanishi (2014) proposes that ergative Case is a type of Case which is assigned by a phase head to the highest Case-less DP within the Spell-Out domain of a phase. In (1), therefore, ergative Case is assigned to the otherwise Case-less subject by the phase head, Voice. On the other hand, Imanishi (2014) assumes that absolutive Case is assigned by T via Agree (Chomsky 2000). See also Imanishi (2020).
4. Data from weak crossover effects make the same point. It has been known since Postal (1971) that an object wh-operator cannot cross over a bound pronoun contained in a structurally higher subject DP. For instance, (ia), which involves no crossover configuration, can be understood as a question asking the identity of the person x such that x respected x's mother, whereas (ib), in which the object wh-operator crosses over the subject DP containing the pronoun *his*, does not allow such a bound variable interpretation.

(i)   a. Who$_1$ t_1 respected his$_1$ mother?
       b. Who$_1$ did his$_{*1/2}$ mother respect t_1?

The corresponding Kaqchikel examples in (ii) show the exactly similar pattern, which suggests that the subject is structurally higher than the object in the language.

(ii) a. Achike$_1$ x-Ø-kamela-n   ru$_1$-te' t_1?
         who   CP-ABS3sg-respect-AF GEN3sg-mother

       b. Achike$_1$ x-Ø-u-kamelaj t_1 ru$_{*1/2}$-te'?
         who   CP-ABS3sg-ERG3sg-respect   GEN3sg-mother

5. We stipulate that specifiers are located to the right, *except for CP*. We suspect that this is because the CP domain is closely related to discourse/information structure, and it might be the case that UG requires elements related to discourse/information structure to appear to the left. This is consistent with the fact that rightward *wh*-movement is virtually unattested in spoken languages (cf. Richards 2010, 2016).
6. In Kaqchikel embedded clauses, a complementizer such as *chin* "that" appears as an independent lexical item, as shown below.

(i)   X-Ø-in-rayij   [chin x-Ø-tzaq   ri   achin].
        CP-B3sg-A1sg-desire COMP CP-B3sg-fall DET Man
        'I wanted the man to fall.'   (Clemens 2013)

Note that this fact does not preclude V-to-C movement in Kaqchikel once a split CP structure (cf. Rizzi 1997) is adopted: the complementizer is located in the topmost category, Force, which specifies clause types, and V moves to a lower category, presumably Topic or Fin(ite).
7. In Kaqchikel, the SVO order is possible in matrix clauses and certain subordinate clauses. Again, we assume a split CP structure for the left periphery.
8. Unlike the Spec,TP subject position, which is considered to have A-properties, the scrambled object in (9) is located in a TP adjoined position, resulting in showing A-bar properties. This is similar to the case where sentence-internal scrambling

12.4 Conclusion

adjoining to TP can be A-bar movement in Japanese, as shown in the following example (no condition C violation is triggered).

(i) Zibun-zishin$_1$-o Taro$_1$-ga t_1 hihanshita
himself Taro-NOM criticized
"Taro criticized himself."

9. Since no examples with an overt subject are provided in Coon (2010), there remains a possibility that the sentence in (16a) has the underlying V-S-Adv-O order and the V-Adv-S-O order is actually ungrammatical. If that is the case, the V-Adv-S-O order will no longer be problematic for the right-specifier analysis of Chol without assuming V-to-C movement (see discussion in Section 12.3.3).
10. Although the time adverb *abi* "yesterday" is adjoined to VoiceP in (17) following the analysis by Coon (2010), we posit in our analysis of Chol and Kaqchikel that time adverbs are adjoined to TP/T', as their interpretations are related to tense, not to voice.
11. We assume that definite objects obligatorily undergo object shift to Spec,VoiceP in both Chol and Kaqchikel, following the Mapping Hypothesis by Diesing (1992).
12. As an anonymous reviewer points out, it would be interesting to see how other types of adverbs such as manner adverbs behave in VOS sentences. Given that manner adverbs appear low in the structure (adjoined to vP or VP, for example), it seems difficult to obtain the "V OBJ$_{def}$ ADV$_{manner}$ SUB" / "V OBJ SUB ADV$_{manner}$" order. (Whether these orders are possible or not is up to the availability of adverb scrambling in the language.) Imanishi (2014, 2020) reports some facts concerning manner and time adverbs in Kaqchikel, although they are used within nominalized clauses (usually with null pronouns) and it is not clear how they behave in VOS sentences (see also Henderson and Coon 2018, who discuss various adverbs in relation to Agent Focus in Kaqchikel).
13. We thank an anonymous reviewer for suggesting the possibility that the presence/absence of (pseudo-)incorporation could be a locus of parametric differences between Chol and Kaqchikel. As the reviewer suggests, this process is similar to "incorporation antipassive," a phenomenon discussed by Dayley (1981); Coon (2013); among others.

(i) a. Transitive
Tyi k-wuts'-u pisil.
PRFV A1-wash-TV clothes
"I washed clothes."

b. Incorporation antipassive
Tyi k-cha'l-e wuts' pisil.
PRFV A1-do-DTV wash clothes
"I washed clothes." (Coon 2013: 76)

Contrary to transitive objects, objects in incorporation antipassive may not be a full DP – determiners cannot appear with antipassive objects, for example. We suspect that a similar process is happening in transitive sentences with bare objects in Chol, thus prohibiting them from being used with determiners and other elements (such as adverbs).

14. A recent paper by Clemens and Coon (2018) proposes yet another theory of deriving verb-initial word order in Mayan languages. They argue that, all else being equal, the basic word order of Mayan languages is invariably VSO (which is derived by a sequence of head movement), and VOS is obtained by one of the following strategies (Clemens and Coon 2018: 238):

(i)   a. subject in high right-side topic position
       b. heavy-NP shift of phonologically heavy subjects
       c. prosodic reordering of bare NP objects

Of relevance to Kaqchikel VOS is (ia), which assumes that the VOS order is derived by moving a subject to a right-side topic position, as illustrated in (ii).

(ii)   [$_{TopicP}$ [$_{CP}$ V-Complex [$_{TP}$ t_S O]] S]

This proposal, however, is incompatible with the experimental data reported in Chapter 3 to Chapter 6, which clearly show that VOS sentences induce less processing load than VSO/SVO sentences for Kaqchikel speakers, suggesting that VOS is syntactically simpler than the other two. If VSO is the basic word order and VOS is derived by movement to the higher right-side functional projection, it is not clear why VOS has a processing advantage over VSO.

15. Erlewine (2016) also argues that ergative subjects in Kaqchikel move to Spec,TP, based on the facts that ergative subjects in Kaqchikel trigger Agent Focus in constructions involving A-bar dependencies.

13 Syntax and Processing Load

We have seen in the previous chapters that the relative difficulty during the comprehension of Kaqchikel transitive sentences with the four commonly used word orders can be schematically summarized as in (1).

(1) Relative processing costs in Kaqchikel
    VOS < SVO < VSO < OVS

The easiest word order to process during sentence comprehension in Kaqchikel is VOS, which is associated with the simplest syntactic structures among grammatically possible word orders in this language. This observation is compatible with the individual grammar view rather than the universal cognition view. That is, word orders other than VOS should be associated with an extra processing cost due to the presence of an extra filler-gap dependency that is absent in VOS. How, then, should the relative processing difficulty among word orders other than VOS be explained? SVO, VOS, and OVS all involve a filler-gap dependency, and their relative difficulty cannot simply be attributed to the *presence* of a filler-gap dependency. Rather, the *nature* of the dependencies must be considered. It is generally held that such dependencies should be resolved as quickly as possible to minimize the distance between the filler and the gap (e.g., Frazier and d'Arcais 1989). The question is, precisely how should this distance be calculated? In this chapter, we will consider representative theories to see how they fare in accounting for the ranking of the Kaqchikel sentences shown in (1) above (Section 13.1) and the corresponding ranking in Japanese (Section 13.2).

13.1 Kaqchikel

We consider three theories of processing cost associated with a filler-gap dependency to determine whether they correctly account for the ranking of the Kaqchikel sentences shown in (1) above: the Dependency Locality Theory (Gibson 2000), the Structural Distance Hypothesis (O'Grady 1997), and the Minimize Filler-Gap Domain (Hawkins 2004). In addition, we also consider an experience-based (frequency-based) account because the relative processing costs of constructions tend to be inversely correlated with their production frequencies.

13.1.1 Experience-Based Hypothesis

It has been demonstrated that frequency has a strong influence on processing cost (Arnon and Snider 2010; Bybee 2010; Gennari and MacDonald 2009; MacDonald 2013; MacDonald, Pearlmutter, and Seidenberg 1994; Reali and Christiansen 2007; Trueswell 1996; Trueswell, Tanenhaus, and Garnsey 1994). According to experience-based theory, human parsers learn how to process sentences efficiently based on their experiences. That is, speakers of a language are more proficient in sentence structures and words that are used frequently, and they are more likely to process these with speed and accuracy. In terms of word order and processing load, it has been observed in many languages that the syntactically simplest word order, which triggers the lowest processing load, is also the most frequently used word order within each language. It is thus interesting to observe how well production frequency predicts the relative processing difficulty among the four word orders in Kaqchikel.

As we saw in Chapter 8, the relative production frequency of Kaqchikel transitive sentences with four commonly used word orders can be schematically summarized as in (2).

(2)   Relative production frequency in Kaqchikel
        SVO > VOS > VSO > OVS

According to Kubo et al.'s (2015) Experiment 1, for example, of all the sentences with a transitive verb and nominal subject and object produced in their sentence-production experiment with a picture-description task, sentences with the SVO, VOS, VSO, and OVS orders constitute approximately 81 percent, 17 percent, 1 percent, and 0 percent, respectively, of the structures used.

If it is the case that a higher production frequency of a construction renders the production easier to process, the frequency ranking in (2) would predict the relative processing load ranking shown in (3).

(3)   Relative processing cost in Kaqchikel predicted by production frequency
        SVO < VOS < VSO < OVS

Compare the predicted ranking in (3) with the actually observed ranking in (1), repeated here as (4).

(4)   Relative processing cost in Kaqchikel
        VOS < SVO < VSO < OVS

The two rankings displayed in (3) and (4) are similar in that they both effectively include the partial hierarchy of [SVO < VSO < OVS]. However, there is a crucial difference between (3) and (4) in that VOS is predicted to be more difficult to process than SVO ((3), contrary to fact (4)). Thus, production frequency alone is not sufficient to account for the relative processing load of Kaqchikel transitive sentences with different word orders.[1] Grammar sometimes overrides frequency (cf. Bornkessel, Schlesewsky, and Friederici 2002; Kempen and Harbusch 2005).

13.1.2 Linear Distance Hypothesis

A recurrent theory regarding the source of the difficulty of filler-gap dependencies is that they can be predicted by the *linear distance* between the filler and the gap (Hawkins 1989; Tarallo and Myhill 1983). Gibson's (1998, 2000) Dependency Locality Theory (DLT) is an example of this type of proposal. According to the DLT, the difficulty of dependencies can be predicted by the linear distance between the filler and the gap. In particular, new discourse referents, such as lexical NPs and verbs, that occur between fillers and gaps increase the processing cost and thus create difficulty.

The DLT holds that cognitive resources are consumed by two aspects of sentence comprehension: (i) *integration* of the current word into the structure built thus far, and (ii) *storage* of the structure built thus far, which includes keeping track of incomplete dependencies. Gibson (1998, 2000) assumes that integration and storage access the same pool of resources.

The integration cost may be affected by many factors, of which the following two are specifically discussed by Gibson (2000):

(5)   *DLT simplified discourse processing cost* (the cost associated with accessing or constructing the discourse structure for the maximal projection of the input word head h_2)
    1 energy unit (EU) is consumed if h_2 is the head of a new discourse referent; 0 EUs otherwise.   (Gibson 2000: 104)

(6)   *DLT structural integration cost*
    The structural integration cost associated with connecting the syntactic structure for a newly input head h_2 to a projection of a head h_1 that is part of the current structure for the input is dependent on the complexity of the computations that took place between h_1 and h_2. For simplicity, it is assumed that 1 EU is consumed for each new discourse referent in the intervening region.   (Gibson 2000: 105)

The storage cost component is calculated according to the hypothesis in (7).

(7)   *DLT storage costs*
        1 memory unit (MU) is associated with each syntactic head required to complete the current input as a grammatical sentence.
        (Gibson 2000: 114)

We next consider how to calculate discourse processing, structural integration, and storage cost, taking the following subject-extracted relative clause (RC) in English as an example:

(8)   Subject-extracted RC
        the reporter who attacked the senator

During the comprehension of the RC in (8), a new discourse referent is introduced upon encountering *reporter*, *attacked*, and *senator*, and 1 EU is consumed at each of these three points, in accordance with (5). All structural integrations in (8) occur between two adjacent constituents (e.g., *the* and *reporter*). Thus, no structural integration cost is incurred, according to (6). As for storage cost, when the sentence-initial determiner *the* is processed, two syntactic heads are needed to form a grammatical sentence: a noun and a verb (e.g., "*The boy left*."). Therefore, a cost of 2 MUs is incurred at this point. After processing *reporter*, only one head is needed to complete a sentence: a verb. Therefore, the storage cost is 1 MU, as dictated by (7). At the point of the relative pronoun *who*, it is clear that the rest of the RC and the verb of the matrix clause must follow. The RC requires two more heads, a verb and an empty category, to be associated with *who*. Thus, the total storage cost at this point is 3 MUs. After processing *attacked*, two heads are needed to form a grammatical sentence: a noun for the object of *attacked* and a verb for the matrix clause. Therefore, the storage cost is 2 MUs. When the second instance of *the* is processed (after *attacked*), two heads are needed to form a complete sentence: a noun and a verb. The noun *senator* satisfies one of the two requirements (i.e., the former), leaving the cost of 1 MU corresponding to the prediction of the matrix verb. This is summarized in Table 13.1, in which the total processing costs are calculated based on the simplified assumption that the magnitude of 1 EU equals that of 1 MU.

Next, consider the object-extracted relative clause in (9).

(9)   Object-extracted RC
        the reporter who the senator attacked

As with the subject-extracted RC in (8), the processing of the object-extracted RC in (9) also involves the introduction of a new discourse referent at the points of *reporter*, *senator*, and *attacked*, consuming 1 EU for each. The maximal structural integration cost is incurred when processing *attacked*. Three structural integrations occur at this point. The verb *attacked* is integrated as the verb for the subject NP, *the senator*. No new discourse referents intervene. Consequently, this integration step is free of cost. An empty category to be

13.1 Kaqchikel

Table 13.1 *Word-by-word predictions of the DLT for the subject-extracted RC in (8)*

Cost types	the	reporter	who	attacked	the	senator
Discourse processing	0	1	0	1	0	1
Structural integration	0	0	0	0	0	0
Storage	2	1	3	2	2	1
Total	2	2	3	3	2	2

Table 13.2 *Word-by-word predictions of the DLT for the object-extracted RC in (9)*

Cost types	the	reporter	who	the	senator	attacked
Discourse processing	0	1	0	0	1	1
Structural integration	0	0	0	0	0	2
Storage	2	1	3	4	3	1
Total	2	2	3	4	4	4

coindexed with the relative pronoun *who* is integrated as the object of *attacked*. This attachment step is also local, with no EUs consumed. The empty category in the object position is coindexed with the preceding relative pronoun *who*. There are two discourse referents in the intervening region: the NP *the senator* and the event referent *attacked*, leading to an integration cost of 2 EUs at this step. The storage costs for the first three words in the object-extracted RC (9) are the same as those in the subject-extracted RC (8). After processing the second *the* in (9), four heads are needed to form a grammatical sentence: two verbs (a verb in RC and a matrix verb), an empty category to be associated with *who*, and a noun for the determiner *the*, thus consuming 4 MUs. The noun *senator* satisfies the last of these requirements, resulting in an ultimate cost of 3 MUs. The verb *attacked* then satisfies the prediction of a verb in RC. At this point, an empty category can also be created in the object position of the verb *attacked*, satisfying another prediction. The storage cost after processing *attacked* is, therefore, 1 MU for the prediction of the matrix verb. This analysis is summarized in Table 13.2.

As shown above, the number of EUs and MUs consumed in processing is larger for the object-extracted RC (nineteen units in total) than for the subject-extracted RC (fourteen units in total). Thus, the former is predicted to be more difficult by the DLT than the latter, which is consistent with the experimental results reported by Gibson (2000) and others.

Table 13.3 *Predictions of the DLT for VOS in Kaqchikel*

Cost types	V	O	S
Discourse processing	1	1	1
Structural integration	0	0	1
Storage	2	1	0
Total	**3**	**2**	**2**

We now turn to Kaqchikel. Predictions of the DLT for simple transitive sentences with four different word orders are shown in Tables 13.3–13.6. For the sake of exposition, we consider simplified cases where V, O, and S each consists of just one head. In VOS (Table 13.3), a new discourse referent, the event referent indicated by V, is introduced at the sentence-initial position, consuming 1 EU. V being a transitive verb, two heads are needed to complete a grammatical Kaqchikel sentence: a noun for the object and another noun for the subject. The storage cost after processing V is therefore 2 MUs. Upon encountering O, a new discourse referent is introduced (consuming 1 EU), and O is locally attached to V (with no EUs consumed). O satisfies one of the two requirements imposed by V, resulting in a cost of 1 MU. Finally, at the point of S, a new discourse referent is introduced (consuming 1 EU), and S is integrated with V across one discourse referent introduced by the object (consuming 1 EU), completing a grammatical sentence. Therefore, there is no storage cost for sentence completion. Thus, the total processing cost for the VOS sentence is seven units (4 EUs and 3 MUs), as summarized in Table 13.3.

In SVO (Table 13.4), a new discourse referent is introduced upon encountering S, V, and O, and 1 EU is consumed at each of these three points. The storage cost after processing S is 2 MUs, corresponding to the predictions of a verb and an empty category to be associated with the preposed S. After the processing of V, it is clear that a noun for the object is needed in addition to the subject empty category, yielding a cost of 2 MUs. When O is processed, the empty category (ts) to be coindexed with S is integrated with V across one discourse referent O, consuming 1 EU. The subject-position empty category is coindexed with the clause-initial S. Two discourse referents corresponding to V and O intervene between them, leading to an integration cost of 2 EUs. Therefore, the total processing cost for the SVO sentence is ten units (6 EUs and 4 MUs), as summarized in Table 13.4.

In VSO (Table 13.5), a new discourse referent is introduced upon encountering V, S, and O, consuming 1 EU at each point. Two MUs are incurred at the point of processing V because two nouns, one for each of the subject and object,

13.1 Kaqchikel

Table 13.4 *Predictions of the DLT for SVO in Kaqchikel*

Cost types	S	V	[O (ts)]
Discourse processing	1	1	1
Structural integration	0	0	3
Storage	2	2	0
Total	**3**	**3**	**4**

Table 13.5 *Predictions of the DLT for VSO in Kaqchikel*

A.

Cost types	V	S	[O (to)]
Discourse processing	1	1	1
Structural integration	0	0	2
Storage	2	2	0
Total	**3**	**3**	**3**

B.

Cost types	V	S	O
Discourse processing	1	1	1
Structural integration	0	0	1
Storage	2	2	0
Total	**3**	**3**	**2**

are required to complete a grammatical transitive sentence. One of them is satisfied upon encountering S, which creates an additional prediction of an empty category for the shifted object. The storage cost after processing S is thus 2 MUs. The object in the VSO underwent rightward movement across the subject. The calculation of the structural integration cost at the point of processing O is unclear because the handling of rightward movement is not discussed in Gibson (1998, 2000). Two possible scenarios can be considered. In one scenario, as shown in Table 13.5A, reflecting the temporal sequence of parsing, an empty category (*to*) to be coindexed with O is generated linearly

Table 13.6 *Predictions of the DLT for OVS in Kaqchikel*

Cost type	O	[V (to)]	S
Discourse processing	1	1	1
Structural integration	0	1	0
Storage	2	1	0
Total	**3**	**3**	**1**
(Reanalysis		?	)

after O in the mental representation relevant to the calculation of resource consumption. The empty category is then integrated with V across two discourse referents, S and O, a process that consumes 2 EUs. In the other scenario, shown in Table 13.5B, the empty category for the object (to) is inserted between V and S, conforming to the canonical word order in Kaqchikel. In this case, the empty category is locally attached to V and is associated with O across one discourse referent, S, consuming 1 EU. The total processing cost for the VSO sentence is, therefore, nine (5 EUs and 4 MUs) or eight (4 EUs and 4 MUs) units, depending on the scenario.

OVS (Table 13.6) also incurs 3 EUs in introducing new discourse referents corresponding to O, V, and S. When the first noun (O) is processed, it is unclear whether it is a subject or object. If it is taken by the parser as a subject, the storage cost is 2 MUs, as in the case of S in SVO, as discussed above. If it is taken as an object, 3 MUs are incurred, corresponding to the predictions of a transitive verb, a subject noun, and an empty category to be associated with the preposed object. On the assumption of the DLT, namely that "(i)n choosing among ambiguous structures, two of the factors that the processor uses to evaluate its choices are DLT storage and structural integration cost" (Gibson 2000: 115), the processor chooses to take the sentence-initial noun as the subject, resulting in a cost of only 2 MUs. Upon encountering V, it may be evident that the sentence-initial noun is an object rather than a subject. An object position empty category was created and locally integrated with V. Furthermore, the object empty category is coindexed with the clause-initial object O across the event referent V, leading to the consumption of 1 EU. After processing V, a noun for the subject is needed to complete a transitive sentence, incurring a storage cost of 1 MU. The total integration and storage cost for OVS is, therefore, seven units (4 EUs and 3 MUs). Furthermore, an additional cost must be incurred upon encountering V due to reanalysis, when the first noun, initially analyzed as a subject, is reanalyzed as an object.

13.1 Kaqchikel

Given the exposition above, the DLT predicts the relative processing difficulty among the four types of Kaqchikel transitive sentences, as summarized in (10).

(10) Relative processing cost in Kaqchikel predicted by the DLT
VOS (7) < OVS (7+?) < VSO (8 or 9) < SVO (10)

The DLT correctly predicts that the VOS is the easiest order to process. However, other aspects of the DLT prediction are problematic. Notably, the most difficult order, OVS, is incorrectly predicted to be easier to process than VSO and SVO if the cost of the reanalysis is not considered. If we assume that the reanalysis incurs a cost comparable to, say, 1 EU, OVS is still predicted to be relatively easy to process, contrary to fact. In addition, the predicted relative difficulty of [VSO < SVO] is the opposite of the observed ranking of [SVO < VSO]. Therefore, it is safe to conclude that the DLT, which was developed based on data from SVO and SOV languages, fails to account for the processing of Kaqchikel, a VOS language.

13.1.3 Structural Distance Hypothesis

The basic idea of the DLT, as shown above, is that the difficulty of linguistic expressions with filler-gap dependencies can be predicted by the *linear distance*. A rather different approach to filler-gap dependencies attributes their relative difficulty to differences in the depth of embedding of the gap, which may be referred to as the *structural distance* account (Collins 1994; O'Grady 1997; O'Grady, Lee, and Choo 2003; see also Pesetsky 1982). In the subject-extracted RC in (11a), for example, the relative pronoun *who* has moved across two projections, IP and C', whereas in the object-extracted RC in (11b), there are four projections, VP, I', IP, and C', intervening hierarchically between *who* and its trace. Because the structural distance, as measured by the number of intervening projections, is larger in the object-extracted RC than in the subject-extracted RC, the former is predicted to be more difficult to process than the latter by the structural distance hypothesis.

(11) a. Subject-extracted RC
the reporter [$_{CP}$ who$_i$ [$_{C'}$ [$_{IP}$ t_i [$_{I'}$ [$_{VP}$ attacked the senator]]]

b. Object-extracted RC
the reporter [$_{CP}$ who$_i$ [$_{C'}$ [$_{IP}$ the senator [$_{I'}$ [$_{VP}$ attacked t_i]]]

Turning to Kaqchikel, consider the syntactic structure of a VOS sentence, as shown in (12), which we proposed in Chapter 11. In calculating the structural distance in Kaqchikel, we disregard, for the sake of exposition, the movement of the subject from Spec,VoiceP to Spec,TP, and all the head movements because they are commonly involved in all four types of sentences discussed here.[2] The structure of a VOS sentence, as shown in (12), therefore, involves no filler-gap dependencies (except for those mentioned in the previous sentence). Thus, the structural distance associated with this structure is zero.

(12)   Kaqchikel VOS

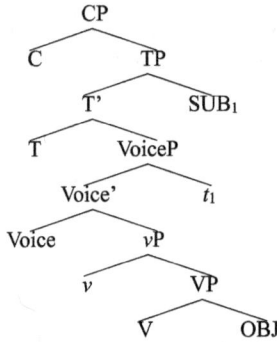

The structure of an SVO sentence, as shown in (13), contains the movement of the subject from Spec,TP to Spec,CP. This movement crosses the TP and C'. Therefore, the structural distance is two in the SVO.

(13)   Kaqchikel SVO

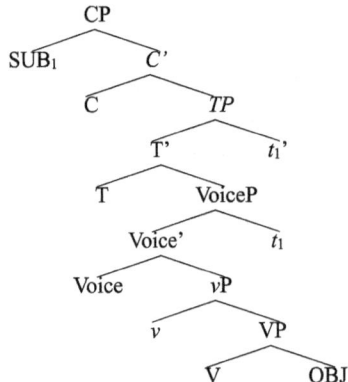

The VSO clause, as shown in (14), involves the movement of the object. This movement crosses six projections (VP, vP, Voice', VoiceP, T', and T'). Therefore, the structural distance of the dependency is six.

(14) Kaqchikel VSO

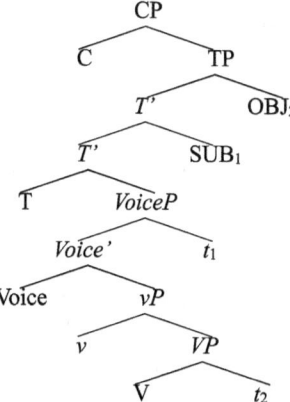

Finally, consider the structure of the OVS, as shown in (15). The OVS sentence contains the movement of the object to Spec,CP. It has crossed seven projections (VP, vP, Voice', VoiceP, T', TP, and C'). Thus, the structural distance is seven in the OVS.

(15) Kaqchikel OVS

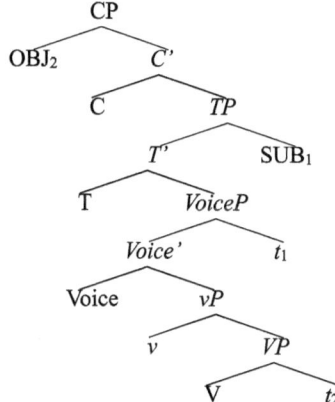

To summarize, the structural distances of the movements involved in the clauses with the four different word orders are as shown in (16).

(16) Structural distances for Kaqchikel sentences
VOS = 0
SVO = 2 {TP, C'}
VSO = 6 {VP, vP, Voice', VoiceP, T', T'}
OVS = 7 {VP, vP, Voice', VoiceP, T', TP, C'}

Given this, the structural distance hypothesis predicts VOS to be the easiest word order to process in Kaqchikel, followed by SVO, VSO, and then OVS as the most difficult word order among the four.

(17) Relative processing cost in Kaqchikel predicted by structural distance hypothesis
VOS < SVO < VSO < OVS

This is consistent with the observations discussed in the previous chapters.

13.1.4 Minimize Filler-Gap Domain

Hawkins' (2004) Minimize Domains Approach is a variant of the structural distance hypothesis. Hawkins (2004) accounts for the relative processing demands of linguistic expressions with a filler-gap dependency from the perspective of an efficiency principle called Minimize Domains (MiD), which is outlined in (18). MiD defines a preference for the minimal structural domains sufficient for processing each dependency relation. The relevant domain for filler-gap dependencies is defined as the Filler-Gap Domain (FGD), as shown in (19).

(18) Minimize Domains (MiD)

The human processor prefers to minimize the connected sequences of linguistic forms and their conventionally associated syntactic and semantic properties in which relations of domination and/or dependency are processed. The degree of this preference is proportional to the number of relations whose domains can be minimized in competing sequences or structures, and to the extent of the minimization difference in each domain. (Hawkins 2004: 31)

(19) Filler-Gap Domain (FGD)

An FGD consists of the smallest set of terminal and non-terminal nodes dominated by the mother of a filler and on a connected path that must be accessed for gap identification and processing; for subcategorized gaps the path connects the filler to a co-indexed subcategorizor and includes, or is extended to include, any additional arguments of the subcategorizor on which the gap depends for its processing; for non-subcategorized gaps the path connects the filler to the head category that constructs the mother node containing the co-indexed gap; all constituency relations and co-occurrence requirements holding between these nodes belong in the description of the FGD. (Hawkins 2004: 175)

With MiD and FGD in mind, we consider the schematic structures of subject-extracted and object-extracted relative clauses, as shown in (20) and (21), which are constructed after Hawkins's (2004: 178) structure (7.10).

13.1 Kaqchikel

(20)   Schematic structure of a subject-extracted RC

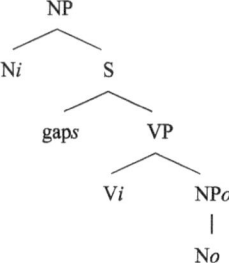

(21)   Schematic structure of an object-extracted RC

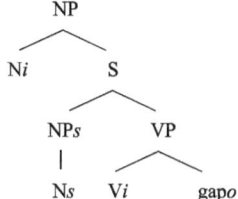

In (20), the minimal FGD consists of five nodes: the filler Ni and its maximal projection NP; the co-indexed subcategorizor of Ni's gap, Vi; and dominating VP and S. In (21), the minimal FGD includes seven nodes: the filler Ni and its maximal projection NP; the co-indexed subcategorizor of Ni's gap, Vi; dominating VP and S; and the co-argument required by the relativized object, that is, Ns and NPs. Note that a subject does not require a co-occurring object, and it is not dependent on a direct object if there is one. In contrast, an object requires and is dependent on the co-occurrence of a subject. Hawkins (2004: 176) assumes that if a gap is in a position that requires the co-occurrence of another argument, then that argument must be in the FGD of the gap as well. Thus, the object is not included in the FGD in (20), whereas the subject is in the FGD in (21). This is summarized in (22).

(22)   Minimal FGDs for relativization
       SU = 5   {Ni, NP, Vi, VP, S}
       DO = 7   {Ni, NP, Vi, VP, S, Ns, NPs}

Because the number of nodes in the FGD is larger in the object-extracted RC (seven) than in the subject-extracted RC (five), MiD predicts that the object-extracted RC is more difficult to process than the subject-extracted RC, which is generally the case in English and many other languages.

154   Syntax and Processing Load

Now consider the clause structures associated with the four word orders in Kaqchikel, shown in (23) to (26), which are simplified in a way similar to the structures shown in (20) and (21) for the sake of comparison.

(23)   Schematic structure of a VOS sentence in Kaqchikel

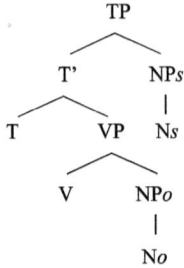

(24)   Schematic structure of an SVO sentence in Kaqchikel

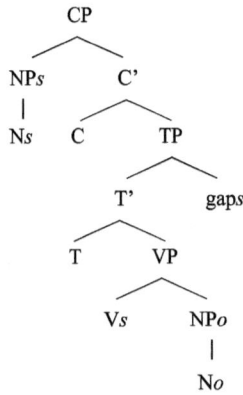

(25)   Schematic structure of a VSO sentence in Kaqchikel

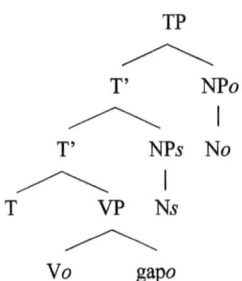

13.1 Kaqchikel

(26) Schematic structure of an OVS sentence in Kaqchikel

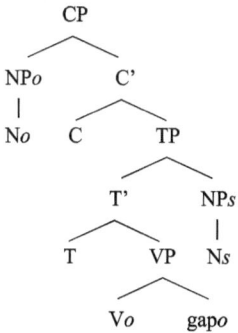

The VOS sentence as represented in (23) does not involve any filler-gap dependency. The FGD in the SVO sentence (24) includes eight nodes: Ns, NPs, CP, Vs, VP, T' TP, and C'. The FGD in the VSO sentence (25) contains nine nodes: No, NPo, TP, Vo, VP, T', T', Ns, and NPs. The FGD in the OVS sentence (26) includes ten nodes: No, NPo, CP, Vo, VP, T', TP, C', Ns, and NPs. This is summarized in (27).

(27) Minimal FGDs for Kaqchikel sentences
VOS = 0
SVO = 8   {Ns, NPs, CP, Vs, VP, T' TP, C'}
VSO = 9   {No, NPo, TP, Vo, VP, T', T', Ns, NPs}
OVS = 10 {No, NPo, CP, Vo, VP, T', TP, C', Ns, NPs}

Given the figures in (27), MiD predicts that the order of relative processing demands of the four types of sentences in Kaqchikel is as shown in (28).

(28) Relative processing cost in Kaqchikel predicted by the Minimize Filler-Gap Domain
VOS < SVO < VSO < OVS

This is consistent with the observations in the previous chapters, as summarized in (1).

13.1.5 Summary

In this section, we have observed that the relative processing difficulty of sentences with the four different word orders (SOV, SVO, VSO, and OVS) in Kaqchikel is consistent with the predictions made by the Structural Distance Hypothesis and the Minimize Filler-Gap Domain, but not the Experience-Based Hypothesis or the Dependency Locality Theory. What is common between the Structural Distance Hypothesis and the Minimize Filler-Gap Domain is that they both calculate the processing cost of dependencies based on *hierarchical distance* determined by syntactic structure, in contrast to the Experience-Based Hypothesis, which predicts processing difficulty based on production frequency, or the Dependency Locality Theory, which computes processing cost based on *linear distance* determined by syntactic structure. Thus, as far as the Kaqchikel data considered in this book are concerned, we can conclude that the hierarchical distance of syntactic dependencies best predicts relative processing difficulty. In the next section, we consider whether the same conclusion can be drawn for Japanese.

13.2 Japanese

As discussed in Chapter 9, Kaqchikel sentences with the four different word orders, VOS, SVO, VSO, and OVS, seem to correspond to the four transitive constructions in Japanese in terms of syntactic structure and discourse function, as shown in (29).

(29) Correspondence between Kaqchikel and Japanese transitive constructions

Kaqchikel	Japanese	Syntax/Function
VOS	[S-NOM O-ACC V]	Basic
SVO	[S-TOP O-ACC V]	S topicalized
VSO	[O-ACC S-NOM V]	O scrambled
OVS	[O-TOP S-NOM V]	O topicalized

Kaqchikel VOS and Japanese [S-NOM O-ACC V] are similar in that they are both syntactically basic transitive sentences. The subject is topicalized in Kaqchikel SVO and Japanese [S-TOP O-ACC V]. The object is scrambled across the subject in Kaqchikel VSO and Japanese [O-ACC S-NOM V]. Finally, in Kaqchikel OVS and Japanese [O-TOP S-NOM V], the object is topicalized. These Kaqchikel and Japanese constructions are parallel to each other in terms of production frequency as well. In Kaqchikel, SVO is the most frequently used, followed by VOS, which ranks as the second. The other two, VSO and OVS, are far less frequently employed. Similarly, in Japanese, the most frequently used word order is [S-TOP O-ACC V], followed by [S-NOM O-ACC V]. The production frequencies of [O-ACC S-NOM V] and [O-TOP S-NOM V] are fairly low (Imamura and Koizumi 2011).

It is interesting, therefore, to observe that, whereas VOS is easier to process than SVO in Kaqchikel, the processing costs of [S-NOM O-ACC V] and [S-TOP O-ACC V] are roughly the same in Japanese (Imamura, Sato, and Koizumi 2016).

(30) Relative processing costs in Kaqchikel
VOS < SVO < VSO < OVS

(31) Relative processing costs in Japanese
[S-NOM O-ACC V] = [S-TOP O-ACC V] < [O-ACC S-NOM V] < [O-TOP S-NOM V]

13.2 Japanese

In the following sections, we will consider whether the Japanese ranking in (31) can be accounted for by the four approaches discussed in the previous sections.

13.2.1 Experience-Based Account

As mentioned, Imamura and Koizumi (2011) revealed that, among the four types of Japanese transitive sentences in question, [S-TOP O-ACC V] (82.5 percent) occurs much more frequently than [S-NOM O-ACC V] (14.7 percent) in Japanese novels. [O-TOP S-NOM V] (1.8 percent) and [O-ACC S-NOM V] (1 percent) are used relatively infrequently.

(32)   Relative production frequency in Japanese
        [S-TOP O-ACC V] > [S-NOM O-ACC V] > [O-TOP S-NOM V] > [O-ACC S-NOM V]

If frequent constructions are processed more easily than infrequent ones, the relative processing difficulty of the four constructions should be as stated in (33).

(33)   Relative processing cost in Japanese predicted by production frequency
        [S-TOP O-ACC V] < [S-NOM O-ACC V] < [O-TOP S-NOM V] < [O-ACC S-NOM V]

The ranking in (33) correctly captures the fact that the two SOV constructions are easier to process than the two OSV constructions. However, it incorrectly predicts that [S-TOP O-ACC V] should be easier to process than [S-NOM O-ACC V] and that [O-TOP S-NOM V] should be easier to process than [O-ACC S-NOM V]. Therefore, production frequency alone cannot account for the relative processing load of Japanese transitive sentences with different word order.

13.2.2 Linear Distance Hypothesis

Predictions of the DLT for the four transitive constructions in Japanese are shown in Tables 13.7–13.10. During the processing of [S-NOM O-ACC V] (Table 13.7), a new discourse referent is introduced upon encountering S-NOM, O-ACC, and V, respectively, and 1 EU is consumed at each of these three points. The storage cost after processing S-NOM is 1 MU, corresponding to the predictions of a(n intransitive) verb. After processing O-ACC, the storage cost is still 1 MU, because a transitive verb is required to complete a sentence. Upon encountering V, S is integrated with V across one discourse referent introduced by the object. This integration operation consumes 1 EU. Therefore, the total processing cost for [S-NOM O-ACC V] is six units (4 EUs and 2 MUs), as summarized in Table 13.7.

The processing of [S-TOP O-ACC V] proceeds in the same way as the processing of [S-NOM O-ACC V] from the viewpoint of the DLT, as summarized in Table 13.8. Thus, the total processing cost for [S-TOP O-ACC V] is six units (4 EUs and 2 MUs).

Table 13.7 *Predictions of the DLT for [S-NOM O-ACC V] in Japanese*

Cost types	[S-NOM]	[O-ACC]	[V]
Discourse processing	1	1	1
Structural integration	0	0	1
Storage	1	1	0
Total	2	2	2

Table 13.8 *Predictions of the DLT for [S-TOP O-ACC V] in Japanese*

Cost types	[S-TOP]	[O-ACC]	[V]
New discourse referent	1	1	1
Structural integration	0	0	1
Storage	1	1	0
Total	2	2	2

Table 13.9 *Predictions of the DLT for [O-ACC S-NOM V] in Japanese*

Cost-types	[O-ACC]	[S-NOM (to)]	[V]
New discourse referent	1	1	1
Structural integration	0	1	0
Storage	3	1	0
Total	4	3	1

In [O-ACC S-NOM V] (Table 13.9), the object is scrambled leftward across the subject. At the beginning of the sentence, a new discourse referent represented by O-ACC is introduced, consuming 1 EU. Three MUs are incurred at this point because a noun for the subject, a transitive verb, and an object empty category are needed to complete a grammatically transitive sentence. Upon encountering S-NOM, a new discourse referent is introduced, consuming 1 EU. At the same time, an object empty category (*to*) is created and coindexed with O-ACC across one discourse referent, S-NOM, incurring an integration cost of 1 EU. The storage cost is 1 MU for the prediction of a verb at this point. Subsequently, one discourse referent is introduced at V, where S-NOM and the object empty

Table 13.10 *Predictions of the DLT for [O-TOP S-NOM V] in Japanese*

Cost types	[O-TOP]	[S-NOM (to)]	[V]
New discourse referent	1	1	1
Structural integration	0	1	0
Storage	3	1	0
Total	**4**	**3**	**1**
(Reanalysis		?	)

category (*to*) are integrated with V locally. Therefore, the total processing cost for [O-ACC S-NOM V] is eight units (4 EUs and 4 MUs).

The processing of [O-TOP S-NOM V] (Table 13.10) parallels that of [O-ACC S-NOM V] in terms of the DLT, except that, like O of OVS in Kaqchikel, O-TOP may initially be taken as the subject, and later reanalyzed as an object upon encountering S-NOM, which may tax some processing cost.

To summarize, the DLT predicts the relative processing difficulty among the four constructions in Japanese, as shown in (34).

(34) Relative processing cost in Japanese predicted by the DLT
 [S-NOM O-ACC V] = [S-TOP O-ACC V] < [O-ACC S-NOM V] < [O-TOP S-NOM V]
  6   6   8   8+?

This is consistent with the actual relative processing cost in Japanese, as summarized in (31).

13.2.3 Hierarchical Distance Hypothesis

Both the Structural Distance Hypothesis (e.g., O'Grady 1997) and the Minimize Filler-Gap Domain (Hawkins 2004) calculate the processing cost incurred by filler-gap dependencies based on the hierarchical structural distance between the filler and gap. Therefore, they make the same prediction for the relative processing difficulty between the four Japanese constructions under discussion. Thus, we discuss only one of them here, that is, the Structural Distance Hypothesis, chosen purely for expository purposes.

As in Section 13.1.3 for Kaqchikel, when calculating structural distance in Japanese sentences, we disregard the movement of the subject from its base position to Spec,TP, and all the head movements because they are commonly involved in all four constructions discussed here. The simplified schematic structure of [S-NOM O-ACC V], as shown in (35), therefore, involves no filler-gap dependencies. Thus, the structural distance associated with this structure is zero:

(35)   [$_{CP}$ [$_{TP}$ S-NOM [$_{T'}$ [$_{VP}$ O-ACC V] T]] C]

The structure of [S-TOP O-ACC V], as shown in (36), contains the movement of the subject from Spec,TP to Spec,CP (Kishimoto 2009: 481; Shibatani 1990: 274). This movement crosses TP and C'. Therefore, the structural distance is two in [S-TOP O-ACC V].

(36)   [$_{CP}$ S-TOP$_1$ [$_{C'}$ [$_{TP}$ t_1 [$_{T'}$ [$_{VP}$ O-ACC V] T]] C]]

The [O-ACC S-NOM V] clause, as shown in (37), involves the movement of the object. This movement crosses three projections (VP, T', and T'). Therefore, the structural distance of the dependency is three.

(37)   [$_{CP}$ [$_{TP}$ O-ACC$_1$ [$_{T'}$ S-NOM [$_{T'}$ [$_{VP}$ t_1 V] T]]] C]

Finally, consider the structure of [O-TOP S-NOM V], as shown in (38). [O-TOP S-NOM V] contains the movement of the object to Spec,CP. It has crossed four projections (VP, T', TP, and C'). Thus, the structural distance is four in [O-TOP S-NOM V].

(38)   [$_{CP}$ O-TOP$_1$ [$_{C'}$ [$_{TP}$ S-NOM [$_{T'}$ [$_{VP}$ t_1 V] T]] C]]

To summarize, the structural distances of the movements involved in the four Japanese transitive constructions are as shown in (39).

(39)   Structural distances for Japanese sentences
         [S-NOM O-ACC V] = 0
         [S-TOP O-ACC V] = 2   {TP, C'}
         [O-ACC S-NOM V] = 3   {VP, T', T'}
         [O-TOP S-NOM V] = 4   {VP, T', TP, C'}

Given this, the structural distance hypothesis predicts that the easiest word order to process in Japanese is [S-NOM O-ACC V], followed by [S-TOP O-ACC V] and [O-ACC S-NOM V], while [O-TOP S-NOM V] is the most difficult among the four. This is schematically shown in (40).

(40)   Relative processing cost in Japanese predicted by the Structural Distance Hypothesis
         [S-NOM O-ACC V] < [S-TOP O-ACC V] < [O-ACC S-NOM V] < [O-TOP S-NOM V]

Although the predicted ranking in (40) is similar to the actual ranking in (31), repeated here as (41), it is incorrectly predicted that [S-TOP O-ACC V] is more difficult to process than [S-NOM O-ACC V].

(41)   Relative processing costs in Japanese
         [S-NOM O-ACC V] = [S-TOP O-ACC V] < [O-ACC S-NOM V] < [O-TOP S-NOM V]

13.2.4 Summary

In this section, we have observed that the relative processing difficulty of the four transitive constructions in Japanese is consistent with the predictions of the Dependency Locality Theory but not with those by the Experience-Based Hypothesis or the Hierarchical Distance Hypothesis. This suggests that the linear distance of syntactic dependencies is the best predictor of relative processing difficulty in Japanese.

13.3 General Discussion

We have seen above that the relative processing difficulty among the Kaqchikel transitive sentences with four different word orders is compatible with the prediction by the Hierarchical Distance Hypothesis but not with those predicted by the Experience-Based Hypothesis or the Linear Distance Hypothesis. In contrast, the relative processing difficulty among the four transitive constructions in Japanese is best predicted by the Linear Distance Hypothesis. Does this mean that Kaqchikel is sensitive only to hierarchical distance, whereas Japanese is sensitive to structural distance? Although it may be logically possible, it is not probable, given that the human cognitive system is basically uniform across all populations. Furthermore, it is unlikely that experience (production frequency) does not affect the processing load in these languages. A more plausible hypothesis, therefore, seems to be that the three factors, that is, production frequency, linear distance, and hierarchical distance, all play a role in determining the total processing cost in both languages (cf. Brennan et al. 2016; Shain et al. 2020). Let us consider this scenario.

Recall that the relative ranking of the processing cost between the four word orders in Kaqchikel is as shown in (42), and the three theories of processing cost generate the predictions shown in (43) to (45).

(42) Ranking of relative processing cost in Kaqchikel observed in experiments:
VOS < SVO < VSO < OVS

(43) Ranking of relative processing cost in Kaqchikel predicted by the Experience-Based Hypothesis (EBH):
SVO < VOS < VSO < OVS
 1   2   3   4

(44) Ranking of relative processing cost in Kaqchikel predicted by the Linear Distance Hypothesis (LDH):
VOS < OVS < VSO < SVO
 1   2   3   4

(45) Ranking of relative processing cost in Kaqchikel predicted by the Hierarchical Distance Hypothesis (HDH):
VOS < SVO < VSO < OVS
 1   2   3   4

Table 13.11 *Ranking of relative processing cost in Kaqchikel predicted by the three factors combined*

Factors	VOS	<	SVO	<	VSO	<	OVS
				Cost			
EBH	2		1		3		4
LDH	1		4		3		2
SDH	1		2		3		4
Total	**4**		**7**		**9**		**10**

We suggest calculating the total processing cost by combining the three rankings in (43), (44), and (45). For the sake of simplicity, let us assume that the effects of the three factors on sentence processing load are of the same magnitude. Then, we can simply add the numbers shown in the three rankings, which reflect the predicted relative processing cost among the four constructions, to calculate the total processing cost of the four constructions, as shown in Table 13.11.

The total costs obtained by summation correctly account for the ranking of the relative processing cost in Kaqchikel, as shown in (42).

Let us now consider the Japanese language. The relative ranking of the processing cost between the four Japanese transitive constructions is as shown in (46), and the three theories make the predictions shown in (47) to (49).

(46) Ranking of relative processing cost in Japanese observed in experiments
[S-NOM O-ACC V] = [S-TOP O-ACC V] < [O-ACC S-NOM V] < [O-TOP S-NOM V]

(47) Ranking of relative processing cost in Japanese predicted by the Experience-Based Hypothesis (EBH):
[S-TOP O-ACC V] < [S-NOM O-ACC V] < [O-TOP S-NOM V] < [O-ACC S-NOM V]
        1   2   3   4

(48) Ranking of relative processing cost in Japanese predicted by the Linear Distance Hypothesis (LDH):
[S-NOM O-ACC V] = [S-TOP O ACC V] < [O-ACC S-NOM V] < [O-TOP S-NOM V]
        1   1   2   3

(49) Ranking of relative processing cost in Japanese predicted by the Hierarchical Distance Hypothesis (HDH):
[S-NOM O-ACC V] < [S-TOP O-ACC V] < [O-ACC S-NOM V] < [O-TOP S-NOM V]
        1   2   3   4

If we sum the numbers in the three rankings in (47) to (49), we obtain the result shown in Table 13.12, which is in accordance with the ranking of actual relative processing costs in Japanese.

Table 13.12 *Ranking of relative processing costs in Japanese predicted by the three factors combined*

Factors	[S-NOM O-ACC V] = [S-TOP O-ACC V] < [O-ACC S-NOM V] < [O-TOP S-NOM V]			
		Cost		
EBH	2	1	4	3
LDH	1	1	2	3
SDH	1	2	3	4
Total	4	4	9	10

13.4 Conclusion

The relative processing costs associated with Kaqchikel transitive sentences with the four different word orders are correctly predicted by the Hierarchical Distance Hypothesis, whereas the relative processing costs associated with the corresponding four transitive constructions in Japanese are correctly predicted by the Linear Distance Hypothesis. However, the relative processing costs in these languages are also consistent with the assumption that they are shaped by the combined effects of the three factors: production frequency, linear distance, and hierarchical distance, suggesting the cognitive uniformity of the human parser.

NOTES

1. As far as the simple transitive sentences considered in this book are concerned, finer-grained experience-based accounts such as Hale's (2001) and Levy's (2008) also make basically the same prediction, and hence fail to account for the ranking in (4).
2. The conclusion regarding the predicted relative processing difficulty of the four word orders to be discussed below remains the same if we take these movements into consideration.

14 Concluding Remarks

Language is a module of the human cognitive faculty. It interacts with the other modules, such as memory. Central to language are its generative processes, often called the faculty of language in the narrow sense (FLN). A prominent view of language holds that FLN may approximate a kind of "optimal solution" to the problem of linking the sensory-motor and conceptual-intentional systems (Hauser, Chomsky, and Fitch 2002: 1574). In other words, FLN may provide a near-optimal solution that satisfies the interface conditions to the faculty of language in the broad sense (FLB), which includes at least the conceptual-intentional and the sensory-motor systems. The research reported in this book can be considered an attempt to elucidate the relationship between the generative processes of the language system, the conceptual-intentional system, and the sensory-motor system, with special reference to constituent order in language and thought. We investigated constituent order preference in language and thought, using different approaches to shed light on this topic from a variety of perspectives.

14.1 Field-Based Comparative Psycholinguistics

We considered preferred constituent orders in both language and thought, as well as their relationship, examining not only comprehension but also production. Moreover, we explored the effects of both grammatical factors and grammar-independent cognitive factors on this preference, as well as their interaction. In this multidimensional enterprise, we benefited from a number of different research methods, such as linguistic fieldwork, theoretical linguistic analysis, corpus research, questionnaire surveys, behavioral experiments, eye tracking, event-related brain potentials, functional magnetic resonance imaging, and near-infrared spectroscopy. Above all, the most noteworthy aspect of this endeavor was its target language Kaqchikel, an endangered Mayan language that we investigated as a representative example of OS languages, which are less studied than familiar SO languages (Moseley (ed.) 2010). The present study clarifies the importance of field-based cross-linguistic cognitive neuroscientific research in uncovering universal and language-particular aspects of the human language faculty.

14.2 Major Findings and Implications

Some of our major findings are as follows. First, other things being equal, a language's syntactically determined basic word order, be it SO or OS, is easier to process than other grammatically possible word orders in that language. The preference for SO word orders in sentence comprehension reported in previous studies (of SO languages) may not be universal, as processing complexities are closely tied to syntactic complexities. In Kaqchikel, the word order that is easiest to process is its syntactically simplest word order, VOS.

Second, agent–patient is the natural order of non-verbal event descriptions, and indeed might be universal across speakers of typologically different languages, including Kaqchikel. The prevalence of SO word orders in the world's languages may arise in part because these orders, which correspond to agent–patient order in thought, are most compatible with how we conceptually represent transitive events.

Third, in both OS and SO languages, sentences with a topicalized subject tend to be more frequently used than those with a non-topicalized subject. Grammar-independent universal cognitive features play a relatively larger role in word order selection in sentence production than in sentence comprehension. The preference for SO order in sentence production might be a plausible candidate for a language universal, although this is not a logical conclusion of our proposed analysis, and there are indeed apparent exceptions that need to be investigated in future research.

Fourth, in OS languages, there is a discrepancy between (i) the syntactically simplest, most easily processed word order and (ii) the most frequently used word order. The most frequently used order requires a relatively higher processing load in OS languages. Thus, OS languages might be less optimal/economical for linguistic performance, which might be one of the reasons they are rare. It may also offer a plausible explanation of why most (possibly all) OS languages are pro-drop, as this lowers the processing load of SO sentences (by making the topicalization of S unnecessary or less frequent).

Finally, the right-specifier analysis of Kaqchikel syntactic structure not only is supported by syntactic theoretical considerations but also is most compatible with the experimental data reported in this book.

14.3 Future Work

The research reported in this book has revealed two new challenges: (1) As the present research focused on the Mayan language Kaqchikel, it is not clear to what extent the results/findings apply to other OS languages, and (2) as the present research focused on the processing of isolated sentences, it is not clear to what extent the results/findings apply to sentences in natural coherent discourse. To solve these challenges and to build a more plausible model of the language processing mechanisms in the mind/brain, we are undertaking, in the FALCOHN (Field-Based Approaches to Language, Cognition, and Human Nature) project, research along the following lines: (1) In addition to examining Mayan languages, we are investigating Austronesian languages (in particular, Truku in Taiwan), which differ from Mayan languages geographically, genetically, and typologically (see Appendix B for its initial results), and (2) we are examining the effects of verbal as well as non-verbal context and word order on sentence comprehension and production in natural discourse (cf. Imamura, Sato, and Koizumi 2016; Koizumi and Imamura 2016; Yano and Koizumi 2018, 2021). We hope to report the results of these studies in the future.

ically, and cartographically, exposing hidden patterns across multiple scales.

Appendix A Spatial Frames of Reference of Kaqchikel Speakers: A Comparative Study with Japanese Speakers

A.1 Introduction

The relationship between language and thought has been a key research topic in linguistics since the hypothesis of linguistic relativity was first proposed by Edward Sapir and Benjamin Lee Whorf (Heider 1972; Kay and Kempton 1984; Whorf 1956). Among the subsequent research projects, a series of studies on the spatial perception of the body's surroundings by Stephen C. Levinson of the Max Planck Institute and his colleagues has been the subject of much debate (Inoue 1998; Levinson 2003; Li et al. 2011; Pinker 2007) because various linguistic communities have been shown to have different preferred spatial coordinate systems, contrary to the common assumption in Western culture that every human being innately prefers using egocentric coordinates when describing the positional relationships of objects. It is within this context that this study was conducted to examine the spatial perception of speakers of Kaqchikel, a Mayan language from Guatemala, which has not previously been studied from this perspective. The study utilized an experiment based on the research of Levinson et al. A similar experiment was then conducted with Japanese speakers to provide context for comparison. The results reaffirm that there are differences in the preferred spatial frames of reference between linguistic and cultural communities, consistent with the Sociotopographic Model (Palmer et al. 2017).

A.2 Spatial Frames of Reference

In general, the location of an object in space is identified in relation to another object. The former is referred to as the "figure," and the latter is referred to as the "ground" or "reference object." The coordinate axis used to determine the relationship between the figure and the ground is known as the "spatial frame of reference" or, simply, the "frame of reference" (FoR). Spatial FoRs can be categorized into three types according to their properties: relative, absolute, and intrinsic. For example, consider the situation shown in Figure A.1.

Figure A.1 A perceiving subject (a human) sees a ball and a car.

The relative FoR is a way of interpreting positionality from the perspective of the perceiving subject, who locates the figure (in this case, the ball) relative to the position of the ground (in this case, the car). The situation in Figure A.1 may be described in Japanese using the relative FoR, as shown in (1).

(1)   Booru ga   kuruma no   hidarigawa ni aru.
       ball NOM car   GEN left side   in exist
       "The ball is to the left of the car."

In contrast, using the absolute FoR involves perceiving spaces using external directional axes such as the cardinal directions (north, south, east, and west) or geographic features ("by the mountains," "by the sea," etc.). The situation shown in Figure A.1 is demonstrated in Japanese using the absolute FoR in (2).

(2)   Booru ga   kuruma no   nisigawa ni aru.
       ball NOM car   GEN west side in exist
       "The ball is to the west of the car."

Finally, we must consider the fact that there is a directional axis inherent in the choice of reference object. The FoR using this directional axis is the intrinsic FoR. For example, the shape and function of a car determine its directional axis, and the direction of travel is considered the "front" side. For humans, the area where our major sensory organs (eyes, nose, and mouth) are concentrated is considered the "front." Using the intrinsic FoR, the situation in Figure A.1 can be described in Japanese as in (3).

(3)   Booru ga   kuruma no   mae ni aru.
        ball NOM car   GEN   front in exist
        "The ball is in front of the car."

In the intrinsic FoR, terms such as "front" and "back" or "left" and "right" are often used as in the relative FoR. However, the use of the directional terms "front," "back," "left," and "right" differs between the intrinsic and relative FoRs. In the intrinsic FoR, these directional terms are determined by the properties of the reference object, whereas in the relative FoR, they are determined by those of the perceiving subject.

Of the three types of FoRs mentioned above, the relative FoR is also referred to as the "egocentric" coordinate system. If the perceiving subject changes its position and moves to the opposite side of the object, a different expression of positionality is required ("The ball is to the right of the car."). In contrast, the absolute and intrinsic FoRs are said to be based on "allocentric" coordinate systems. Even if the perceiving subject changes position, no change is required to express the relationship between the figure and the ground ("The ball is to the west of the car." "The ball is in front of the car.").

No single language necessarily makes use of only one type of FoR. For instance, as shown in examples (1) to (3), the same situation can be expressed using several FoRs in Japanese, and the preferred FoR can depend on the situation and spatial scale involved. Different linguistic communities have also been found to prefer different FoRs when expressing or recalling the positional relationships of objects within a relatively small spatial context, such as that of a tabletop (Levinson 2003; Pederson et al. 1998).

A.3 Previous Studies

The spatial perception of humans derives from the idea of a plane that passes through the human body; thus, it is believed that humans perceive space in terms of an egocentric coordinate system, which has long been the dominant conceptualization of human spatial perception in Western philosophy and psychology (Kant 1991; Miller and Johnson-Laird 1976). However, the results of a large-scale study conducted by Levinson et al. showed that the preferred FoRs differed by language (Brown and Levinson 1993a, 1993b; Levinson 1996a, 1996b, 2003;

Majid et al. 2004). For example, speakers of Japanese, Dutch, and English typically use the relative FoR to express the positional relationships of objects. On the other hand, speakers of Balinese (Austronesian, Indonesia), Guugu Yimithirr (Pama-Nyungan, Australia), and Tzeltal (Mayan, Mexico) primarily use the absolute FoR. Of the languages whose speakers prefer using the absolute FoR, some, including Guugu Yimithirr and Tzeltal, lack words to express relative direction (e.g., "left," "right," "front," and "behind") in the first place. Instead, in Guugu Yimithirr, absolute directional terms, such as *naga* "east," *guwa* "west," *jiba* "south," and *gungga* "north," are used to express an object's position (Levinson 2003). In Tzeltal, the words for "uphill," "downhill," and "across" are used similarly (Brown and Levinson 1992).

Levinson and his colleagues then investigated which FoRs speakers of various languages used to interpret, recall, and recreate the positional relationships of objects without using language (see Section A.5 for specific examples of such tasks). The results revealed that the preferred FoRs for verbal expression within a cultural group coincided with those that were used for non-verbal comprehension of a space by the same group (Levinson 2003; Levinson et al. 2002; Pederson et al. 1998; Wassmann and Dasen 1998). For example, Japanese speakers who primarily used the relative FoR in their verbal representation also used the relative FoR in non-verbal tasks. In addition, Tzeltal speakers who used the absolute FoR in their language also preferred the absolute FoR in non-verbal tasks.

It should be noted that speakers of Tzeltal and other languages that do not have linguistic expressions for the relative FoR are not necessarily incapable of understanding the space within it. When explicitly instructed to use the relative FoR when working on a non-verbal spatial recognition task or when otherwise implicitly encouraged to do so, Tzeltal speakers showed the ability to use the relative FoR to solve a task without issue (Li et al. 2011). Conversely, English speakers who preferred the relative FoR were also more likely to complete a task using the absolute FoR if they were made aware of the scenery or guided by landmarks (Li and Gleitman 2002). In other words, the choice of which FoR to use in spatial perception is a matter of cultural preference, but all of the frames are biologically available for use by all human beings.

Which factors, then, determine a person's preference for a specific spatial FoR? As seen above, the preferred FoR for language use and non-verbal spatial perception varies depending on the language being spoken. As previously mentioned, speakers of Tzeltal, a Mayan language, tend to use the absolute FoR; however, according to Pederson et al. (1998), speakers of Mopan (Mayan, Belize), which is also from the Mayan language family and seems to have much in common phylogenetically and culturally with Tzeltal, mainly use the intrinsic FoR. In addition, speakers of Yucatec (Mayan, Mexico) use both intrinsic and relative FoRs. Considering these findings, Levinson and his colleagues argued that the lexical system of a language has a causal influence on spatial perception (see Majid et al. 2004 for a summary). Speakers who, even before their birth, are exposed to languages like Tzeltal, which do not have words for constructing the relative FoR, do not use it even in non-verbal spatial recognition tasks. This phenomenon suggests a causal relationship between the lexical system of a language and its speakers' preferences for specific spatial FoRs. However, why the lexical system of a particular language is the way it is (e.g., why Tzeltal lacks words for "left" and "right") is a question that invites further exploration. Additionally, there are cases of linguistic populations, such as speakers of Balinese, that have expressions indicating the relative FoR yet appear to prefer the absolute FoR in language use and non-verbal spatial recognition. In addition, there are cases in which speakers of the same language show different preferences regarding FoRs. For example, in the case of Tamil, it has been reported that speakers from urban areas tend to use the relative FoR, while speakers from rural areas tend to use the absolute FoR (Pederson et al. 1998). Even in Japanese, which is believed to prioritize the relative FoR, the absolute FoR was once widely used in Kochi Prefecture, Japan (Inoue 2002). It has also been reported that university students born and raised in Kobe, Japan, used the absolute FoR more frequently than those born and raised in Osaka, Japan, and that, even among those born in Osaka, the preference for the absolute FoR increased the longer they lived in Kobe (Matsumoto et al. 2010). These phenomena suggest that factors other than a language's lexical system should be considered when examining preferences regarding spatial FoRs.

An extralinguistic factor that has been repeatedly identified is the population's living environment, including the geographical features of the locale. The absolute FoR is more likely to be used in small, rural communities where landmarks, such as mountains and hills, are visible, while large, urban communities, where such landmarks are less visible, are more likely to rely on the relative FoR (Inoue, 2002, 2005; Li and Gleitman 2002; Li et al. 2011; Mishra, Dasen, and Niraula 2003; Pinker 2007). Tzeltal speakers live on sloped terrain where they need to be directionally aware, and, in both Kochi and Kobe, there are mountains along the seaside. These cases are consistent with the living environment theory. On the contrary, however, some researchers have noted that urban dwellers who move within large spaces are more likely to use the absolute FoR (Brown 1983), and some researchers have questioned the causal relationship between geographical factors and spatial FoRs (Levinson 2003; Majid et al. 2004).

As mentioned above, several factors, such as language and living environment, may influence preferences regarding FoR, but the extent to which these factors predominate requires further investigation (Bohnemeyer et al. 2014).

A.4 Setting of the Problem

Building on the research outlined in the previous section, we conducted an experiment involving the use of non-verbal tasks to investigate the preferences of speakers of Kaqchikel, a Mayan language spoken in Guatemala that has yet to be studied in this capacity, regarding spatial FoRs. Kaqchikel is a language from the Mayan language family. This family includes about thrity languages spoken in Central America, including Guatemala, Mexico, and Belize. According to Campbell and Kaufman (1985: 188), the Mayan languages can be phylogenetically classified as shown in (4). Kaqchikel is part of the Greater Quichean branch of the Quichean-Mamean languages (4eii).

(4)   Mayan language classification
(The languages referred to in this appendix are shown in italics)

   a. **Huastecan**: Wastek, Chicomuceltec [extinct]
   b. **Yukatekan**: *Yukatek*, Lakantun; Itza', *Mopan*
   c. **Greater Tseltalan**:
      i. **Cholan**: Ch'orti', Cholti [extinct]; Chontal, Chol
      ii. **Tseltalan**: Tzotzil, *Tseltal*
   d. **Greater Q'anjob'alan**:
      i. **Chujean**: Tojolabal, Chuj
      ii. **Q'anjob'alan**: Mocho (Motocintlec); Jakaltek, Akatek, Q'uanjob'al
   e. **K'ichean-Mamean** (or Eastern Mayan):
      i. **Mamean**: Ixil, Awakatek; Mam, Teco
      ii. **K'ichean**: Sipakapense, Sakapultek, Tz'utujil, *Kaqchikel*, K'ichee';
      Poqomam, Poqomchi'; Uspantek; Q'eqchi'

(Adapted from Campbell and Kaufman 1985: 188)

The speakers of Kaqchikel live mainly in the central highland region that extends from Guatemala City, the capital of Guatemala, to Lake Atitlan (Figure A.2). This area is situated between 1,500 and 3,000 meters above sea level. The exact number of speakers is unknown but is estimated to be approximately 500,000 (Brown, Maxwell, and Little 2006; Eberhard, Simons, and Fennig (eds.) 2020; England 2003; Tay Coyoy 1996; Yasugi 1996;).

Kaqchikel has words for "left" and "right": *xokon* and *ijqi*, respectively. There are also expressions corresponding to "north," *releb'al kaq'iq'* (*lit.* "the exit of the wind"); "south," *ruq'ajb'al kaq'iq'* (the setting place of the wind); "east," *releb'al q'ij* (*lit.* "the exit of the sun); and "west," *ruqajb'al q'ij* (*lit.* "the setting place of the sun"). Thus, in Kaqchikel, as in Japanese, expressions based on both relative and absolute FoRs can be used.

A.4 Setting of the Problem 173

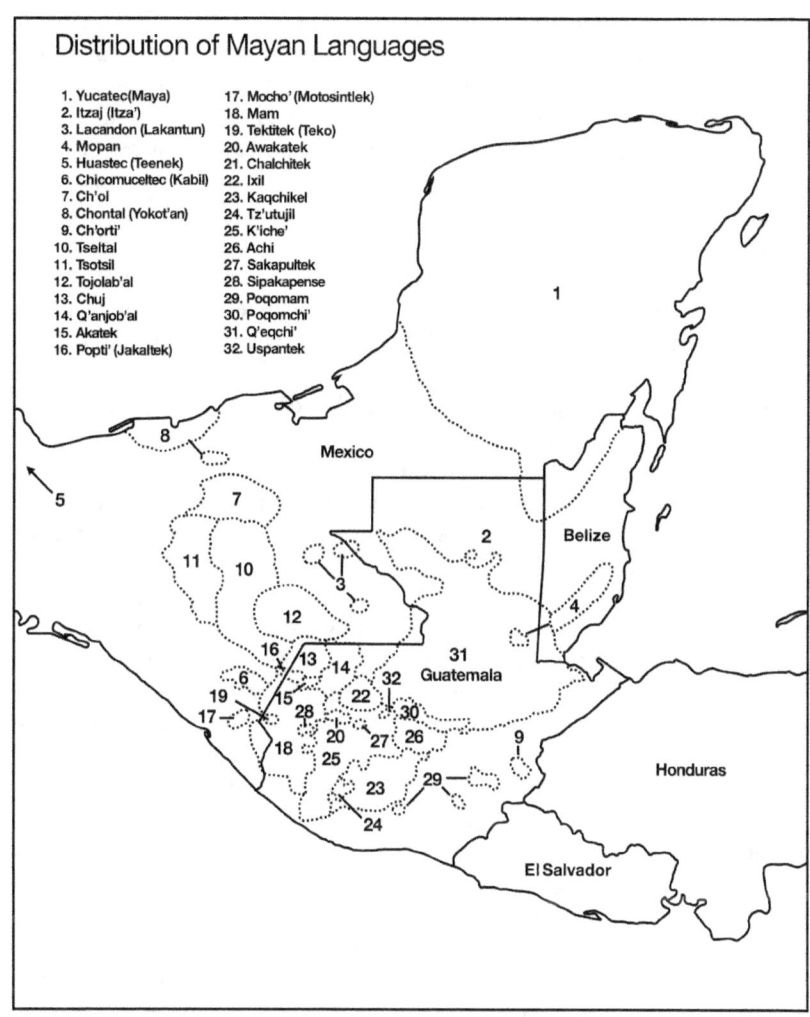

Figure A.2 Geographic distribution of Mayan languages.
(Based on Map 4 in Law 2014, with modification by Bennett, Coon, and
Henderson 2016, used with permission.)

Many Kaqchikel speakers are bilingual, speaking Spanish as a second language. Spanish, like Japanese and Kaqchikel, also possesses words to express both "left, right" and "north, east, south, and west" (*izquierdo*, "left"; *derecho*, "right"; *norte*, "north"; *este* "east"; *sur*, "south"; and *oeste*, "west").

There are two main reasons that Kaqchikel was chosen as the subject of this study. First, in the study of spatial FoRs, Mayan languages have played a prominent and symbolic role in demonstrating that relative FoRs are not universally preferred and that the distribution of preferences regarding FoRs cannot be understood simply by focusing on broad categories such as language families. However, only three Mayan languages have been investigated so far: Tzeltal, Yucatec, and Mopan. Not only is this number small, but this combination of languages is also non-representative. Tzeltal is from the Greater Tseltalan branch of the Mayan language family, while Mopan and Yucatec are both from the Yucatecan branch (see (4) above). In other words, only two of the five branches of the Mayan language family have been investigated regarding the use of spatial FoRs, with three branches left unexamined. In addition, when considering the speakers of each language by country, while Tzeltal and Yucatec speakers are concentrated in Mexico and Mopan speakers in Belize, Guatemala remains unexplored despite being the country where approximately two-thirds of the Mayan languages are spoken (Figure A.2). In exploring the factors that determine preferences regarding spatial FoRs, a more diverse range of languages must be examined. This gap can be addressed by surveying speakers of Kaqchikel, a language belonging to the K'ichean-Mamean branch spoken in Guatemala.

Another reason for examining Kaqchikel speakers in this study was the need to test the Sociotopographic Model, which attempts to model the complex interaction of environment, sociocultural factors, and language (Palmer et al. 2017). Kaqchikel speakers traditionally live in a mountainous region between 1,500 and 3,000 meters above sea level, where they lead an agricultural lifestyle. If the absolute FoR is more suitable for use in areas in which landmarks that can serve as directional markers, such as mountains, are visible, then Kaqchikel speakers should be more likely to use this FoR.

In this study, the same experiment that was conducted on Kaqchikel speakers was also conducted on Japanese speakers. The objectives of this experiment were to determine whether the results would indeed demonstrate a prioritization of the relative FoR by Japanese speakers, confirm the validity of these tasks and their implementation, and provide a basis for comparison when interpreting the results of the experiment conducted on Kaqchikel speakers.

A.5 Experiment

To examine systems of spatial perception among Kaqchikel and Japanese speakers, the Animal Recall Task, Chips Recognition Task, and Transitive Inference Task from the non-verbal experiments conducted by Brown and Levinson (1993b) were selected and conducted using a methodology similar to theirs.

A.5 Experiment

A.5.1 Experimental Method

A.5.1.1 Participants The following experiments were conducted with the participation of twenty native Japanese speakers (nine males, eleven females; average age, 21.45 years) and twenty native Kaqchikel speakers (nine males, eleven females; average age, 33.65 years). The Kaqchikel-speaking participants were all bilingual and used Spanish daily.

A.5.1.2 Instructions The instructions were communicated verbally to the Japanese-speaking participants. The Kaqchikel speakers received the original instructions translated from Japanese into Kaqchikel and printed on sheets of A4-sized paper, which they read for themselves.

A.5.1.3 Method of Evaluating Results The resulting placements and indications from each participant were recorded verbatim at the time of the experiment. These recorded results were then examined to evaluate whether the relative or absolute FoR was used. The evaluation standards were based on Brown and Levinson (1993b).

A.5.2 Task Outline and Experiment Procedure

A.5.2.1 Animal Recall Task (ART) In this task, the participants were shown various stuffed animals and asked to memorize their positions. The participants were then rotated 180 degrees to replicate the original order of the stuffed animals (Figure A.3).

The participants were asked to stand between two tables arranged in the middle of a room. Each participant first faced Table 1. Three stuffed animals were arranged in a row on top of the table, and each participant was asked to memorize their order. The stuffed animals were removed after fifteen seconds. The participants were then asked to turn 180 degrees to face Table 2. On this table, six stuffed animals were arranged, from which the participants were asked to correctly select the three that had been present earlier. They were then instructed to arrange the stuffed animals the "same" as before. After three practice rounds, the participants were asked to perform this task five times. The practice rounds were all conducted using Table 1.

For the stimuli, stuffed toys representing six types of animals known to both cultures were used: a cow, tiger, rabbit, horse, chicken, and pig. All of the participants were asked if they recognized each animal and understood the direction it was facing.

It was expected that if the participant had interpreted and memorized the animals' positions on Table 1 in relation to the position of their own body, they

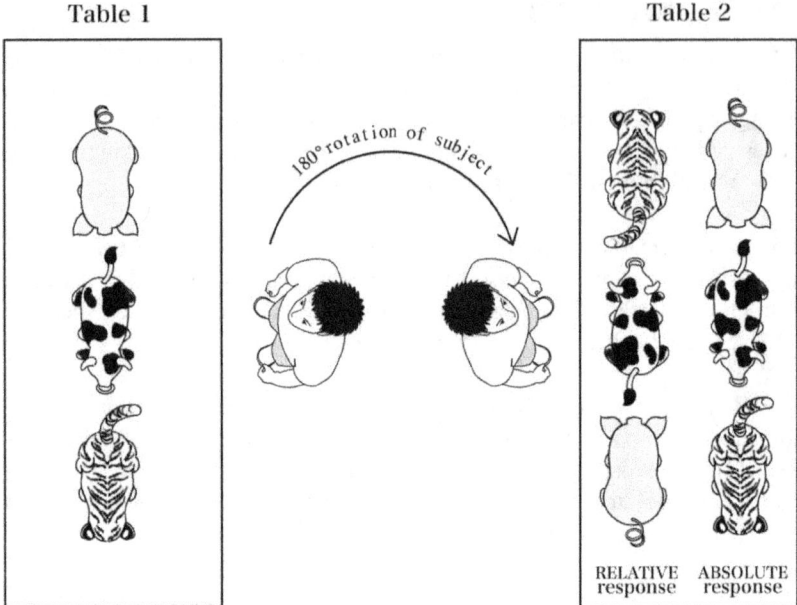

Figure A.3 RELATIVE and ABSOLUTE responses to the Animal Recall Task.

would replicate the animals' positions as they had been before but rotated 180 degrees, as they themselves had rotated 180 degrees when turning to face Table 2. This was the RELATIVE response, as shown in Figure A.3. Conversely, it was expected that those who had interpreted the animals' positions and memorized them in accordance with their surroundings would replicate the animals' positions without rotating them, as in the ABSOLUTE response shown in Figure A.3.

A.5.2.2 Chips Recognition Task (CRT) In this task, each participant was shown a card and then asked to turn 180 degrees and choose the card that was the "same" as the previous one from a selection of cards (Figure A.4).

First, the participants were asked to stand between two tables arranged in the middle of a room. The participants were originally situated facing Table 1. They were shown a single card on top of Table 1 and asked to memorize the card's design. The card was removed after three seconds. The participants were then asked to turn 180 degrees to face Table 2. On Table 2, there were four cards with the same design, which were facing different directions, and the participants were asked to select the card that was the "same" as before. After three

A.5 Experiment

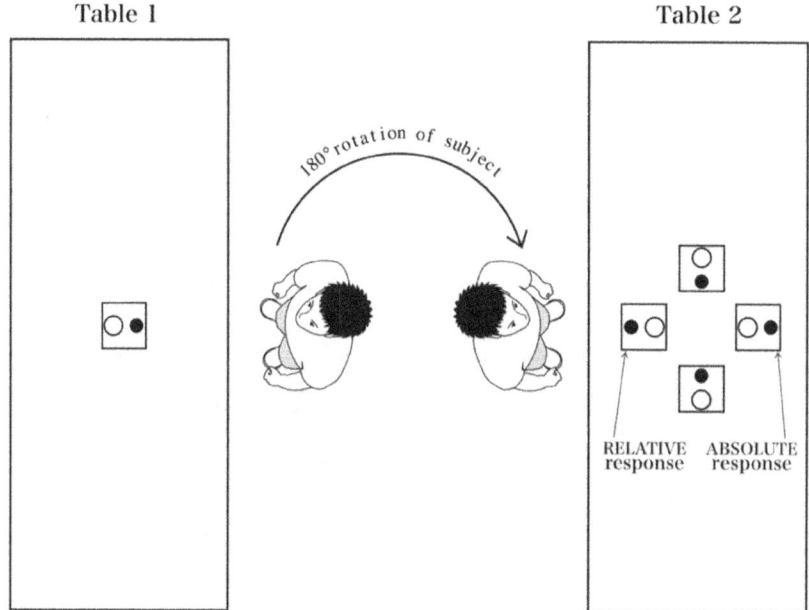

Figure A.4 RELATIVE and ABSOLUTE responses to the Chips Recognition Task.

practice rounds, each participant performed the task five times. The practice rounds were all conducted on Table 1.

As stimuli, five types of cards with various shapes, such as circles and squares, were used. All participants recognized that a card facing a different direction would be considered a different card.

The participants who had used the relative FoR to memorize the shapes were expected to select the shapes that had been rotated 180 degrees (the RELATIVE response in Figure A.4), while the participants who had used the absolute FoR were expected to choose the shapes that had not been rotated (the ABSOLUTE response in Figure A.4).

A.5.2.3 Transitive Inference Task (TIT) In this task, the participants viewed two figures, A and B, arranged in a particular configuration on Table 1, and were then rotated 180 degrees to Table 2, where they saw two figures, B and C. Finally, they were rotated back to Table 1, where Figure A was standing alone. Their task was to place Figure C next to Figure A, keeping the location consistent with what they had seen before (Figure A.5).

Appendix A

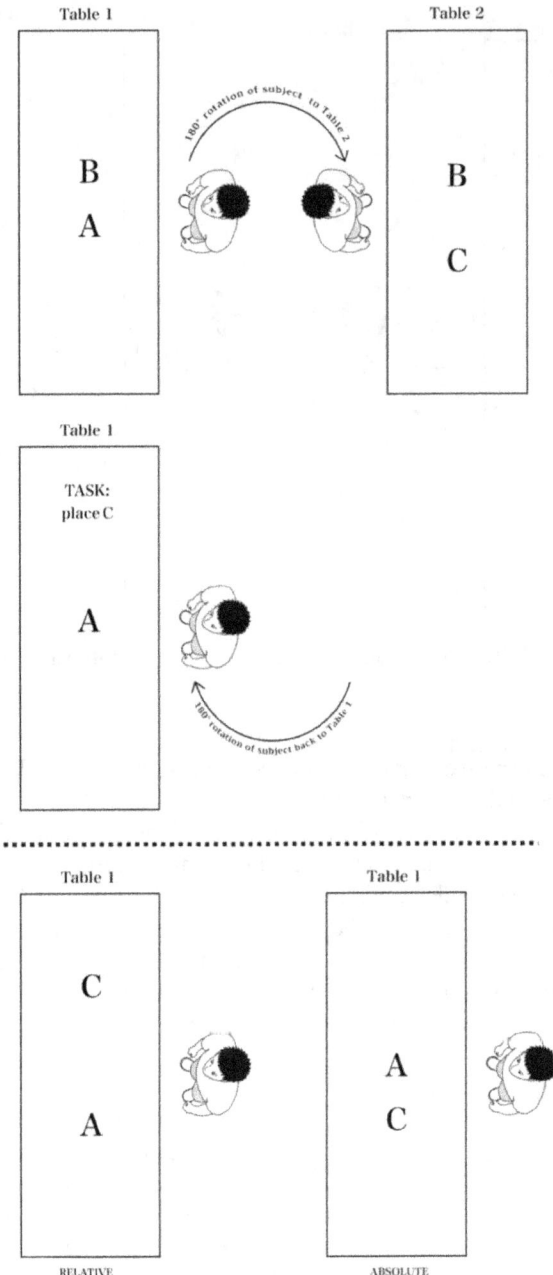

Figure A.5 RELATIVE and ABSOLUTE responses to the Transitive Inference Task.

A.5 Experiment

First, each participant was asked to stand between two tables arranged in the middle of a room. The participants were originally situated facing Table 1. They were shown two shapes on top of Table 1 (A and B) and asked to memorize them. The shapes were removed after ten seconds. The participants were then asked to turn 180 degrees to face Table 2. On Table 2, the participants were presented with two shapes. Only one of the shapes matched a shape from Table 1. The other shape was a new one (B and C). As before, the participants were instructed to memorize the shapes. The shapes were removed after ten seconds. Finally, the participants turned to face Table 1 again, where Figure A had already been placed. The participants were asked to recall both of the arrangements that they had memorized and position Figure C accordingly. Three practice rounds were conducted before the participants were asked to perform the task five times. The practice rounds were all conducted on Table 1.

For the stimuli, small bottles featuring blue cones, green cones, blue cubes, red cubes, and transparent cylinders were used. All participants recognized each figure as distinct from the others.

In this task, the participants had to combine their memory of the positions of the objects on both Tables 1 and 2 to create a new mental image. Nonetheless, as in the other tasks, when coming up with answers, the participants' logic differed when they used the relative FoR and when they used the absolute one. A solution based on the relative FoR places C on the "right side" of A. A solution based on the absolute FoR places C on the (for example) "south side" of A.

A.5.3 Experimental Results

Table A.1 shows the results of the three tasks conducted with twenty Japanese-speaking and twenty Kaqchikel-speaking participants. All of the answers in the "Others" category of the Animal Recall Task, which corresponded to neither a RELATIVE (REL) nor an ABSOLUTE (ABS) response, were answers in which the stuffed animals had been selected or ordered incorrectly.

Table A.1 *Japanese and Kaqchikel speakers' responses (RELative, ABSolutive, or Others) to the three tasks*

	Animal Recall Task			Chips Recognition Task			Transitive Inference Task		
	REL	ABS	Others	REL	ABS	Others	REL	ABS	Others
Japanese	85	13	2	95	5	0	83	16	1
Kaqchikel	18	73	9	52	48	0	55	45	0

180 Appendix A

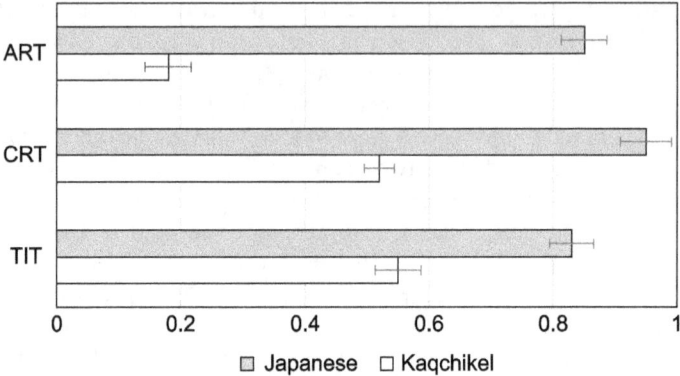

Figure A.6 Mean relative response ratios by native language.
Note: The error bar indicates the standard error for each condition.

The "Others" category of the Transitive Inference Task represented a trial in which the participant did not provide a response.

The relative response ratio was defined as the number of relative responses to each task for each participant divided by five (the number of trials). For example, a participant who responded to the Animal Recall Task with four relative responses over five trials had a relative response ratio of 0.8. The mean relative response ratios for each task by native language are shown in Figure A.6.

A 2 × 3 analysis of variance was conducted on native language (Japanese, Kaqchikel) and task type (ART, CRT, TIT) with the mean relative response ratio as the dependent variable. The results showed that the main effect of native language was significant ($F_{1,114} = 59.434$, $p < .001$), with Japanese speakers having a higher relative response rate than Kaqchikel speakers. The main effect of task type was also significant ($F_{2,114} = 5.059$, $p = .008$). A pairwise comparison between the two conditions using Tukey's method to correct for the significance of task factors showed that the Animal Recall Task had a lower relative response rate than did the other two tasks (ART vs. CRT: $p = .009$; ART vs. TIT: $p = 0.48$). However, there was no significant difference between performance on the Chips Recognition Task and that on the Transitive Inference Task ($p = .812$). Furthermore, the interaction between the two factors was significant ($F_{2,114} = 3.623$, $p = .030$). This was due to the fact that the Japanese speakers did not differ significantly in their performance on the tasks (ART vs. CRT: $p = .927$; ART vs. TIT: $p = 1.000$; CRT vs. TIT: $p = .854$), whereas the Kaqchikel speakers differed significantly. The Kaqchikel speakers had lower relative response rates for the Animal Recall Task, compared to the other two tasks (ART vs. CRT: $p = .016$; ART vs. TIT: $p = .007$), but showed no significant difference in their relative response rates for the Chips Recognition Task and the Transitive Inference Task ($p = 1.000$).

A.6 Discussion

A.6.1 Speakers of Japanese and Kaqchikel

We conducted an experiment comprising three tasks to investigate whether there were differences in the spatial FoRs that Japanese and Kaqchikel speakers subconsciously adopted when making sense of and remembering positional relationships without the intervention of language. The results showed that the Japanese speakers performed all three tasks using the relative FoR in most of the trials. Conversely, a larger proportion of the Kaqchikel speakers responded using the absolute FoR than did the Japanese speakers when completing all tasks.

These results demonstrate that Japanese and Kaqchikel speakers differ in their preferred FoR for spatial recognition, at least under conditions similar to those in this study. Traditionally, the Kaqchikel people led agrarian lifestyles in mountainous areas where it was easy to identify one's position from the surrounding landscape. Perhaps having been born and raised in such an environment led the Kaqchikel speakers to use the absolute FoR at a higher rate than their predominantly urban Japanese counterparts. These results are consistent with the Sociotopographic Model, which suggests that those in rural societies are more likely to use the absolute FoR than their urban counterparts.

A.6.2 Differences by Task

Japanese speakers preferred the same FoR (i.e., the relative one) when completing all tasks. In contrast, Kaqchikel speakers differed in their preferred FoR depending on the task. More than 80 percent of the responses to the Animal Recall Task were absolute, while only approximately half of the responses to the other two tasks were absolute. In previous studies, researchers have not reported any significant differences in FoR preferences among these three types of tasks; thus, the results for the Kaqchikel speakers in this study are noteworthy.

Why, then, did the Animal Recall Task elicit this high absolute response rate? This task revolved around the positions of stuffed animals. Although they were only toys, animals were still involved in the task. Many Kaqchikel speakers live in an environment in which they see animals out in the open daily. It may be that the Kaqchikel speakers, when seeing the stuffed animals, recalled large outdoor spaces instead of the confines of a desk, leading them to use the absolute FoR, which would be easier to use when attempting to recognize positions in large spaces. In contrast, it is uncommon for Japanese speakers to live in areas surrounded by animals and an open outdoor environment. As a result, the sight of stuffed animals would be unlikely to evoke in them the image of a large outdoor space. Even among the Japanese speakers who did think of a farm, they (except for those who lived in a farm-like environment) still used the relative FoR when describing the space of that scale. Japanese speakers tend to rely on the absolute FoR when attempting to grasp positional relationships within larger spaces, as when describing a long road trip (e.g., "From the Miyagi IC, drive north on the Tohoku Expressway for about forty-five minutes, then exit at the Furukawa IC and take the prefectural road west for thirty minutes to the hot spring district of Kawatabi Town."). For this reason, we assumed that Japanese speakers would use the relative FoR in the Animal Recall Task.

A.6.3 *Tendencies of Individual Kaqchikel Speakers*

There were roughly equal numbers of absolute and relative responses from Kaqchikel speakers to both the Chips Recognition Task and the Transitive Inference Task. According to a somewhat simplistic analysis, it appears that there are two main reasons for these results. One possibility is that, under the conditions that prevailed when these two tasks were being carried out, there was a group of speakers who preferred the absolute FoR and a group of speakers who preferred the relative FoR. Based on the total results, it appears that both FoRs were used at approximately the same rate. In this case, the speakers who used the absolute FoR more often in the Chips Recognition Task should have used the same FoR more often in the Transitive Inference Task. Conversely, speakers who used the relative FoR more often in the Chips Recognition Task should have used the same FoR more often in the Transitive Inference Task. Another conceivable reason for the observed outcome could be that the extent to which each Kaqchikel speaker preferred the absolute or relative FoR was not especially significant and that the FoR that was used was selected essentially randomly in each instance. In this case, it does not necessarily follow that a speaker who used one of the FoRs (e.g., the relative one) more frequently in the Chips Recognition Task automatically used the same one more often in the Transitive Inference Task, which could have resulted in variation.

To examine which of these possible reasons is a more likely explanation for the results, we determined the correlation between the number of times each speaker used the relative FoR in the Chips Recognition Task and the number of times that they used the relative FoR in the Transitive Inference Task and found a trend toward weak correlation with $r = .399$ and $p = .081$ (Figure A.7).

A.6 Discussion

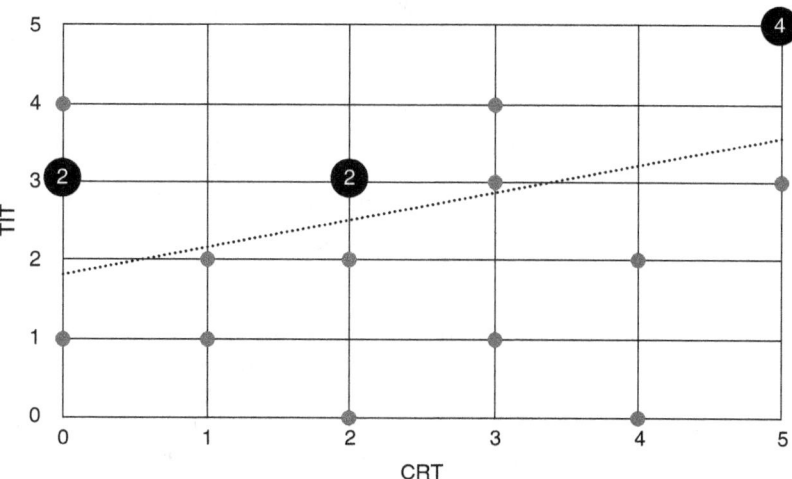

Figure A.7 The number of times the relative FoR was used in the Chips Recognition Task and Transitive Inference Task and the responses' correlations ($r = .399, p = .081$). The numbers within the black circles indicate the number of speakers in the category. A black circle without a number indicates a single speaker.

Four of the speakers used the relative FoR in both tasks (five times each) and never selected the absolute FoR. These four speakers also did not use the absolute FoR when carrying out the Animal Recall Task. For convenience, we refer to these four speakers as "consistent relative speakers." When looking at the other sixteen speakers, there was no correlation between the number of relative responses to the Chips Recognition Task and that of the Transitive Inference Task ($r = -.131, p = .628$). That is, the weak correlation found in the data when all twenty speakers were included appears to have been caused mainly by the responses of the four consistent relative speakers. The responses of the other sixteen participants showed no correlation in terms of the selection of an FoR for the two tasks. This supports the latter of the two possibilities discussed earlier in this section, namely, the hypothesis that, for the majority of Kaqchikel speakers, "the extent to which each Kaqchikel speaker preferred the absolute or relative FoR was not especially significant, and the FoR that was used was selected essentially randomly."

A.6.4 Variations within the Mayan Language Family

Regarding the three Mayan languages for which the speakers' spatial FoR preferences have already been examined, the absolute FoR appears to predominate in Tzeltal, the intrinsic FoR appears to predominate in Mopan, and the intrinsic and relative FoRs appear to predominate in Yucatec. The results of this study demonstrate that, unlike in any of the three languages mentioned, both the relative and absolute FoRs are used relatively often in Kaqchikel. Of the three languages mentioned, Tzeltal exhibits an FoR preference that aligns most closely with that of Kaqchikel. Tzeltal speakers exhibit a preference for the absolute FoR in both speech and non-verbal spatial cognition. Most of the Tzeltal speakers provided responses reflecting the absolute FoR to the same three tasks used in this study (Brown and Levinson 1993b). Unlike the Kaqchikel speakers, the Tzeltal speakers rarely used the relative FoR. One possible explanation for this difference may be related to differences in vocabulary. As mentioned in the section on previous studies, Tzeltal possesses words that correspond to the absolute FoR but not to the relative FoR. In contrast, Kaqchikel possesses expressions that correspond to both the absolute and relative FoRs. It is possible that this difference in vocabulary may have influenced the differences in the degrees of preference for the absolute FoR between the two languages' speakers. Another possible factor that should be considered is the influence of bilingualism and the Spanish language. Latin America is largely Spanish-speaking, and the Mayan languages have all been influenced to some degree by the Spanish language. Among these languages, Kaqchikel is believed to exhibit the most pronounced Spanish influence (England 2003). Although no research has been conducted on FoR preferences in Spanish, it seems likely that, at least in Castilian Spanish, the relative FoR would be preferred, considering the language's genealogy and the characteristics of its associated region and culture. There is an impression that "left" and "right" are used more often than "north," "east," "south," and "west" in the everyday Spanish heard in Guatemala as well. If Latin American Spanish can be considered a relative-FoR language, then it is possible that Kaqchikel has been influenced by this tendency and is shifting from having originally been an absolute-FoR language to becoming a relative-FoR language. The differences seen among Kaqchikel speakers regarding the extent to which they preferred the absolute FoR when completing the three tasks may also be related to this factor. When a language community changes from absolute FoR dominance to relative FoR dominance, the use of the relative FoR begins with the description of a narrow space and gradually expands to the description of a wide space (Inoue 2005). If this is the case, it is expected that the number of Kaqchikel speakers who use the relative FoR in the Animal Recall Task will increase in the future.

Appendix B Syntax and Processing in Seediq: A Behavioral Study*

B.1 Introduction

B.1.1 Word Order and Sentence Comprehension

It has been well established in the sentence processing literature that various syntactic properties, such as word order and the type/length of syntactic dependency, have a major influence on the processing cost of a sentence (Aoshima et al. 2004; Fiebach et al. 2002; Frazier 1987; Nakano et al. 2002; Phillips et al. 2005; Phillips and Wagers 2007; Schlesewsky et al. 2000; among many others). For instance, in languages where the subject (S) precedes the object (O) in their canonical word order, which we call "SO-type languages," it has been repeatedly observed that the native speakers need more time to comprehend sentences when they are presented in a non-canonical word order, such as the OS word order, where the object comes before the subject (Bornkessel et al. 2002; Erdocia et al. 2009; Hagiwara et al. 2007; Imamura and Koizumi 2008; Kim et al. 2009; Matzke et al. 2002; Mazuka, Itoh, and Kondo 2002; Sekerina 2003; Tamaoka et al. 2003). In the pair of sentences in (1), taken from Mazuka, Itoh, and Kondo (2002), native speakers of Japanese took more time to read the scrambled sentence in (1b) than the canonical word order sentence in (1a).

(1) a. SO word order (canonical)
   Mariko-ga otooto-o yonda
   Mariko-NOM brother-ACC called

  b. OS word order (scrambled, non-canonical)
   Otooto-o Mariko-ga yonda
   brother-ACC Mariko-NOM called
   "Mariko called her brother."

Further, Bader and Meng (1999) presented stimulus sentences in German, those in (2), to the native speakers of German in a speeded grammaticality judgment task, where the participants were instructed to judge as quickly and accurately as possible whether or not the sentence was grammatically acceptable. The sentences shown in (2) involve a relative clause structure, in which the noun phrase *die Eltern* "the parents" is locally ambiguous between the subject or the object in the relative clause until the reader reads the clause-final auxiliary verb *hat* or *haben*. This auxiliary verb indicates whether the subject is singular or plural, which disambiguates the structure.

(2)   a. Subject gap in the relative clause
Maria   erzählte   mir   von   der   Frau,   [CP   die   die   Eltern
Maria   told   me   about   the   woman   who   the   parents
angerufen   hat]
phoned   has
"Maria told me about the woman, who has phoned the parents."

       b. Object gap in the relative clause
Maria   Erzählte   mir   von   der   Frau,   [CP   die   die   Eltern
Maria   told   me   about   the   woman   who   the   parents
angerufen   haben]
phoned   have
"Maria told me about the woman, who the parents have phoned."

Bader and Meng (1999) found that the participants in their experiment were slow to judge (2b) to be "acceptable," compared to (2a). Furthermore, they were less accurate in making a judgment for (2b) than (2a). This showed that the native speakers of German have a bias in which the relative pronoun *die* "who" corresponds to the subject in the relative clause, so the first noun phrase they encounter in the relative clause is assumed to be the object. They have a subject-first/agent-first preference.

The observations from Mazuka, Itoh, and Kondo (2002) and others suggest that syntactic complexity is one major factor for determining the processing cost of a given sentence. When readers encounter a sequence of noun phrases in a non-canonical word order, they must map those phrases into a structure with an extra layer of projection to accommodate the scrambled noun phrase (Saito 1989; Saito and Fukui 1998; but see Miyagawa 2005 for a different approach). In this sense, the sentences that use the canonical word order have a simpler syntactic structure, hence they require a smaller amount of processing resources for comprehension (e.g., O'Grady 1997). Furthermore, the German examples in (2) suggest that sentences with a longer syntactic dependency are costly to process. The example in (2b) involves a dependency between the relative pronoun and the object position in the relative clause, which is longer than the dependency in (2a) (Gibson 2000; Grodner and Gibson 2005). In terms of dependency, it is possible to regard the processing cost in (1b) of the non-canonical word order as the cost for a filler-gap dependency. The displaced object functions as a filler that has to be encoded in the working memory until it

B.1 Introduction

is eventually interpreted at the gap-position; the storage and integration of a filler require a cognitive cost (Gibson 2000). Therefore, the presence of a filler-gap dependency and its length are factors that increase the processing cost of a given sentence.[1]

There is another approach to the processing costs associated with the OS word order. It has been observed in many sentence production studies that a perceptual property in an event, often noted as saliency, has an effect on word order preferences. Saliency, or properties connected to conceptual accessibility or animacy, is related to the thematic roles in an event, and some have suggested that the agent-before-patient or animate-before-inanimate order is preferred (Bock 1982; Bock and Warren 1985; Branigan et al. 2008; McDonald et al. 1993; Tanaka et al. 2011). For instance, Tanaka et al. (2011) used a sentence recall task, and asked the participants to recall Japanese sentences such as those shown in (3).

(3)   a. SO word order
          Minato-de ryoosi-ga booto-o hakonda
          port-at fisherman-NOM boat-ACC carried
    b. OS word order
          Minato-de booto-o ryoosi-ga hakonda
          port-at boat-ACC fisherman-NOM carried
          "At the port, the fisherman carried the boat."

Tanaka et al. (2011) observed that, when the participants recalled the sentences, they were more likely to invert the word order and produce an SO word order such as (3a). One interpretation of this result is that, in addition to syntactic factors, native speakers of Japanese prefer to produce sentences in which the agent comes before the patient. Such an ordering preference may stem from an idea that the agent is more salient than the theme in an event, because the agent has more control over the event's progress.

Similarly, Sauppe et al. (2013) observed the agent preference over the patient in their picture-description experiment using Tagalog, a language spoken in the Philippines. They presented participants with a picture depicting a transitive event, and measured eye gaze patterns while the participants produced a sentence. In the time-window of the first 600 milliseconds (ms) after the presentation of the stimulus picture on the screen, participants looked at the agent in the picture more often and longer than the patient in the picture. Also, Hwang (2017) found the tendency among native speakers of Korean to place agent nouns in the sentence-initial position in a sentence-assembly task. Crucially, this effect was also present when animacy was controlled. These observations suggest that there is a universal tendency to place a salient element, such as an agent noun, before a less salient element. Similar ideas based on some notions related to human cognitive features and/or discourse features are found in MacWhinney (1977),

Primus (1999), Kemmerer (2012), Cohn and Paczynski (2013), and Cohn et al. (2017), among others.

The above discussion should make clear that the word order preference of SO over OS (or agent–theme order over theme–agent order) is observed in a wide range of paradigms, but at the same time it should also be noted that data samples are quite limited in terms of the linguistic diversity. Most of the languages that have been studied and found to have SO and/or agent-before-theme preferences are heavily biased toward socially, economically, and/or politically "rich" languages (see related discussions in Anand et al. 2011; Jaeger and Norcliffe 2009; Norcliffe et al. 2015). With this in mind, it is important to investigate a much wider range of languages, to examine to what extent the SO and agent-before-theme preferences are universal features of language. In particular, in terms of this word order preference, it is important to investigate those that we call "OS-type languages," in which the object comes before the subject in their underlying basic word order.

Koizumi et al. (2014) conducted one of the few studies investigating the nature of the SO preference, using an OS-type language (see also Kiyama et al. 2013; Yasunaga et al. 2015). They examined the word order preference in Kaqchikel, a Mayan language spoken in Guatemala. In Kaqchikel, the canonical word order is VOS (Ajsivinac Sian et al. 2004: 162; García Mátzar and Rodríguez Guaján 1997: 333; Rodríguez Guaján 1994: 200; Tichoc Cumes et al. 2000: 195; see also England 1991 and Aissen 1992), but the language also allows SVO word order. Like other Mayan languages, Kaqchikel is a head-marking language, in which the verb carries agreement markers of the dependent elements such as subject and object (with respect to person and number), in addition to tense/aspect markers. Sentences in (4) are a sample set of their target sentences; in an auditory semantic anomaly detection task, they measured participants' response times in making a plausibility judgment. In the following examples, the verb shows the person and number agreement markers; one for the ergative NP (subject), and the other for the absolutive NP (object).

(4)   a.   VOS word order (canonical)
X-∅-u-chöy   ri   chäj   ri   ajanel
CP-ERG.3SG-ABS.3SG-cut   DET   pine.tree   DET   carpenter

   b.   SVO word order (the subject is fronted to the sentence-initial position)
Ri   ajanel   x-∅-u-chöy   ri   chäj
DET   carpenter   CP-ERG.3SG-ABS.3SG-cut   DET   pine.tree
"The carpenter cut the pine tree."

Koizumi et al. (2014) observed that VOS sentences were responded to significantly faster than SVO sentences, at a rate of roughly 150 ms. These results suggest that the SO preference is not a universal feature of language. Instead, they suggest that syntactic properties of a given language greatly affect the processing cost in sentence comprehension, and note that it took more time for native speakers of Kaqchikel to process sentences with non-canonical word orders, like that in (4b). Yasunaga et al. (2015) also observed a similar effect in their event-related potential (ERP) study. Comparing the SVO and VOS sentences, the object in SVO word order sentences elicited a P600 effect, suggesting that SVO sentences are more costly than VOS sentences. These studies suggest that, both in SO- and OS-type languages, sentences that are syntactically more complex, due to the presence of a filler-gap dependency, require more processing resources than those sentences with no filler-gap dependency.

Building upon the findings from Koizumi et al. (2014), this paper reports on an experiment conducted in the Truku dialect of the Seediq language, which is spoken in Taiwan. Truku is an OS-type language, in which the canonical word order is claimed to be VOS (Aldridge 2004; Tsukida 2009). Truku is typologically different from Kaqchikel, and is not a head-marking language. As is demonstrated in the next section, verbs in Truku do not carry any person/number agreement markers of the dependent elements, but the verb is required to have one voice marker indicating which element in the event is treated as the subject. One might suggest a processing advantage in the verb-initial structure, due to the agreement markers on the verb. In fact, Sauppe (2016) conducted an experiment using the visual-world eye-tracking paradigm in Tagalog and found that, while listening to sentences, native speakers of Tagalog used verbal semantics to anticipate the upcoming referents and their thematic roles as soon as the verb was heard. Studying Truku allows us to examine the role of verbs whose morphological properties are widely different from those in a head-marking language such as Kaqchikel.

Furthermore, it is important to investigate the word order preferences in Truku, because such an inquiry allows us to determine to what extent the widely observed processing preferences, namely the SO and agent-before-theme preferences, are grounded in properties of the linguistic system or somewhat more general human cognitive properties (Koizumi et al. 2014; Kubo et al. 2015). Truku allows SVO word order, but it has also been claimed that SVO is a word order derived from the more basic VOS word order in this language (Aldridge 2004). In the following sections, we will see a more detailed discussion of the grammatical properties of Truku. Under the syntactic complexity hypothesis, that the syntactic complexity has an impact on the word order preferences for sentences (i.e., it is reflected in processing costs), the SVO word order should be more costly than the VOS order in Truku. By contrast, one could propose that, being in the privileged position, the subject is universally salient over objects. Given a typical transitive event, a subject is often associated with the agent role, while the object is associated with the theme role, which accounts for the subject preference. Under this universal saliency hypothesis, the SO word order preference should also be favored in Truku, irrespective of its basic word order. Of course, these two accounts of syntactic complexity and saliency are not in an exclusive relationship, and it is possible that both of them are found to have a certain effect on the word order preferences in Truku.

Finally, we should note that the SO word order preference discussed above is, nevertheless, often conflated with the "agent-before-theme preference" noted in the previous studies. Using various SO-type languages or even Kaqchikel, it has been difficult to tease apart the possible source of the saliency noted above. It is possible that being a subject is an important property to be counted as salient, but it is also possible that being an agent is important and the agent is taken to be salient. Then, we have a case in which the agent is more likely to be promoted to the subject, yielding the subject preference. As will be seen in greater detail below, Truku has a symmetrical voice system in which the agent and patient are equally likely to be promoted to the subject of the sentence (Foley 2008). Given this grammatical characteristic of Truku, along with other grammatical characteristics, it is possible to investigate how these two properties, being a subject and being an agent, interact in comprehending Truku sentences.

B.1.2 Truku Grammar

Truku, a dialect of the Seediq language, is spoken in East Taiwan. Seediq is an indigenous language and the Seediq people are one of Taiwan's sixteen nationally recognized tribes. Seediq belongs to the Atayal group of the Austronesian language family, and is spoken by approximately 20,000–30,000 people (Eberhard et al. 2019). Some grammatical properties of Truku are introduced below, as these are relevant to the design of the current experiment.

Truku, like many other Austronesian languages, uses the symmetrical voice system (Aldridge 2004; Foley 2008; Riesberg 2014; Tsukida 2009). Verbs need to carry one of the three voice markers (agent voice, goal voice, or conveyance voice). This system is described as "symmetrical" because there is no default or unmarked voice among the three voice markers (cf., English and Japanese, where the active voice is clearly unmarked syntactically and morphologically, compared to the passive voice). The following examples show the basic voice patterns. The two example sentences in (5) basically represent the same event. The verb carries different voice markers, and the agent "the cook" is promoted to the subject in (5a), while the theme "this pineapple" is promoted to the subject in (5b). Truku also has a third type of voice marker, conveyance voice; in sentences with the verb in the conveyance voice, elements such as instrument phrases or benefactive NPs are promoted to the subject position. Examples of the conveyance voice are not shown here, because sentences of this voice type

B.1 Introduction

are not used in the current study. In the VOS word order, the subject is marked with *ka*, which is glossed as NOM, following Tsukida (2009), but a slightly different terminology is used in other works (Aldridge 2004; Holmer 2005).

(5) a. Agent voice, VOS word order
q⟨m⟩nilis kalat niyi ka emphapuy
AV-peels pineapple this NOM cook

b. Goal voice, VOS word order
qnlis-an emphapuy ka kalat niyi
peels-GV cook NOM pineapple this
"The cook peels this pineapple."

Another relevant feature in Truku is the word order variation. As shown in (5), the language allows the VOS word order. It also allows the SVO word order, as shown in (6).

(6) a. Agent voice, SVO word order
emphapuy o q⟨m⟩nilis kalat niyi
cook TOP AV-peels pineapple this

b. Goal voice, SVO word order
kalat niyi o qnlis-an emphapuy
pineapple this TOP peels-GV cook
"The cook peels this pineapple."

In (6), the nominal phrase appearing along with the particle *ka* in (5) is now placed in the clause-initial position. When the subject is fronted, the particle *ka* can no longer appear, but another particle, *o*, appears after the fronted subject. It has been claimed that the VOS word order is the syntactically basic word order, and the SVO order is syntactically derived from the VOS word order (Aldridge 2004; Tsukida 2009). In this paper, we follow Aldridge (2004) and assume that the VOS word order is derived by predicate fronting. As for the SVO word order, Yano et al. (2019) have shown that the SVO order is derived from the VOS, and the subject is in a higher position, as evidenced by the observation that the fronted subject can leave its associated quantifier after VO (see the relevant discussion in Sportiche (1988)). Assuming that the subject fronting involves more functional categories in the CP domain (Rizzi 1997), the SVO structure is a syntactically more complex one.

The present study investigates the word order preference in Truku, manipulating voice and word order at the same time. We are particularly interested in whether SVO sentences produce a large processing cost. In Truku, SVO is a derived word order, and the syntactic complexity hypothesis predicts that SVO is more costly than VOS in Truku, because SVO involves a filler-gap dependency. By contrast, if subject is universally salient over object, and if saliency is a major factor responsible for the processing cost of the sentence, native speakers of Truku should process SVO sentences faster than VOS ones. Given that Truku is a symmetrical voice language, we can manipulate whether the agent role is assigned to the subject or object, which allows us to examine the interaction of voice and word order (saliency order) fully. Then, the saliency hypothesis predicts that the SVO word order is preferred in Agent Voice (AV) sentences, while the VOS is preferred in Goal Voice (GV) sentences in our auditory semantic anomaly detection experiment, which is introduced in the next section.

B.2 Experiment

B.2.1 Participants

Forty-two native speakers of the Truku dialect of Seediq (nine males and thirty-three females; $M = 60.1$ years, $SD = 11.1$) were paid to participate in the experiment; all signed a written informed consent document. All reported no hearing or other language-related disorders. They live in a village near Hualien City, Taiwan, and all of them also speak Chinese daily.[2]

B.2.2 Materials

The materials for our experiment consist of forty-eight sets of sentences. Each set crossed two types of the verb voice (AV and GV) and two word orders (VOS and SVO), making four conditions. Among the forty-eight sets of sentences, twenty-four sets used a proper name in the agent phrase, such as *Rabay* and *Abis*, which are commonly used names in Truku, according to our consultants. The other twenty-four sets used a common noun in the agent phrase. Those included *emphapuy* "cook" or *knsat* "policeman," etc. In the AGENT VOICE condition, the verb had the agent voice marker, and the NP with the agent role appeared as the subject of the sentence. In the GOAL VOICE condition, however, the verb was marked with the goal voice marker, and the NP with the theme role appeared as the subject. As for the word order factor, we prepared the VOS word order, which had the subject at the end of the clause with the nominative marker *ka*. The SVO word order was also prepared, in which the subject was fronted to the sentence-initial position. Each set of target stimuli thus had four versions, and half of the target stimuli used a proper name, while the other half used a common name. Those 192 sentences were distributed into four lists by crossing voice and word order in a Latin-squared design, so that no participant saw more than one version from each set. Therefore, three factors (voice of the verb, word order, and noun type) are within-subjects factors. A sample set of the target sentences of the common noun type is shown below.

(7) a. Agent voice, VOS word order
m-n-hapuy begu niyi ka empsapuh
AV-PRF-cook soup this NOM doctor
"The doctor cooked this soup."

b. Agent voice, SVO word order
empsapuh o m-n-hapuy begu niyi
doctor TOP AV-PRF-cook soup this

c. Goal voice, VOS word order
n-puy-an empsapuh ka begu niyi
PRF-cook-GV doctor NOM soup this
"Lit. This soup was cooked by the doctor."

d. Goal voice, SVO word order
begu niyi o n-puy-an empsapuh
soup this TOP PRF-cook-GV doctor

In addition to the target sentences, forty-eight filler sentences were prepared. Those filler sentences were all semantically anomalous, such as #*Simaw planted the bag*; #*the chopsticks steamed the vegetables*, etc. We made filler sentences in this way because, as will be seen below, we used a semantic anomaly detection task, and all of the target sentences should be acceptable to the native speakers of Truku, while the filler sentences should be responded to as anomalous.[3]

One male native speaker of Truku from the village read the sentences aloud and we recorded him. After the recording, the audio files were trimmed so that the total length of the sentences was closely matched with respect to the voice and word order factor. The mean length of sentences was about three seconds(s), and there was a significant difference according to the noun-type factor ($F(1, 46) = 31.54, p < 0.01$), indicating that the mean length of sentences with a proper name was shorter than that with a common noun (the proper name condition, 2589 ms ($SD = 311$); the common noun condition, 3077 ms ($SD = 408$)). There was no other significant main effect or interaction.

B.2.3 Task and Procedure

The participants were tested individually. They sat in front of a laptop computer and wore a headset in a quiet room, and were told to relax. They were instructed by an experimenter, who is a native speaker of Truku, to listen to the sentences through the headset, and to decide, as quickly and accurately as possible, whether the sentences they heard made sense or not (Caplan et al. 2008). Two keys on the keyboard ("J" and "F") were assigned for the responses ("yes" and "no"). The participants were instructed to use both hands to make their responses. All target sentences should have been judged as "yes," and all filler sentences should have been judged as "no." The number of "yes" responses, then, was counterbalanced with the number of "no" responses. After the experimenter provided the instructions to the participant, there was a practice session with seven trials. In each trial, the participants briefly saw a small fixation cross in the middle of the screen for 1,000 ms, and the sentence was presented auditorily through their headset. Stimulus sentences were presented in a randomized order for each participant. While the stimulus sentence was presented auditorily, a pair of the smiley face and non-smiley face icons was shown on the screen, which would help the participants press the response keys as they intended. In the practice session, the experimenter provided feedback to the participants' responses, to ensure they understood the task and felt familiar with the procedure. This practice session was repeated if the participants wanted to practice more. During the experimental session, no feedback was given for wrong answers. The participant could make a judgment before the sentence ended, but they usually made their response after the end of the sentence. We recorded the responses (i.e., "yes" or "no" for the accuracy) and measured the response times (RTs) from the onset of the sentence. The whole experiment took about fifteen minutes.

This task required participants to judge the semantic plausibility of each sentence. The underlying assumption of using RTs is that the length of time it took to complete the task reflected sentence processing difficulties or complexities, such as sentences with relatively long syntactic dependencies (Grodner and Gibson 2005) or ones with a non-canonical word order (Kaiser and Trueswell 2004). Self-paced measurements have been widely used in various fields, and measuring response times of the full sentences may not allow us to draw strong conclusions regarding exactly which word or from what region of the sentence such processing difficulty has emerged. To assess the time-course of language comprehension, a word-by-word or phrase-by-phrase self-paced listening task can be set up as a more fine-grained measurement of processing efficiency (Ferreira et al. 1996). We, however, employed a whole-sentence measurement, due to concerns for the ecological validity (Kaiser 2013); that is, people do not hear a sentence segment by segment at their own pace in a natural setting. Instead, they have to process it as speakers produce their utterances. Because most, if not all, native speakers of Truku do not regularly read in Truku, we had to rely on a task measuring their auditory sentence comprehension, rather than reading.

B.2.4 Analysis

We removed data gathered from four participants from the analyses because they only used one hand to make their responses, and such responses are not reliable. The remaining data from thirty-eight participants were analyzed further. As for the analyses of the response times, data from the trials in

B.2 Experiment

which the participants made an incorrect response were excluded. In those incorrect responses for the target sentences the participants answered "no," and we removed those data from the response time analysis because such negative responses are known to be disproportionally longer. We analyzed our remaining data using the lme4 package (Bates et al. 2015a, 2015b) for the R software (R Core Team 2019). We used logistic mixed-effect models for the accuracy data (Jaeger 2008), as the dependent measure was categorical, and linear mixed-effect models for the RT data (Baayen et al. 2008). Following Barr et al. (2013), the model was initially fit with the maximal random effects structure, including random slopes for the repeated measures factors and random intercepts for participants and items. Three repeated measures factors, VOICE, WORD ORDER, and NOUN TYPE, were entered into the model as fixed factors. For the RT analyses, the mean correct response rate for each participant, and for each item, were entered as covariates. The trial order was also included initially, but was later eliminated because it did not significantly contribute to the improvement of the model's performance. Converged models were evaluated, and the optimal model was selected using backward elimination. Once the optimal model was chosen, we eliminated the data points that were more than 2.5 SD away from the estimation by the model, and the model was re-fit to determine the final model. The model summary and p-values were obtained using the lmerTest package (Kuznetsova et al. 2017).

While we were preparing for the data analysis, we noticed that the RT patterns from the stimuli with a proper name and those with a common name were largely different. Roughly, the sentences used in our experiment have three phrases/words: subject, verb, and object. Although the participants could sometimes detect anomalous meanings at the second phrase of the filler sentences, they usually needed to listen to the third phrase. The participants then needed to listen to the third phrase to decide whether the stimulus sentence made sense or not. It seemed that the onset time for the third phrase and its duration had some major influence on the response time, in addition to the different length of the total sentence. We then suspected that the length of the third phrase was one of the reasons why the RT patterns differed depending on the type of agent (a proper name or a common noun). Proper names used in the stimuli were relatively short, so the onset and the length of the third phrase differed across conditions. Three research assistants listened to the audio files and measured the length of the third phrases; they also measured the onset of the third phrase. We calculated the means of those measurements for each stimulus. Then, for the RT analyses, the onset time of the third phrase and the length of the third phrase were also entered into the model as covariates.[4]

B.2.5 Results

The overall correct response rate was 75 percent. The mean accuracy data by condition is shown in Figure B.1, and a summary of the statistical analyses of the response accuracy data is shown in Table B.1.

There was a significant main effect of WORD ORDER, showing that the mean accuracy rate for the SVO condition was lower than that for the VOS condition. Also, a significant main effect of NOUN TYPE showed that the common noun condition was more difficult than the proper name condition. There was a three-way interaction (almost significant) among the three within-subject factors, and further pairwise comparisons indicated that there was a WORD ORDER × NOUN TYPE interaction only in the AV condition, but not in the GV condition. This interaction was driven by the contrast within the common noun condition, showing that the AV-SVO condition was more difficult than the AV-VOS condition. There was no such word order effect in the GV condition.

The overall mean response times are shown in Figure B.2, and a summary of the statistical analysis is shown in Table B.2.

Table B.2 shows that the mean RT patterns for the proper name and the common noun conditions were different, as indicated by a significant NOUN TYPE factor and a marginally significant three-way interaction among WORD ORDER,

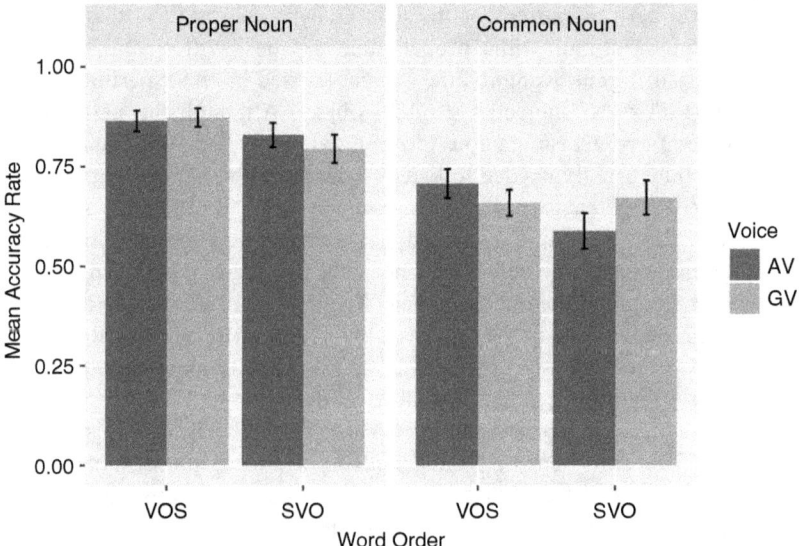

Figure B.1 The mean response accuracy rates for each condition. The error bars indicate standard errors of the mean.

Table B.1 *Summary of the statistical analysis on the response accuracy data*

	Estimate	S.E.	Z	p-value
Overview				
(Intercept)	1.462	0.189	7.727	<.001 ***
Word Order	− 0.399	0.124	− 3.205	<.010 **
Voice	− 0.033	0.125	− 0.266	.790
Noun Type	− 1.212	0.305	− 3.973	<.001 ***
Word Order * Voice	0.243	0.250	0.972	.331
Word Order * Noun Type	0.207	0.249	0.834	.404
Voice * Noun Type	0.113	0.250	0.451	.652
Word Order * Voice * Noun Type	0.983	0.500	1.967	<.050 *
Within AV				
Word Order * Noun Type	− 0.699	0.352	− 1.987	<.050 *
Within AV, Common Noun				
Word Order	− 0.616	0.271	− 2.275	<.030 *

Note: *p < .05, **p < .01, ***p < .001

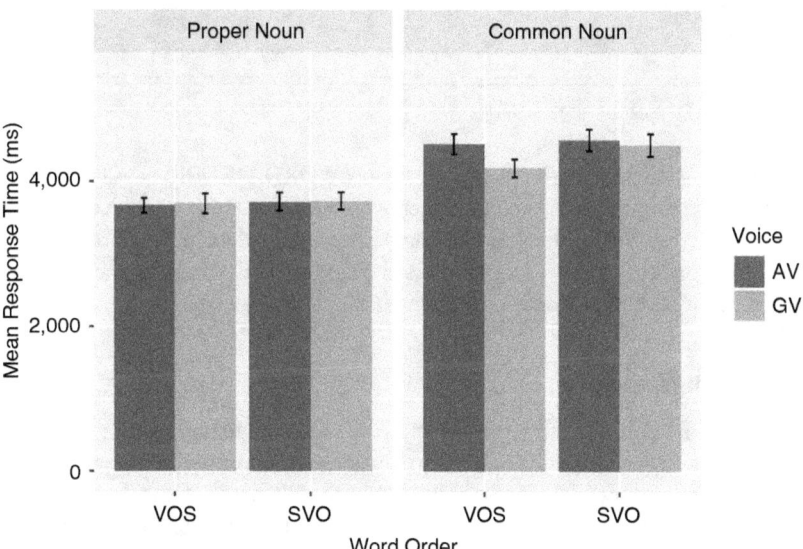

Figure B.2 The mean response time (ms) for each condition. The error bars indicate standard errors of the mean.

VOICE, and NOUN TYPE. In general, the mean RT for the common noun condition was slower than that for the proper name condition, which is correlated with the low accuracy for the common noun condition discussed above. Pairwise

Table B.2 *Summary of the statistical analysis on the response time data*

	Estimate	S.E.	t-value	p-value
Overview				
(Intercept)	6,331.54	564.77	11.21	<.001 ***
Word Order	22.19	27.91	0.80	.427
Voice	−18.27	28.09	−0.65	.516
Noun Type	253.45	49.76	5.09	<.001 ***
Onset 3rd Phrase	315.80	19.67	16.06	<.001 ***
Length 3rd Phrase	210.66	21.73	9.70	<.001 ***
Accuracy Rate (Participant)	−2,431.99	728.06	−3.34	<.010 **
Accuracy Rate (Item)	−708.68	148.32	−4.78	<.001 ***
Word Order * Voice	74.73	71.29	1.05	.295
Word Order * Noun Type	37.15	56.52	0.66	.511
Voice * Noun Type	−171.54	56.43	−3.04	<.010 **
Word Order * Voice * Noun Type	274.53	143.71	1.91	<.060
Within Common Noun				
Word Order * Voice	228.38	84.80	2.69	<.010 **
Within AV Word Order	−72.42	60.82	−1.19	.234
Within GV Word Order	155.97	58.93	2.65	<.010 **
Within Proper Name				
Word Order * Voice	46.15	111.89	0.41	.680

Note: *p < .05, **p < .01, ***p < .001

comparisons suggest that while there was no WORD ORDER × VOICE interaction in the proper name condition, there was a significant interaction of such in the common noun condition. Further comparisons show that, in the GV condition, the VOS condition was significantly faster than the SVO condition, but no such difference was found in the AV condition.

B.3 Discussion

The mean response accuracy rates indicated that sentences with a common noun agent were more difficult than those with a proper name agent. As demonstrated below, this is also reflected in the RT data. The lower accuracy rates in the common noun condition indicated that the participants were more willing to reject the common noun target sentences. In the common noun target sentences, for instance, they had to decide whether "the carpenter looked for the eggs" was a likely event. We suspect that some participants thought that there was a more likely agent who would look for the eggs – a cook, for instance. By contrast, in the proper name target sentences, they may not have had to examine in too much detail whether a given agent was a plausible entity to initiate the action, because the agent was just a name. Of course, they still had

B.3 Discussion

to decide whether the eggs are something people look for in general, but the task demand seemed lower in the proper name condition. We also observed the general pattern that sentences presented in the SVO word order were more difficult than those in the VOS word order. This contrast in the accuracy data was clearly visible in the common noun-AV conditions, suggesting that the derived SVO sentences were more costly to process than the VOS sentences.

The results of the RT measure suggest a few major patterns. First, the mean RT in the proper name condition was faster than that in the common noun in general. Second, there was no WORD ORDER × VOICE interaction in the proper name condition, but those two factors do interact in the common noun condition. Basically, there was no RT difference by condition within the proper name condition; in the common noun condition, the RT for the GV-VOS was faster than the other three conditions. With respect to the noun type contrast, we suggest the same account as discussed above; the RT for the proper name condition was faster because it required less processing demand, compared to the common noun condition, to judge whether the sentence was semantically plausible or not. Further, the total length of the sentences with a proper name was shorter than that with a common noun, which is also likely to be responsible for the RT difference. It seems that the participants made a response very soon after the sentence finished, so the lack of WORD ORDER × VOICE interaction might be due to the ease of comprehension for the sentences.

As for the WORD ORDER × VOICE interaction in the common noun condition, in Section B.1, we introduced the syntactic complexity account and the universal saliency account, but the predictions regarding these are hard to tease apart when testing SO-type languages. In languages like Truku, the syntactic complexity account predicts that the SVO word order should take longer to process in general because it is a derived word order from the more basic VOS word order. Assuming that the SVO word order involves a more complex syntactic structure (Aldridge 2004; Yano et al. 2019), it is, in general, more costly to process sentences in that word order. Furthermore, the saliency account suggests that sentences in which the agent comes before the theme are processed quickly. Among the conditions in this experiment, sentences in the AV-SVO and the GV-VOS conditions have the agent before the theme, and are predicted to be processed more quickly.

To account for the patterns from the accuracy and the response time data together, we suggest that there is a general VOS preference in Truku. Based on the common noun conditions, a VOS advantage was found in AV conditions in the accuracy data. A similar contrast was not seen in the response time data, but we propose that this exhibits a pattern of speed-accuracy trade-off. The response time in the AV-VOS condition seemed no faster than that in the AV-SVO condition, but this could be due to the relatively high accuracy rate. Participants made a better response by taking a slightly longer time to make a response. So, possibly, the response time in AV-SVO would be faster and the accuracy rate would be slightly lower. Then, the contrast between the SVO and the VOS word orders would have been much clearer, showing the VOS advantage. With respect to the pattern in GV conditions, in a similar way, we would expect a slightly higher accuracy rate for the GV-VOS condition, if there is a general VOS advantage. We suppose that this "lower-than-expected" accuracy rate in the GV-VOS is related to the faster response time in this condition. In sum, although we have to rely on the speed-accuracy trade-off, it is plausible to hypothesize that Truku has a general VOS preference, because this can explain the combined pattern of accuracy and response time data.

These interpretations of the results suggest that the often-observed SO preference is not a universal feature of language (Kiyama et al. 2013; Koizumi and Kim 2016; Koizumi et al. 2014; Yano et al. 2019; Yano, Yasunaga, and Koizumi 2017; Yasunaga et al. 2015). The SO preference has been observed in the sentence processing literature, and, most of the time, the SO-type languages are the targets of investigation. In those languages, the SO word order is the canonical/basic order, implying that it involves a syntactically less complex structure than the non-canonical OS word order. In languages like Truku, the SO word order necessarily involves a more complex structure, so there is no general preference of the SO word order.

There seems to be an apparent alternative account for the common noun condition that employs an interaction between syntactic complexity and saliency (see the relevant illustration in Table B.3). This "interaction" account would suggest that both syntactic complexity and saliency are needed in order to explain the full picture of the response time results. According to this account, the GV-SVO sentences took longer time to process than the GV-VOS sentences because: (a) the SVO word order involves a more complex syntactic structure, and (b) the theme NP is the subject and placed in the sentence-initial position in the SVO word order condition. It then precedes the agent NP, which is in the object position. In other words, the GV-SVO

Table B.3 *The relationship between the two accounts (the Universal Saliency and the Syntactic Complexity) with respect to the processing cost, and the four sentence patterns based on voice and word order*

	Universal Saliency Salient order	Syntactic Complexity Subject stay
GV.VOS	✓	✓
GV.SVO	Costly	Costly
AV.VOS	Costly	✓
AV.SVO	✓	Costly

sentence is a costly structure both under the syntactic complexity account and the saliency account. On the other hand, in the AV sentences, the AV-SVO sentence is costly to process because it has a more complex structure than the AV-VOS sentence. The AV-VOS sentence, however, is costly to process because the agent NP is the subject and placed at the end of the clause. The theme NP then precedes the agent NP in this sentence type. Assuming that the magnitude of the costs coming from the syntactic complexity and the saliency are not largely different from each other, it may be possible to claim that those two costs cancel each other out. Then, the reaction times from the two conditions did not show a significant difference.[5] This account may successfully explain the response time pattern, but it requires some extra assumptions with respect to the pattern found in the accuracy data, where there is a clear difference within the AV condition, but not within the GV condition.

The results from the present study have some implications for the role of head-marking morphology in sentence processing. Recall that Koizumi et al. (2014) and their related work indicated that word order preference is largely determined by the syntactic properties of a given language. They examined Kaqchikel, a Mayan language, which shares a certain syntactic characteristic with Truku. Both have VOS as the canonical word order and SVO as a derived word order. Although Kaqchikel and Truku are typologically different, it is noteworthy that both languages show the OS word order preference. This indicates that the OS word order preference is not limited to certain languages that belong to a particular language family, such as Mayan, but rather this seems to be a property of languages whose canonical word order is VOS. Some might speculate that, because the verbs in Kaqchikel carry a lot of agreement morphemes about the dependent nouns, the head-marking properties in Kaqchikel play a large role for the OS preference. Our current results suggest that having such a head-marking property is not a necessary condition for the OS word order preference, because Truku verbs do not have agreement markers analogous to those in Kaqchikel, yet the language still shows an OS word order preference.

As discussed in Section B.2.3, we decided to employ a task to measure the response time at the end of the sentence, not a word-by-word self-paced listening task, for example. Therefore, it is difficult to point out exactly at what stage the processing cost emerges in comprehending sentences, but nevertheless, we would predict that the processing cost arises at the sentence-initial NP, because it signals that the sentence is not in the VOS word order (see Yano et al. 2019).

Our results also suggest that properties like saliency often have an influence on the sentence processing costs, but to a different extent in SO- versus OS-type languages. In quite a few production studies of SO-type languages, it has been found that cognitive properties such as saliency have an effect on the word order selections (Branigan et al. 2008; Tanaka et al. 2011). However, our results suggest that saliency is not a major factor explaining the response pattern in Truku. Note that Truku is a language that has a rich voice system. It has been claimed that the goal voice in which a theme argument is promoted to the subject is no more marked than the agent voice, in terms of frequency (Tsukida 2009). Such a distributional tendency with respect to the construction types is not common in SO-type languages (Japanese, English, etc.). Sentences in passive voice are often morphologically more marked, and arguably less frequent (e.g., Roland et al. 2007). The lack of clear indication of the agent-before-theme preference suggests a correlation between the voice property of a given language and the importance of the saliency factor (see Sauppe 2016 for a relevant discussion). Of course, the availability of the symmetrical voice system is not restricted to OS-type languages, and the patterns are much more complicated.

B.4 Conclusion

Previous experimental results have shown that there is a processing bias whereby sentences are processed more quickly and easily when the subject appears before the object. We pointed out that this bias is widespread, but most of the data come from languages in which the subject precedes the object in their canonical word order. It is often also confounded that the agent argument precedes the theme argument in a sentence. The question of whether the SO word order bias is based on the syntactic complexity of the sentence or on its saliency can be solved by investigating Truku, whose canonical word order is VOS. The results showed that, with respect to the response time, there was, superficially, no word order effect in AV sentences with a common noun agent, but the SVO sentences are processed significantly slower than the VOS sentences in GV sentences. We argued, however, that there was a general VOS preference in Truku, further indicating that the syntactic complexity account is better suited for explaining the pattern found in both response accuracy and response time data.

In sum, our auditory comprehension experiment suggests that the often-observed SO preference in SO-type languages is not fully grounded in the universal properties of human cognition. In Truku, an OS-type language, the OS word order was preferred. We suggest that the lack of (or at least very weak) saliency effect in this language may relate to the symmetrical voice system, where promoting a theme argument to subject does not require a more marked structure, with respect to the verbal morphology and syntax, than promoting an agent argument. Finally, we should point out that investigating a typologically wide set of languages is not only interesting but also necessary for determining the nature of various preferences found in the psycholinguistic literature. It is not always easy to find a way to conduct research as we do in our own institutions, but in a way, just looking at languages that are spoken and used within an easily accessible range will invite unwanted "bias" in our minds.

Acknowledgments

We thank anonymous reviewers and Jim Huang for their insightful comments and suggestions. Various portions of this research were presented at the thirty-fourth Annual Meeting of the Japanese Cognitive Science Society, and the International Workshop on Seediq and Related Languages held at Harvard-Yenching Institute. We would especially like to thank Colin Phillips and Norvin Richards for serving as the commentators for the workshop. We also appreciate the kind support from collaborators and participants in Hualien. Remaining errors are obviously our own. This study was supported by Grant-in-Aids for Scientific Research from the Japan Society for the Promotion of Science (#15H02603, #19H05589, PI: Masatoshi Koizumi, #15K02529, #19K00586, PI: Hajime Ono).

NOTES

* This appendix is a reprint of Ono et al. (2020), which is licensed under a Creative Commons Attribution 4.0 International License.
1. We should also note that Yano and Koizumi (2018) and Yano et al. (2019) argue that discourse context is yet another factor for the increased processing cost of the non-canonical word orders, demonstrating that the processing cost for the non-canonical word order decreases when the sentence is placed in a supportive discourse context for such a word order. See also Kaiser and Trueswell (2004) for the effect of discourse factors.
2. This study was approved by the Ethics Committee of the Graduate School of Arts and Letters, Tohoku University.
3. The entire set of experimental stimuli can be found at: https://osf.io/fzagc/ [last accessed August 24, 2022].
4. We included these two measures, instead of the total length of the sentence, because they are more fine-grained, compared to the total length, and should influence the RT more directly.
5. A similar interaction among multiple factors can be found in the previous literature, although the relevant factors are slightly different. Polinsky et al. (2012) investigated the processing difficulties in various relative clause (RC) structures in Avar, an ergative language in the Caucasian language family. They concluded that syntactic structure and case play an important role in comprehending relative clause structures in Avar (see also Polinsky 2016).

References

Aissen, J. L. (1992). Topic and focus in Mayan. *Language*, 68, 43–80. https://doi.org/10.1353/lan.1992.0017.

Aissen, J. L. (1996). Pied-piping, abstract agreement, and functional projections in Tzotzil. *Natural Language and Linguistic Theory*, 14, 447–491. https://doi.org/10.1007/BF00133596.

Aissen, J. L. (2017). Information structure in Mayan. In Aissen J. L., England N. C., and Maldonado, R. Z. (Eds.). *The Mayan languages*, 293–324. Philadelphia, PA: Taylor and Francis.

Aissen, J., England, N. C., and Maldonado, R. Z. (Eds.). (2017). *The Mayan languages*. Philadelphia, PA: Taylor and Francis.

Ajsivinac Sian, J. E., García Mátzar, L. P. O., Cutzal, M. C., et al. (2004). *Gramática descriptiva del idioma maya Kaqchikel: Rutzijoxik rucholik ri Kaqchikel ch'ab'äl. Antigua.* Guatemala: Academia de las Lenguas Mayas de Guatemala, Comunidad Lingüística Kaqchikel.

Aldridge, E. (2004). Ergativity and word order in Austronesian languages. *Doctoral dissertation*, Cornell University, Ithaca, NY.

Altmann, G. T., and Kamide, Y. (1999). Incremental interpretation at verbs: Restricting the domain of subsequent reference. *Cognition*, 7(3), 247–264. https://doi.org/10.1016/S0010-0277(99)00059-1.

Anand, P., Chung, S., and Wagers, M. (2011). Widening the net: Challenges for gathering linguistic data in the digital age. In *NSF SBE 2020: Rebuilding the mosaic: Future research in the social, behavioral and economic sciences at the National Science Foundation in the next decade*. Alexandria, Virginia: National Science Foundation.

Aoshima, S., Phillips, C., and Weinberg, A. (2004). Processing filler-gap dependencies in a head-final language. *Journal of Memory and Language*, 51, 23–54. https://doi.org/10.1016/j.jml.2004.03.001.

Arnon, I., and Snider, N. (2010). More than words: Frequency effects for multi-word phrases. *Journal of Memory and Language*, 62(1), 67–82. https://doi.org/10.1016/j.jml.2009.09.005.

Baayen, H., Davidson, D. J., and Bates, D. M. (2008). Mixed-effects modeling with crossed random effects for subjects and items. *Journal of Memory and Language*, 59(4), 390–412. https://doi.org/10.1016/j.jml.2007.12.005.

Bader, M., and Meng, M. (1999). Subject-object ambiguities in German embedded clauses: An across-the-board comparison. *Journal of Psycholinguistic Research*, 28, 121–143. https://doi.org/10.1023/A:1023206208142.

Baker, M. (1985). The Mirror Principle and morphosyntactic explanation. *Linguistic Inquiry*, 16, 373–416.

References

Barr, D. J., Levy, R., Scheepers, C., et al. (2013). Random effects structure for confirmatory hypothesis testing: Keep it maximal. *Journal of Memory and Language*, 68(3), 255–278. https://doi.org/10.1016/j.jml.2012.11.001.

Bates, E. (1976). *Language and context: The acquisition of pragmatics*. New York, NY: Academic Press.

Bates, D., Kliegl, R., Vasishth, S., et al. (2015a). Parsimonious mixed models. Available online at: https://arxiv.org/abs/1506.04967.

Bates, D., Maechler, M., Bolker, B., et al. (2015b). Fitting linear mixed-effects models using lme4. *Journal of Statistical Software*, 67(1), 1–48. https://doi.org/10.18637/jss.v067.i01.

Bennett, R. (2016). Mayan phonology. *Language and Linguistics Compass*, 10(10), 469–514. https://doi.org/10.1111/lnc3.12148.

Bennett, R., Coon, J., and Henderson, R. (2016). Introduction to Mayan linguistics. *Language and Linguistics Compass*, 10(10), 455–468. https://doi.org/10.1111/lnc3.12159.

Bickerton, D. (1981). *Roots of language*. Ann Arbor, MI: Karoma.

Boatman, D., Gordon, B., Hart, J., et al. (2000). Transcortical sensory aphasia: Revisited and revised. *Brain*, *123*(8), 1634–1642. https://doi.org/10.1093/brain/123.8.1634.

Bock, J. K. (1982). Toward a cognitive psychology of syntax: Information processing contributions to sentence formulation. *Psychological Review*, 89(1), 1–47. https://doi.org/10.1037/0033-295X.89.1.1.

Bock, K., and Loebell, H. (1990). Framing sentences. *Cognition*, 35(1), 1–39. https://doi.org/10.1016/0010-0277(90)90035-I.

Bock, K., Loebell, H., and Morey, R. (1992). From conceptual roles to structural relations: Bridging the syntactic cleft. *Psychological Review*, 99(1), 150. https://doi.org/10.1037/0033-295X.99.1.150.

Bock, J. K., and Warren, R. K. (1985). Conceptual accessibility and syntactic structure in sentence formulation. *Cognition*, 21(1), 47–67. https://doi.org/10.1016/0010-0277(85)90023-X.

Boersma, P., and Weenink, D. (2010). Praat: Doing phonetics by computer. Version 5.1.31. Available online at: www.praat.org.

Bohnemeyer, J., Donelson, K. T., Tucker, R. E., et al. (2014). The cultural transmission of spatial cognition: Evidence from a large-scale study. *Proceedings of the Annual Meeting of the Cognitive Science Society*, 36, 213–217.

Bornkessel, I., Schlesewsky, M., and Friederici, A. D. (2002). Grammar overrides frequency: Evidence from online processing of flexible word order. *Cognition*, 85, B21–B30. https://doi.org/10.1016/S0010-0277(02)00076-8.

Bornkessel, I., Schlesewsky, M., and Friederici, A. D. (2003). Eliciting thematic reanalysis effects: The role of syntax-independent information during parsing. *Language and Cognitive Processes*, 18(3), 269–298. https://doi.org/10.1080/01690960244000018.

Bornkessel-Schlesewsky, I., and Schlesewsky, M. (2009a). The role of prominence information in the real-time comprehension of transitive constructions: A cross-linguistic approach. *Language and Linguistics Compass*, 3(1), 19–58. https://doi.org/10.1111/j.1749-818X.2008.00099.x.

Bornkessel-Schlesewsky, I., and Schlesewsky, M. (2009b). *Processing syntax and morphology: A neurocognitive perspective*. Oxford: Oxford University Press.

Bornkessel-Schlesewsky, I., Schlesewsky, M., and von Cramon, D. Y. (2009). Word order and Broca's region: Evidence for a supra-syntactic perspective. *Brain and Language*, 111(3), 125–139. https://doi.org/10.1016/j.bandl.2009.09.004.

Branigan, H. P., and Feleki, E. (1999). Conceptual accessibility and serial order in Greek language production. In Hahn, M., and Stones, S. C. (Eds.). *Proceedings of the 21st Annual Conference of the Cognitive Science Society*, 96–101. Mahwah, NJ: Erlbaum

Branigan, H. P., Pickering, M. J., and Tanaka, M. (2008). Contributions of animacy to grammatical function assignment and word order during production. *Lingua*, 118, 172–189. https://doi.org/10.1016/j.lingua.2007.02.003

Brennan, J., Nir, Y., Hasson, U., et al. (2012). Syntactic structure building in the anterior temporal lobe during natural story listening. *Brain and Language*, 120(2), 163–173. https://doi.org/10.1016/j.bandl.2010.04.002.

Brennan, J., and Pylkkänen, L. (2012). The time-course and spatial distribution of brain activity associated with sentence processing. *NeuroImage*, 60(2), 1139–1148. https://doi.org/10.1016/j.neuroimage.2012.01.030.

Brennan, J. R., and Pylkkänen, L. (2017). MEG evidence for incremental sentence composition in the anterior temporal lobe. *Cognitive Science*, 41(Suppl. 6), 1515–1531. https://doi.org/10.1111/cogs.12445.

Brennan, J., Stabler, E., Wagenen, S. V., et al. (2016). Abstract linguistic structure correlates with temporal activity during naturalistic comprehension. *Brain and Language*, 157–158, 81–94. https://doi.org/10.1016/j.bandl.2016.04.008.

Brody, J. (1984). Some problems with the concept of basic word order. *Linguistics*, 22, 711–736. https://doi.org/10.1515/ling.1984.22.5.711.

Brown, C. H. (1983). Where do cardinal direction terms come from? *Anthropological Linguistics*, 25(2), 121–161.

Brown, P., and Levinson, S. C. (1992). 'Left' and 'right' in Tenejapa: Investigating a linguistic and conceptual gap. *Zeitschrift für Phonetik, Sprachwissenschaft und Kommunikationsforschung*, 45(6), 590–611.

Brown, P., and Levinson, S. C. (1993a). "Uphill" and "downhill" in Tzeltal. *Journal of Linguistic Anthropology*, 3(1), 46–74. https://doi.org/10.1525/jlin.1993.3.1.46.

Brown, P., and Levinson, S. C. (1993b). *Linguistic and nonlinguistic coding of spatial arrays: Explorations in Mayan cognition* (Working Paper 24). Cognitive Anthropology Research Group, Max Planck Institute for Psycholinguistics, Nijmegen.

Brown, R. M., Maxwell, J. M., and Little, W. E. (2006). *¿La ütz awäch?: Introduction to Kaqchikel Maya language*. Austin, TX: University of Texas Press.

Bybee, J. (2010). *Language, usage and cognition*. Cambridge: Cambridge University Press.

Campbell, L., and Kaufman, T. (1985). Mayan linguistics: Where are we now? *Annual Review of Anthropology*, 14, 187–198.

Caplan, D., Alpert, N., Waters, G., et al. (2000). Activation of Broca's area by syntactic processing under conditions of concurrent articulation. *Human Brain Mapping*, 9(2), 65–71. https://doi.org/10.1002/(SICI)1097-0193(200002)9:2<65::aid-hbm1>3.0.CO;2-4.

Caplan, D., Chen, E., and Waters, G. (2008). Task-dependent and task-independent neurovascular responses to syntactic processing. *Cortex*, 44(3), 257–275. https://doi.org/10.1016/j.cortex.2006.06.005.

Caplan, D., Stanczak, L., and Waters, G. (2008). Syntactic and thematic constraint effects on blood oxygenation level dependent signal correlates of comprehension of relative clauses. *Journal of Cognitive Neuroscience*, 20(4), 643–656. https://doi.org/10.1162/jocn.2008.20044.

Carnie, A. and Guilfoyle, E. (Eds.) (2000). *The syntax of verb initial languages*. Oxford: Oxford University Press.

Chomsky, N. (1957). *Syntactic structures*. The Hague: Mouton.

Chomsky, N. (1965). *Aspects of the theory of syntax*. Cambridge, MA: MIT Press.

Chomsky, N. (1981). *Lectures on government and binding*. Dordrecht: Foris.

Chomsky, N. (2000). Minimalist inquiries: The Framework. In Martin, R., et al. (Eds.). *Step by step: Essays on minimalist syntax in honor of Howard Lasnik*, 89–155. Cambridge, MA: MIT Press.

Christianson, K., and Ferreira, F. (2005). Conceptual accessibility and sentence production in a free word order language (Odawa). *Cognition*, 98(2), 105–135. https://doi.org/10.1016/j.cognition.2004.10.006.

Chujo, K. (1983). Nihongo tanbun-no rikai katei – Bunrikai sutoratejii no sougo kankei [The interrelationships among strategies for sentence comprehension]. *Japanese Journal of Psychology*, 54, 250–256.

Chung, S. (2017). VOS languages: Some of their properties. In Everaert, M., and Van Riemsdijk, H. C. (Eds.). *The Wiley Blackwell companion to syntax, Second Edition*, 4787–4832. Malden, MA: Wiley-Blackwell.

Clemens, L. E. (2013). Kaqchikel SVO: V2 in a V1 language. In Kenstowicz, M. (Ed.). *Studies in Kaqchikel grammar*, 1–24. Cambridge, MA: MIT Working Papers in Linguistics (MITWPL).

Clemens, L., and Coon, J. (2018). Deriving verb-initial word order in Mayan. *Language*, 94(2), 237–280. https://doi.org/10.1353/lan.2018.0017.

Clemens, L. E., Coon, J., Pedro, P. M., et al. (2015). Ergativity and the complexity of extraction: A view from Mayan. *Natural Language and Linguistic Theory*, 33(2), 417–467. https://doi.org/10.1007/s11049-014-9260-x.

Cohn, N., and Paczynski, M. (2013). Prediction, events, and the advantage of agents: The processing of semantic roles in visual narrative. *Cognitive Psychology*, 67(3), 73–97. https://doi.org/10.1016/j.cogpsych.2013.07.002.

Cohn, N., Paczynski, M., and Kutas, M. (2017). Not so secret agents: Event-related potentials to semantic roles in visual event comprehension. *Brain and Cognition*, 119, 1–9. https://doi.org/10.1016/j.bandc.2017.09.001.

Collins, C. (1994). Economy of derivation and the generalized proper binding condition. *Linguistic Inquiry*, 25(1), 45–61.

Comrie, B. (1989). *Language universals and linguistic typology: Syntax and morphology*. Chicago, IL: University of Chicago Press.

Coon, J. (2010). VOS as predicate fronting in Chol Mayan. *Lingua*, 120, 345–378. https://doi.org/10.1016/j.lingua.2008.07.006.

Coon, J. (2013). *Aspects of split ergativity*. Oxford: Oxford University Press.

Coon, J. (2016). Mayan morphosyntax. *Language and Linguistics Compass*, 10(10), 515–550. https://doi.org/10.1111/lnc3.12149.

Coppola, M., and Newport, E. L. (2005). Grammatical subjects in home sign: Abstract linguistic structure in adult primary gesture systems without linguistic input.

Proceedings of the National Academy of Sciences of the United States of America, 102(52), 19249–19253. https://doi.org/10.1073/pnas.0509306102.

Croft, W. (1991). *Syntactic categories and grammatical relations: The cognitive organization of information*. Chicago, IL: University of Chicago Press.

Croft, W. (1998). Event structure in argument linking. In Butt, M., and Geuder, W. (Eds.). *The projection of arguments: Lexical and compositional factors*, 21–64. Stanford, CA: CSLI Publications.

Dayley, J. (1981). Voice and ergativity in Mayan languages. *Journal of Mayan Linguistics*, 2, 3–82.

De Smedt, K. (1990). IPF: An incremental parallel formulator. In Dale, R., Mellish, C., and Zock, M. (Eds.). *Current research in natural language generation*, 167–192. London: Academic Press.

Diesing, M. (1992). *Indefinites*. Cambridge, MA: MIT Press.

Dryer, M. S. (2002). Case distinctions, rich verb agreement, and word order type (comments on Hawkins' paper). *Theoretical Linguistics*, 28(2), 151–158. https://doi.org/10.1515/thli.2002.28.2.151.

Dryer, M. S. (2013). Order of subject, object and verb. In Dryer, M. S., and Haspelmath, M. (Eds.). *The world atlas of language structures online*. Leipzig: Max Planck Institute for Evolutionary Anthropology. Available online at: http://wals.info/chapter/81 [last accessed August 24, 2022].

Eberhard, D. M., Simons, G. F., and Fennig, C. D. (Eds.). (2019). *Ethnologue: Languages of the world* (22nd ed.). Dallas, TX: SIL International. Online version available at: www.ethnologue.com [last accessed August 24, 2022].

Eberhard, D. M., Simons, G. F., and Fennig, C. D. (Eds.). (2020). *Ethnologue: Languages of the world* (23rd ed.). Dallas, TX: SIL International. Online version at: www.ethnologue.com [last accessed August 24, 2022].

England, N. C. (1991). Changes in basic word order in Mayan languages. *International Journal of American Linguistics*, 57(4), 446–486. https://doi.org/10.1086/ijal.57.4.3519735.

England, N. C. (2003). Mayan language revival and revitalization politics: Linguists and linguistic ideologies. *American Anthropologist*, 105(4), 733–743. https://doi.org/10.1525/aa.2003.105.4.733.

Erdocia, K., Laka, I., Mestres-Missé, A., et al. (2009). Syntactic complexity and ambiguity resolution in a free word order language: Behavioral and electrophysiological evidences from Basque. *Brain and Language*, 109(1), 1–17. https://doi.org/10.1016/j.bandl.2008.12.003.

Erlewine, M. Y. (2016). Anti-locality and optimality in Kaqchikel Agent Focus. *Natural Language and Linguistic Theory*, 34, 429–479. https://doi.org/10.1007/s11049-015-9310-z.

Ferreira, F., Henderson, J. M., Anes, M. D., et al. (1996). Effects of lexical frequency and syntactic complexity in spoken-language comprehension: Evidence from the auditory moving-window technique. *Journal of Experimental Psychology: Learning, Memory, and Cognition*, 22(2), 324–335. https://doi.org/10.1037/0278-7393.22.2.324.

Fiebach, C. J., Schlesewsky, M., and Friederici, A.D. (2002). Separating syntactic memory costs and syntactic integration costs during parsing: The processing of

German wh-questions. *Journal of Memory and Language*, 47(2), 250–272. https://doi.org/10.1016/S0749-596X(02) 00004-9.
Fischer, S. A. (1975). Influences on word-order change in American Sign Language. In Li, C. N. (Ed.). *Word order and word order change, 1–25*. University of Texas, Austin.
Foley, W. A. (2008). The place of Philippine languages in a typology of voice systems. In Austin, P. K., and Musgrave, S. (Eds.). *Voice and grammatical relations in Austronesian languages*, 22–44. Stanford, CA: CSLI Publications.
Forster, K. I., Guerrera, C., and Elliot, L. (2009). The maze task: Measuring forced incremental sentence processing time. *Behavior Research Methods*, 41(1), 163–171. https://doi.org/10.3758/BRM.41.1.163.
Frazier, L. (1987). Theories of sentence processing. In Garfield, J. (Ed.). *Modularity in knowledge representation and natural language processing*, 291–307. Cambridge, MA: MIT Press.
Frazier, L., and Clifton Jr, C. (1989). Successive cyclicity in the grammar and the parser. *Language and Cognitive Processes*, 4(2), 93–126. https://doi.org/10.1080/01690968908406359.
Frazier, L., and d'Arcais, G. B. F. (1989). Filler driven parsing: A study of gap filling in Dutch. *Journal of Memory and Language*, 28(3), 331–344. https://doi.org/10.1016/0749-596X(89)90037-5.
Friederici, A. D. (2017). *Language in our brain: The origins of a uniquely human capacity*. Cambridge, MA: MIT Press.
Friederici, A. D., Chomsky, N., Berwick, R. C., et al. (2017). Language, mind and brain. *Nature Human Behaviour*, 1, 713–722. https://doi.org/10.1038/s41562-017-0184-4.
Futrell, R., Hickey, T., Lee, A., et al. (2015). Cross-linguistic gestures reflect typological universals: A subject-initial, verb-final bias in speakers of diverse languages. *Cognition*, 136, 215–221. https://doi.org/10.1016/j.cognition.2014.11.022.
García Matzar, L. P. O., and Rodríguez Guaján, P. B'. J. O. (1997). *Rukemik ri Kaqchikel chi': Gramática Kaqchikel*. Guatemala City: Cholsamaj and OKMA.
García Matzar, P. O., Cotzajay, V. T., and Tuiz, D. C. (1999). *Gramática del idioma Kaqchikel*. Antigua, Guatemala: Proyecto Lingüistico Francisco Marroquín.
Garzon, S., Brown, M. R., Richards, J. B., et al. (1998). *The life of our language: Kaqchikel Maya maintenance*. Austin, TX: University of Texas Press.
Gell-Mann, M., and Ruhlen, M. (2011). The origin and evolution of word order. *Proceedings of the National Academy of Sciences of the United States of America*, 108(42), 17290–17295. https://doi.org/10.1073/pnas.1113716108.
Gennari, S. P., and MacDonald, M. C. (2009). Linking production and comprehension processes: The case of relative clauses. *Cognition*, 111(1), 1–23. https://doi.org/10.1016/j.cognition.2008.12.006.
Gennari, S. P., Mirković, J., and MacDonald, M. C. (2012). Animacy and competition in relative clause production: A cross-linguistic investigation. *Cognitive Psychology*, 65(2), 141–176. https://doi.org/10.1016/j.cogpsych.2012.03.002.
Gibson, E. (1998). Linguistic complexity: Locality of syntactic dependencies. *Cognition*, 68(1), 1–76. https://doi.org/10.1016/S0010-0277(98)00034-1.
Gibson, E. (2000). Dependency locality theory: A distance-based theory of linguistic complexity. In Marantz, A., Miyashita, Y., and O' Neil, W. (Eds.). *Image, language,*

brain: Papers from the first mind articulation project symposium, 95–126. Cambridge, MA: MIT Press.
Gibson, E., Piantadosi, S. T., Brink, K., et al. (2013). A noisy-channel account of cross-linguistic word-order variation. *Psychological Science*, 24(7), 1079–1088. https://doi.org/10.1177/0956797612463705.
Givón, T. (1979). From discourse to syntax: Grammar as a processing strategy. In Givon, T. (Ed.). *Discourse and syntax*, 81–112. New York, NY: Academic Press. https://doi.org/10.1163/9789004368897_005.
Gleitman, L. R., January, D., Nappa, R., et al. (2007). On the give and take between event apprehension and utterance formulation. *Journal of Memory and Language*, 57(4), 544–569. https://doi.org/10.1016/j.jml.2007.01.007.
Goldin-Meadow, S. (2003). *The resilience of language: What gesture creation in deaf children can tell us about how all children learn language*. New York, NY: Psychology Press.
Goldin-Meadow, S., and Feldman, H. (1977). The development of language-like communication without a language model. *Science*, 197(4301), 401–403. https://doi.org/10.1126/science.877567.
Goldin-Meadow, S., and Mylander, C. (1998). Spontaneous sign systems created by deaf children in two cultures. *Nature*, 391(6664), 279–281. https://doi.org/10.1038/34646.
Goldin-Meadow, S., So, W. C., Özyürek, A., et al. (2008). The natural order of events: How speakers of different languages represent events nonverbally. *Proceedings of the National Academy of Sciences*, 105(27), 9163–9168. https://doi.org/10.1073/pnas.0710060105.
Greenberg, J. H. (1963). *Some universals of grammar with particular reference to the order of meaningful elements*. In Greenberg, J.H. (Ed.). Universals of language, 73–113. Cambridge, MA: MIT Press.Grewe,
Grewe, T., Bornkessel-Schlesewsky, I., Zysset, S., et al. (2007). The role of the posterior superior temporal sulcus in the processing of unmarked transitivity. *NeuroImage*, 35(1), 343–352. https://doi.org/10.1016/j.neuroimage.2006.11.045
Griffin, Z. M., and Bock, K. (2000). What the eyes say about speaking. *Psychological Science*, 11(4), 274–279. https://doi.org/10.1111/1467-9280.00255.
Grodner, D., and Gibson, E. (2005). Some consequences of the serial nature of linguistic input. *Cognitive Science*, 29(2), 261–290. https://doi.org/10.1207/s15516709cog0000_7.
Grodzinsky, Y., Pieperhoff, P., and Thompson, C. (2021). Stable brain loci for the processing of complex syntax: A review of the current neuroimaging evidence. *Cortex*, 142, 252–271, https://doi.org/10.1016/j.cortex.2021.06.003.
Grodzinsky, Y., and Santi, A. (2008). The battle for Broca's region. *Trends In Cognitive Sciences*, 12(12), 474–480. https://doi.org/10.1016/j.tics.2008.09.001.
Hagiwara, H. (1993). The breakdown of Japanese passives and theta-role assignment principle by Broca's aphasics. *Brain and Language*, 45(3), 318–339. https://doi.org/10.1006/brln.1993.1049.
Hagiwara, H., and Caplan, D. (1990). Syntactic comprehension in Japanese aphasics: Effects of category and thematic role order. *Brain and Language*, 38(1), 159–170. https://doi.org/10.1016/0093-934X(90)90107-R.
Hagiwara, H., Soshi, T., Ishihara, M., et al. (2007). A topographical study on the event-related potential correlates of scrambled word order in Japanese complex

sentences. *Journal of Cognitive Neuroscience*, 19(2), 175–193. https://doi.org/10.1162/jocn.2007.19.2.175.
Hagoort, P. (2019). The neurobiology of language beyond single-word processing. *Science*, 366(6461), 55–58. https://doi.org/10.1126/science.aax0289.
Hagoort, P., and Brown, C. M. (2000). ERP effects of listening to speech compared to reading: The P600/SPS to syntactic violations in spoken sentences and rapid serial visual presentation. *Neuropsychologia*, 38(11), 1531–1549. https://doi.org/10.1016/S0028-3932(00)00053-1.
Hakulinen, A., and Karlsson, F. (1980). Finnish syntax in text: Methodology and some results of a quantitative study. *Nordic Journal of Linguistics*, 3(2), 93–129. https://doi.org/10.1017/S0332586500000536.
Hale, J. (2001). A probabilistic Earley parser as a psycholinguistic model. In the *Proceedings of the Second Meeting of the North American Chapter of the Association for Computational Linguistics*, 159–166. https://doi.org/10.3115/1073336.1073357.
Hall, M. L., Mayberry, R. I., and Ferreira, V. S. (2013). Cognitive constraints on constituent order: Evidence from elicited pantomime. *Cognition*, 129(1), 1–17. https://doi.org/10.1016/j.cognition.2013.05.004.
Hall, M. L., Ahn, Y. D., Mayberry, R. I., et al. (2015). Production and comprehension show divergent constituent order preferences: Evidence from elicited pantomime. *Journal of Memory and Language*, 81, 16–33. https://doi.org/10.1016/j.jml.2014.12.003.
Harley, H. (2013). External arguments and the Mirror Principle: On the distinctness of Voice and v. *Lingua*, 125, 34–57. https://doi.org/10.1016/j.lingua.2012.09.010.
Hauser, M. D., Chomsky, N., and Fitch, W. T. (2002). The faculty of language: What is it, who has it, and how did it evolve? *Science*, 298(5598), 1569–1579. https://doi.org/10.1126/science.298.5598.1569.
Haviland, J. B. (2011). Nouns, verbs, and constituents in an emerging 'Tzotzil' sign language. In Gutiérrez-Bravo, R., Mikkelsen, L., and Potsdam, E. (Eds.). *Representing language: Essays in honor of Judith Aissen*, 157–171. Santa Cruz, VS: UC Santa Cruz.
Hawkins, J. A. (2004). *Efficiency and complexity in grammars*. Oxford: Oxford University Press.
Hawkins, R. (1989). Do second language learners acquire restrictive relative clauses on the basis of relational or configurational information? The acquisition of French subject, direct object, and genitive restrictive clauses by second language learners. *Second Language Research*, 5(2), 156–188. https://doi.org/10.1177/026765838900500204.
Heaton, R., Deen, K., & O'Grady, W. (2016). The status of syntactic ergativity in Kaqchikel. *Lingua*, 170, 35–46. https://doi.org/10.1016/j.lingua.2015.10.006.
Heider, E. R. (1972). Universals in color naming and memory. *Journal of Experimental Psychology*, 93(1), 10–20. https://doi.org/10.1037/h0032606.
Hemforth, B. (1993). *Kognitives Parsing: Repräsentation und Verarbeitung sprachlichen Wissens*. Sankt Augustin: Infix.
Henderson, R. (2016). Mayan semantics. *Language and Linguistics Compass*, 10(10), 551–588. https://doi.org/10.1111/lnc3.12187.
Henderson, R., and Coon, J. (2018). Adverbs and variability in Kaqchikel Agent Focus. *Natural Language and Linguistic Theory*, 36, 149–173. https://doi.org/10.1007/s11049-017-9370-3.

Herring, S. C. (2012). Information structure as a consequence of word order type. *Proceedings of the Annual Meeting of the Berkeley Linguistics Society*, 16, 163–174. https://doi.org/10.3765/bls.v16i1.3363.

Hirsh-Pasek, K., and Golinkoff, R. M. (1996). *The origins of grammar: Evidence from early language comprehension*. Cambridge, MA: MIT Press.

Holmer, A. (2005). Seediq: Antisymmetry and final particles in a Formosan VOS language. In Carnie, A., Harley, H., and Dooley, S. A. (Eds.). *Verb first: On the syntax of verb initial languages*, 175–201. Amsterdam: John Benjamins.

Hwang, H. (2017). The role of thematic role accessibility in production: Evidence from Korean. *Language, Cognition and Neuroscience*, 32(1), 117–128. https://doi.org/10.1080/23273798.2016.1237668.

Hyönä, H., and Hujanen, H. (1997). Effects of case marking and word order on sentence parsing in Finnish: An eye fixation analysis. *The Quarterly Journal of Experimental Psychology: Section A*, 50(4), 841–858. https://doi.org/10.1080/713755738.

Imamura, S., and Koizumi, M. (2008). Bunrikai-ni okeru joho kozo-to togo kozo-no kogosayo-ga syojiru taimingu-ni tuite [On the time course of the interaction between information structure and syntactic structure in sentence comprehension]. *Proceedings of the 137th Conference of the Linguistics Society of Japan*, 92–97. Kyoto: Linguistics Society of Japan.

Imamura, S., and Koizumi, M. (2011). A centering analysis of word order in Japanese. *Tohoku Studies in Linguistics*, 20, 59–74.

Imamura, S., Sato, Y., and Koizumi, M. (2016). The processing cost of scrambling and topicalization in Japanese. *Frontiers in Psychology*, 7, 531. https://doi.org/10.3389/fpsyg.2016.00531.

Imanishi, Y. (2014). Default ergative. *Doctoral dissertation*, Massachusetts Institute of Technology, Cambridge, MA.

Imanishi, Y. (2020). Parameterizing split ergativity in Mayan. *Natural Language and Linguistic Theory*, 38(1), 151–200. https://doi.org/10.1007/s11049-018-09440-9.

Inoue, K. (1998). *Moshi migi ya hidari ga nakattara – Gengo jinruigaku heno shotai* [A world without right or left – An introduction to linguistic anthropology]. Tokyo: Taishukan Shoten.

Inoue, K. (2002). Zettai to sotai no hazama de – Kukanshiziwaku ni yoru kominyukeshon [Between absolute and relative: Communication through spatial frame of reference]. In Ohori, T. (Ed.). *Ninchigengogaku II: Kategorika [Cognitive linguistics II: Categorization]*, 11–35. Tokyo: University of Tokyo Press.

Inoue, K. (2005). Kukan ninchi to komyunikeshon [Spatial cognition and communication]. In Ide, S., and Hiraga, M. (Eds.). *Ibunka to komyunikeshon* [Intercultural communication], 118–129. Tokyo: Hituzi Shobo.

Jaeger, F. T. (2008). Categorical data analysis: Away from ANOVAs (transformation or not) and towards Logit Mixed Models. *Journal of Memory and Language*, 59(4), 434–446. https://doi.org/10.1016/j.jml.2007.11.007.

Jaeger, F. T., and Norcliffe, E. (2009). The cross-linguistic study of sentence production: State of the art and a call for action. *Language and Linguistics Compass*, 3(4), 866–887. https://doi.org/10.1111/j.1749-818X.2009.00147.x.

Jarvis, E. D. (2019). Evolution of vocal learning and spoken language. *Science*, 366(6461), 50–54. https://doi.org/10.1126/science.aax0287.

Jasper, H. H. (1958). The ten-twenty electrode system of the international federation. *Electroencephalography and Clinical Neurophysiology*, 10, 371–375.

Kaan, E., Harris, A., Gibson, E., et al. (2000). The P600 as an index of syntactic integration difficulty. *Language and Cognitive Processes*, 15(2), 159–201. https://doi.org/10.1080/016909600386084.

Kaan, E., and Swaab, T. Y. (2003a). Electrophysiological evidence for serial sentence processing: A comparison between non-preferred and ungrammatical continuations. *Cognitive Brain Research*, 17(3), 621–635. https://doi.org/10.1016/S0926-6410(03)00175-7.

Kaan, E., and Swaab, T. Y. (2003b). Repair, revision and complexity in syntactic analysis: An electrophysiological differentiation. *Journal of Cognitive Neuroscience*, 15, 98–110. https://doi.org/10.1162/089892903321107855.

Kaiser, E. 2013. Experimental paradigms in psycholing*uistics*. In Podesva, R. J., and Sharma, D. (Eds.). *Research Methods in Linguistics*, 135–168. Cambridge: Cambridge University Press.

Kaiser, E., and Trueswell, J. C. (2004). The role of discourse context in the processing of a flexible word-order language. *Cognition*, 94(2), 113–147. https://doi.org/10.1016/j.cognition.2004.01.002.

Kanduboda, A. B. P., and Tamaoka, K. (2012). Priority information determining the canonical word order of written Sinhalese sentences. *Open Journal of Modern Linguistics*, 2(1), 26. http://dx.doi.org/10.4236/ojml.2012.21004.

Kant, I. (1991). On the first ground of the distinction of regions in space. In Van Cleve, J., and Frederick, R. E. (Eds.). *The philosophy of right and left*, 27–33. Dordrecht: Springer.

Kay, P., and Kempton, W. (1984). What is the Sapir-Whorf hypothesis? *American Anthropologist*, 86(1), 65–79. https://doi.org/10.1525/aa.1984.86.1.02a00050.

Kayne, R. S. (1994). *The antisymmetry of syntax*. Cambridge, MA: MIT Press.

Keenan, E. L., and Comrie, B. (1977). Noun phrase accessibility and universal grammar. *Linguistic Inquiry*, 8(1), 63–99.

Kemmerer, D. (2012). The cross-linguistic prevalence of SOV and SVO word orders reflects the sequential and hierarchical representation of action in Broca's area. *Language and Linguistics Compass*, 6(1), 50–66. https://doi.org/10.1002/lnc3.322.

Kempen, G., and Harbusch, K. (2005). The relationship between grammaticality ratings and corpus frequencies: A case study into word order variability in the midfield of German clauses. In Kepser, S., and Reis, M. (Eds.). *Linguistic evidence: Empirical, theoretical, and computational perspectives*, 329–349. Berlin: Mouton De Gruyter.

Kempen, G., and Hoenkamp, E. (1987). An incremental procedural grammar for sentence formulation. *Cognitive Science*, 11(2), 201–258. https://doi.org/10.1207/s15516709cog1102_5.

Kempen, G., Olsthoorn, N., and Sprenger, S. (2012). Grammatical workspace sharing during language production and language comprehension: Evidence from grammatical multitasking. *Language and Cognitive Processes*, 27(3), 345–380. https://doi.org/10.1080/01690965.2010.544583.

Kim, J. (2012). Kankokugo kakimazegojyunbun-no puraimingu kooka [Priming effects in scrambled sentences in Korean]. *Culture*, 75, 228–213.

Kim, J., Koizumi, M., Ikuta, N., et al. (2009). Scrambling effects on the processing of Japanese sentences: An fMRI study. *Journal of Neurolinguistics*, 22(2), 151–166. https://doi.org/10.1016/j.jneuroling.2008.07.005.

Kimmelman, V. (2012). Word order in Russian sign language: An extended report. *Linguistics in Amsterdam*, 5(1), 1–56.

King, J., and Just, M. A. (1991). Individual differences in syntactic processing: The role of working memory. *Journal of Memory and Language*, 30(5), 580–602. https://doi.org/10.1016/0749-596X(91)90027-H.

King, J. W., and Kutas, M. (1995). Who did what and when? Using word-and clause-level ERPs to monitor working memory usage in reading. *Journal of Cognitive Neuroscience*, 7(3), 376–395. https://doi.org/10.1162/jocn.1995.7.3.376.

Kinno, R., Kawamura, M., Shioda, S., et al. (2008). Neural correlates of non-canonical syntactic processing revealed by a picture-sentence matching task. *Human Brain Mapping*, 29, 1015–1027. https://doi.org/10.1002/hbm.20441

Kinno, R., Muragaki, Y., Hori, T., et al. (2009). Agrammatic comprehension caused by a glioma in the left frontal cortex. *Brain and Language*, 110(2), 71–80. https://doi.org/10.1016/j.bandl.2009.05.001.

Kishimoto, H. (2009). Topic prominency in Japanese. *The Linguistic Review*, 26(4), 465–513. https://doi.org/10.1515/tlir.2009.017.

Kitagawa, C. (1982). Topic constructions in Japanese. *Lingua*, 57(2–4), 175–214. https://doi.org/10.1016/0024-3841(82)90004-3.

Kiyama, S., Tamaoka, K., Kim, J., et al. (2013). Effect of animacy on word order processing in Kaqchikel Maya. *Open Journal of Modern Linguistics*, 3(3), 203–207. https://doi.org/10.1515/tlir.2009.017

Kiyama, S., Sun, M., Kim, J., et al. (2017). Interference of context and bilinguality with the word order preference in Kaqchikel reversible sentences. *Tohoku Psychologica Folia*, 75, 22–34.

Koizumi, M., and Imamura, S. (2016). Interaction between syntactic structure and information structure in the processing of a head-final language, *Journal of Psycholinguistic Research*, 46, 247–260. https://doi.org/10.1007/s10936-016-9433-3.

Koizumi, M., and Kim, J. (2016). Greater left inferior frontal activation for SVO than VOS during sentence comprehension in Kaqchikel. *Frontiers in Psychology*, 7, 1541. https://doi.org/10.3389/fpsyg.2016.01541.

Koizumi, M., and Saito, T. (2021). Kakuchikerugo washa no kuukan sanshowaku: nihongo washa to no hikaku [Spatial frames of reference of Kaqchikel speakers: A comparative study with Japanese speakers]. *Tohoku Studies in Linguistics*, 29, 1–24.

Koizumi, M., Takeshima, Y., Tachibana, R., et al. (2019). Cognitive loads and time courses related to word order preference in Kaqchikel sentence production: An NIRS and eye-tracking study. *Language, Cognition and Neuroscience*, 35(2), 137–150. https://doi.org/10.1080/23273798.2019.1650945.

Koizumi, M., Yasugi, Y., Tamaoka, K., et al. (2014). On the (non)universality of the preference for subject-object word order in sentence comprehension: A sentence-processing study in Kaqchikel Maya. *Language*, 90(3), 722–736. https://doi.org/10.1353/lan.2014.0068.

Kronmüller, E., and Barr, D. J. (2015). Referential precedents in spoken language comprehension: A review and meta-analysis. *Journal of Memory and Language*, 83, 1–19. https://doi.org/10.1016/j.jml.2015.03.008.

Kubo, T., Ono, H., Tanaka, M., et al. (2015). Kakuchikerugo VOS-gojyun no sanshutsu mekanizumu: yuu-seisei ga gojyun no sentaku ni ataeru kooka o tooshite [Mechanisms for VOS sentence production in Kaqchikel: Evidence from animacy effects on choice of word order]. *Cognitive Studies*, 22 (4), 591–603. https://doi.org/10.11225/jcss.22.591.

Kuno, S. (1978). *Danwa-no bumpo* [Grammar of discourse]. Tokyo: Taishukan.

Kuno, S., and Kaburaki, E. (1977). Empathy and syntax. *Linguistic Inquiry*, 8(4), 627–672.

Kuperberg, G. R., Sitnikova, T., Caplan, D., et al. (2003). Electrophysiological distinctions in processing conceptual relationships within simple sentences. *Cognitive Brain Research*, 17(1), 117–129. https://doi.org/10.1016/S0926-6410(03)00086-7.

Kuroda, S. Y. (1988). Whether we agree or not: A comparative syntax of English and Japanese. *Lingvisticae Investigationes*, 12(1), 1–47. https://doi.org/10.1075/li.12.1.02kur.

Kuznetsova, A., Brockhoff, P. B., and Christensen, R. H. B. (2017). lmerTest package: Tests in linear mixed effects models. *Journal of Statistical Software*, 82(13), 1–26. https://doi.org/10.18637/jss.v082.i13.

Laka, I., and Erdocia, K. (2012). Linearization preferences given "free word order"; Subject preferences given ergativity: A look at Basque. In Torrego, E. (Ed.). *Festschrift for Professor Carlos Piera*, 115–142. Oxford: Oxford University Press.

Langacker, R. W. (1987). *Foundations of cognitive grammar: Theoretical prerequisites* (Vol. 1). Stanford California, CA: Stanford University Press.

Langacker, R. W. (1991). *Foundations of cognitive grammar, vol. 2, descriptive application*. Stanford, CA: Stanford University Press.

Langacker, R. W. (2008). *Cognitive grammar: A basic introduction*. Oxford: Oxford University Press.

Langus, A., and Nespor, M. (2010). Cognitive systems struggling for word order. *Cognitive Psychology*, 60(4), 291–318. https://doi.org/10.1016/j.cogpsych.2010.01.004.

Larsen, T. W. (1988). Manifestations of ergativity in Quiché grammar. *Doctoral dissertation*, University of California Berkeley, Berkeley, CA.

Larsen, T. W., and Norman, W. M. (1979). Correlates of ergativity in Mayan grammar. In Plank, F. (Ed.). *Ergativity: Towards a theory of grammatical relations*, 347–370. London/New York: Academic Press.

Lascaratou, C. (1989). *A functional approach to constituent order with particular reference to Modern Greek. Implications for language learning and language teaching*. Athens: *Parousia Monograph Series*, 5.

Lau, E. F., Phillips, C., and Poeppel, D. (2008). A cortical network for semantics: (De)constructing the N400. *Nature Reviews Neuroscience*, 9, 920–933. https://doi.org/10.1038/nrn2532.

Law, D. (2014). *Language contact, inherited similarity and social difference: The story of linguistic interaction in the Maya lowlands*. Amsterdam: John Benjamins.

Lee, E. K., Brown-Schmidt, S., and Watson, D. G. (2013). Ways of looking ahead: Hierarchical planning in language production. *Cognition*, 129(3), 544–562. https://doi.org/10.1016/j.cognition.2013.08.007.

Levelt, W. J. M. (1989). *Speaking: From intention to articulation*. Cambridge, MA: MIT Press.

Levinson, S. C. (1996a). Language and space. *Annual Review of Anthropology*, 25(1), 353–382. https://doi.org/10.1146/annurev.anthro.25.1.353.

Levinson, S. C. (1996b). Frames of reference and Molyneux's question: Crosslinguistic evidence. In Bloom, P., Peterson, M. A., Nadel, L., et al. (Eds.). *Language and space*, 109–170. Cambridge, MA: MIT Press.

Levinson, S. C. (2003). *Space in language and cognition: Explorations in cognitive diversity*. Cambridge: Cambridge University Press.

Levinson, S. C., Kita, S., Haun, D. B., et al. (2002). Returning the tables: Language affects spatial reasoning. *Cognition*, 84(2), 155–188. https://doi.org/10.1016/S0010-0277(02)00045-8.

Levy, R. (2008). Expectation-based syntactic comprehension. *Cognition*, 106(3), 1126–1177. https://doi.org/10.1016/j.cognition.2007.05.006

Li, P., and Gleitman, L. (2002). Turning the tables: Language and spatial reasoning. *Cognition*, 83(3), 265–294. https://doi.org/10.1016/S0010-0277(02)00009-4.

Li, P., Abarbanell, L., Gleitman, L., et al. (2011). Spatial reasoning in Tenejapan Mayans. *Cognition*, 120(1), 33–53. https://doi.org/10.1016/j.cognition.2011.02.012.

Lindsley, J. R. (1975). Producing simple utterances: How far ahead do we plan? *Cognitive Psychology*, 7(1), 1–19. https://doi.org/10.1016/0010-0285(75)90002-X.

MacDonald, M. C. (2013). How language production shapes language form and comprehension. *Frontiers in Psychology*, 4, 226. https://doi.org/10.3389/fpsyg.2013.00226.

MacDonald, M. C., Pearlmutter, N. J., and Seidenberg, M. S. (1994). The lexical nature of syntactic ambiguity resolution. *Psychological Review*, 101(4), 676. https://doi.org/10.1037/0033-295X.101.4.676.

MacWhinney, B. (1977). Starting points. *Language*, 53(1), 152–168. https://doi.org/10.2307/413059.

MacWhinney, B., Malchukov, A., and Moravcsik, E. (Eds.). (2014). *Competing motivations in grammar and usage*. Oxford: Oxford University Press.

Majid, A., Bowerman, M., Kita, S., et al. (2004). Can language restructure cognition? The case for space. *Trends in Cognitive Sciences*, 8(3), 108–114. https://doi.org/10.1016/j.tics.2004.01.003.

Marantz, A. (1991). Case and licensing. *Proceedings of the Eastern States Conference on Linguistics (ESCOL)*, 9, 234–253.

Marantz, A. (2000). Case and licensing. In Reuland, E. (Ed.). *Arguments and case: Explaining Burzio's generalization*, 11–30. Amsterdam: John Benjamins.

Marantz, A. (2005). Generative linguistics within the cognitive neuroscience of language. *The Linguistic Review*, 22(2–4), 429–445. https://doi.org/10.1515/tlir.2005.22.2-4.429.

Marian, V., and Spivey, M. (2003). Competing activation in bilingual language processing: Within- and between-language competition. *Bilingualism: Language and Cognition*, 6(2), 97–115.

Matsumoto, M. E. (2016). WI as a marker of pragmatic salience in the language of the kaqchikel chronicles. *Transactions of the Philological Society*, 114(1), 51–74.

Matsumoto, Y., Hara, S., and Natsuike, D. (2010). Chiritekikankyo to kukansanshowaku no shiyo: Kobe ni okeru chosa kara [Geographic environment and the use of spatial reference frames: A study in Kobe]. *Proceedings of the Annual Meeting of the Kansai Linguistic Society*, 30, 13–24.

Matzke, M., Mai, H., Nager, W., et al. (2002). The cost of freedom: An ERP-study of non-canonical sentences. *Clinical Neurophysiology*, 113(6), 844–852. https://doi.org/10.1016/S1388-2457(02)00059-7.

Maxwell, J. M., and Little, W. E. (2006). *Tijonïk Kaqchikel oxlajuj aj – Curso de idioma y cultura maya Kaqchikel*. Guatemala: Editorial Junajpu.

Mazuka, R., Itoh, K., and Kondo, T. (2002). Costs of scrambling in Japanese sentence processing. In Nakayama, M. (Ed.). *Sentence processing in East Asian languages*, 131–166. Stanford, CA: CSLI.

McDonald, J. L., Bock, K., and Kelly, M. H. (1993). Word and world order: Semantic, phonological, and metrical determinants of serial position. *Cognitive Psychology* 25(2), 188–230. https://doi.org/10.1006/cogp.1993.1005.

Meir, I., Lifshitz, A., Ilkbasaran, D., et al. (2010). *The interaction of animacy and word order in human languages: A study of strategies in a novel communication task. Paper presented at the 8th International Conference on the Evolution of Language*, Utrecht, Germany.

Meyer, M., Obleser, J., Anwander, A., et al. (2012). Linking ordering in Broca's area to storage in left temporo-parietal regions: The case of sentence processing. *NeuroImage*, 62(3), 1987–1998. https://doi.org/10.1016/j.neuroimage.2012.05.052.

Miller, G.A., and Johnson-Laird, P. N. (1976). *Language and perception*. Cambridge, MA: Harvard University Press.

Mishra, R. C., Dasen, P. R., and Niraula, S. (2003). Ecology, language, and performance on spatial cognitive tasks. *International Journal of Psychology*, 38(6), 366–383. https://doi.org/10.1080/00207590344000187.

Miyagawa, S. (2005). EPP and semantically vacuous scrambling. In Sabel, J., and Saito, M. (Eds.). *The free word order phenomenon*, 181–220. Berlin: Mouton de Gruyter.

Momma, S. M. (2016). *Parsing, generation, and grammar.* Doctoral dissertation, University of Massachusetts, Amherst.

Momma, S., and Phillips, C. (2018). The relationship between parsing and generation. *Annual Review of Linguistics*, 4, 233–254. https://doi.org/10.1146/annurev-linguistics-011817-045719.

Moseley, C. (Ed.). (2010). *Atlas of the world's languages in danger*, 3rd ed. Paris: UNESCO Publishing.

Myachykov, A., and Tomlin, R. S. (2008). Perceptual priming and structural choice in Russian sentence production. *Journal of Cognitive Science*, 9(1), 31–48. https://doi.org/10.17791/jcs.2008.9.1.31.

Nakano, Y., Felser, C. and Clahsen, H. (2002). Antecedent priming at trace position in Japanese long-distance scrambling. *Journal of Psycholinguistic Research*, 31, 531–571. https://doi.org/10.1023/A:1021260920232.

Napoli, D. J., and Sutton-Spence, R. (2014). Order of the major constituents in sign languages: Implications for all language. *Frontiers in Psychology*, 5, 1–18. https://doi.org/10.3389/fpsyg.2014.00376.

Newmeyer, F. J. (2000). *Language form and language function*. Cambridge, MA: MIT Press.

Nichols, J. (1986). Head-marking and dependent-marking grammar. *Language*, 62(1), 56–119. https://doi.org/10.1353/lan.1986.0014.

Norcliffe, E., Harris, A. C., and Jaeger, T. F. (2015). Cross-linguistic psycholinguistics and its critical role in theory development: Early beginnings and recent advances.

Language, Cognition and Neuroscience, 30(9), 1009–1032. https://doi.org/10.1080/23273798.2015.1080373.

Norcliffe, E., Konopka, A. E., Brown, P., et al. (2015). Word order affects the time course of sentence formulation in Tzeltal. *Language, Cognition and Neuroscience*, 30(9), 1187–1208. https://doi.org/10.1080/23273798.2015.1006238.

Nuger, J. (2010). *Architecture of the Palauan verb complex. Doctoral dissertation*, UC Santa Cruz.

O'Grady, W. (1997). *Syntactic development*. Chicago, IL: University of Chicago Press.

O'Grady, W., Lee, M., and Choo, M. (2003). A subject-object asymmetry in the acquisition of relative clauses in Korean as a second language. *Studies in Second Language Acquisition*, 25(3), 433–448. https://doi.org/10.1017/S0272263103000172.

Ohta, S., Koizumi, M., and Sakai, K. L. (2017). Dissociating effects of scrambling and topicalization within the left frontal and temporal language areas: An fMRI study in Kaqchikel Maya. *Frontiers in Psychology*, 8, 748. https://doi.org/10.3389/fpsyg.2017.00748.

Oldfield, R. C. (1971). The assessment and analysis of handedness: The Edinburgh inventory. *Neuropsychologia*, 9(1), 97–113. https://doi.org/10.1016/0028-3932(71)90067-4.

Ono, H., Kim, J., Sato, M., et al. (2020). Syntax and processing in Seediq: A behavioral study. *Journal of East Asian Linguistics*, 29(2), 237–258. https://doi.org/10.1007/s10831-020-09207-7.

Osterhout, L., and Holcomb, P. J. (1992). Event-related brain potentials elicited by syntactic anomaly. *Journal of Memory and Language*, 31(6), 785–806. https://doi.org/10.1016/0749-596X(92)90039-Z.

Osterhout, L., and Mobley, L. A. (1995). Event-related brain potentials elicited by failure to agree. *Journal of Memory and language*, 34(6), 739–773. https://doi.org/10.1006/jmla.1995.1033.

Otaki, K., Sugisaki, K., Yusa, N., et al. (2019). Two routes to the Mayan VOS: From the view of Kaqchikel. *Gengo Kenkyu*, 156, 25–45. https://doi.org/10.11435/gengo.156.0_25.

Otsuka, Y. (2005a). Syntax and/or pragmatics: PP-scrambling in Tongan and the thematic hierarchy. *Proceedings of the Twelfth Annual Meeting of the Austronesian Formal Linguistics Conference*, 343–357.

Otsuka, Y. (2005b). Two derivations of VSO: A comparative study of Niuean and Tongan. In Carnie, A., Dooley, S. A., and Harley, H. (Eds.). *Verb first: On the syntax of verb-initial languages*, 65–90. Amsterdam: John Benjamins.

Otsuka, Y. (2005c). Scrambling and information focus: VSO-VOS alternation in Tongan. In Sabel, J., and Saito, M. (Eds.). *The free word order phenomenon: Its syntactic sources and diversity*, 243–280. Berlin: Mouton de Gruyter.

Palmer, B., Lum, J., Schlossberg, J., et al. (2017). How does the environment shape spatial language? Evidence for sociotopography. *Linguistic Typology*, 21(3), 457–491.

Pederson, E., Danziger, E., Wilkins, D., et al. (1998). Semantic typology and spatial conceptualization. *Language*, 74(3), 557–589. https://doi.org/10.2307/417793.

Pesetsky, D. M. (1982). *Paths and categories. Doctoral dissertation*, Massachusetts Institute of Technology, Cambridge, MA.

Phillips, C., Kazanina, N. and Abada, S. H. (2005). ERP effects of the processing of syntactic long-distance dependencies. *Cognitive Brain Research*, 22(3), 407–428. https://doi.org/10.1016/j.cogbrainres.2004.09.012.

Phillips, C., and Wagers, M. W. (2007). Relating structure and time in linguistics and psycholinguistics. In Gaskell, G. (Ed.). *Oxford handbook of psycholinguistics*, 739–756. Oxford: Oxford University Press.

Pinker, S. (2007). *The stuff of thought: Language as a window into human nature*. London: Allen Lane.

Polinsky, M. (2016). *Deconstructing ergativity: Two types of ergative languages and their features*. Oxford: Oxford University Press.

Polinsky, M., Gallo, C. G., Graff, P., et al. (2012). Subject preference and ergativity. *Lingua*, 122(3), 267–277. https://doi.org/10.1016/j.lingua.2011.11.004.

Postal, P. (1971). *Cross-over phenomena*. New York, NY: Halt, Rinehart and Winston.

Preminger, O. (2011). *Agreement as a fallible operation. Doctoral dissertation*, Massachusetts Institute of Technology, Cambridge, MA.

Preminger, O. (2014). *Agreement and its failures*. Cambridge, MA: MIT Press.

Primus, B. (1999). *Cases and thematic roles*. Tübingen: Niemeyer.

Pritchett, B., and Whitman, J. (1995). Syntactic representation and interpretive preference. In Mazuka, R., and Nagai, N. (Eds.). *Japanese sentence processing*, 65–76. Hillsdale, NJ: Lawrence Erlbaum.

Pullum, G. K. (1977). Word order universals and grammatical relations. *Syntax and Semantics 8: Grammatical relations*, 249–277. New York, NY: Academic Press.

Pye, C. (1992). The acquisition of K'iche' (Maya). In Slobin, D. I. (Ed.). *The crosslinguistic study of language acquisition*, vol. 3, 221–308. Hillsdale, NJ: Lawrence Erlbaum.

Pylkkänen, L. (2002). *Introducing arguments. Doctoral dissertation*, Massachusetts Institute of Technology, Cambridge, MA.

Pylkkänen, L. (2019). The neural basis of combinatory syntax and semantics. *Science*, 366(6461), 62–66. https://doi.org/10.1126/science.aax0050.

Pylkkänen, L., and Marantz, A. (2003). Tracking the time course of word recognition with MEG. *Trends in Cognitive Sciences*, 7(5), 187–189. https://doi.org/10.1016/S1364-6613(03)00092-5.

R Core Team. (2019). *R: A language and environment for statistical computing*. Vienna, Austria: R Foundation for Statistical Computing. Available at: www.R-project.org [last accessed August 24, 2022].

Reali, F., and Christiansen, M. H. (2007). Processing of relative clauses is made easier by frequency of occurrence. *Journal of Memory and Language*, 57(1), 1–23. https://doi.org/10.1016/j.jml.2006.08.014.

Richards, M. (2003). *Atlas lingüístico de Guatemala*. Guatemala: Instituto de Lingüística y Educación de la Universidad Rafael Landívar.

Richards, N. (2010). *Uttering trees*. Cambridge, MA: MIT Press.

Richards, N. (2016). *Contiguity theory*. Cambridge, MA: MIT Press.

Riesberg, S. (2014). *Symmetrical voice and linking in western Austronesian languages*. Berlin: De Gruyter Mouton. https://doi.org/10.1515/9781614518716.

Rizzi, L. (1997). The fine structure of the left periphery. In Haegeman, L. (Ed.). *Elements of grammar*, 281–337. Dordrecht: Springer.

Robinson, S. (2002). Constituent order in Tenejapan Tzeltal. *International Journal of American Linguistics*, 68(1), 51–81. https://doi.org/10.1086/466479.

Rodríguez Guaján, J. O. (1989). *Orden basico del Kaqchikel del siglo XVI*. Paper presented at the XI Taller Maya, Quetzaltenango, Guatemala.

Rodríguez Guaján, J. O. (1994). *Rutz'ib'axik ri Kaqchikel: Manual de redacción Kaqchikel*. Guatemala: Editorial Cholsamaj.

Rogalsky, C., Matchin, W., and Hickok, G. (2008). Broca's area, sentence comprehension, and working memory: An fMRI study. *Frontiers in Human Neuroscience*, 2, 14. https://doi.org/10.3389/neuro.09.014.2008.

Roland, D., Dick, F., and Elman, J. L. (2007). Frequency of basic English grammatical structures: A corpus analysis. *Journal of Memory and Language*, 57(3), 348–379. https://doi.org/10.1016/j.jml.2007.03.002.

Rösler, F., Pechmann, T., Streb, J., et al. (1998). Parsing of sentences in a language with varying word order: Word-by-word variations of processing demands are revealed by event-related brain potentials. *Journal of Memory and Language*, 38(2), 150–176. https://doi.org/10.1006/jmla.1997.2551.

Saito, M. (1985). *Some asymmetries in Japanese and their theoretical implications*. Doctoral dissertation. Cambridge, MA: MIT.

Saito, M. (1989). Scrambling as semantically vacuous A'-movement. In Baltin, M., and Kroch, A. (Eds.). *Alternative conceptions of phrase structure*, 182–200. Chicago, IL: University of Chicago Press.

Saito, M., and Fukui, N. (1998). Order in phrase structure and movement. *Linguistic Inquiry*, 29(3), 439–474. https://doi.org/10.1162/002438998553815.

Sakai, K. L. (2005). Language acquisition and brain development. *Science*, 310(5749), 815–819.

Sakai, H., Kubo, T., Ono, H., et al. (2012). Does word order influence non-verbal event description by speakers of OS language? *The 34th Annual Meeting of the Cognitive Science Society. Sapporo, August* 4, 2012.

Sandler, W., Meir, I., Padden, C., et al. (2005). The emergence of grammar: Systematic structure in a new language. *Proceedings of the National Academy of Sciences*, 102(7), 2661–2665. https://doi.org/10.1073/pnas.040544810.

Santi, A., and Grodzinsky, Y. (2010). fMRI adaptation dissociates syntactic complexity dimensions. *NeuroImage*, 51(4), 1285–1293. https://doi.org/10.1016/j.neuroimage.2010.03.034.

Sauppe, S. (2016). Verbal semantics drives early anticipatory eye movements during the comprehension of verb-initial sentences. *Frontiers in Psychology*, 7, 95. https://doi.org/10.3389/fpsyg.2016.00095.

Sauppe, S., Norchiffe, E., Konopka, A., et al. (2013). Dependencies first: Eye tracking evidence from sentence production in Tagalog. In Knauff, M., Pauen, M., Sebanz, N., et al. (Eds.). *Proceedings of the 35th Annual Meeting of the Cognitive Science Society*, 1265–1270. Austin, TX: Cognitive Science Society.

Schlesewsky, M., Fanselow, G., Kliegl, R., et al. (2000). The subject preference in the processing of locally ambiguous wh-questions in German. In Hemforth, B., and Konieczny, L. (Eds.). *German sentence processing*, 65–93. Dordrecht: Springer.

Scott, S. K. (2019). From speech and talkers to the social world: The neural processing of human spoken language. *Science*, 366(6461), 58–62. https://doi.org/10.1126/science.aax0288.

Sekerina, I. A. (1997). *The syntax and processing of Russian scrambled constructions in Russian*. Doctoral dissertation, City University of New York, New York, NY.

Sekerina, I. A. (2003). Scrambling processing: Dependencies, complexity, and constraints. In Karimi, S. (Ed.). *Word order and scrambling*, 301–324. Oxford: Blackwell.

Senghas, A., Coppola, M., Newport, E. L., et al. (1997). Argument structure in Nicaraguan sign language: The emergence of grammatical devices. *Proceedings of the Boston University Conference on Language Development*, 21(2), 550–561.

Shain, C., Blank, I. A., van Schijndel, M., et al. (2020). fMRI reveals language-specific predictive coding during naturalistic sentence comprehension. *Neuropsychologia*, 138, 107307. https://doi.org/10.1016/j.neuropsychologia.2019.107307.

Shibata, H., Sugiyama, T., Suzuki, M., et al. (2006). Nihongo-setsunai-kakimazebun-no konsekiitishuuhen-ni okeru shorikatei-no kentou [An investigation of processing processes around a trace position in sentences with clause-internal scrambling]. *Cognitive Studies*, 13, 301–315. https://doi.org/10.11225/jcss.13.301.

Shibatani, M. (1990). *The languages of Japan*. Cambridge: Cambridge University Press.

Siewierska, A. (1993). Syntactic weight vs information structure and word order variation in Polish. *Journal of Linguistics*, 29(2), 233–265. https://doi.org/10.1017/S0022226700000323.

Silverstein, M. (1976). Hierarchy of features and ergativity. In Dixon, R. (Ed.). *Grammatical categories in Australian languages*, 112–171. Canberra: Australian Institute of Aboriginal Studies.

Simons, G. F., and Fennig, C. D. (2017). *Ethnologue global dataset*. Dallas, TX: SIL International.

Slobin, D. I. (1991). Learning to think for speaking: Native language, cognition, and rhetorical style. *Pragmatics*, 1(1), 7–25. https://doi.org/10.1075/prag.1.1.01slo.

Slobin, D. I. (1996). From "thought and language" to "thinking for speaking." In Gumperz, J., and Levinson, S. (Eds.). *Rethinking linguistic relativity*, 70–96. Cambridge: Cambridge University Press.

Slobin D. I. (2003). Language and thought online: Cognitive consequences of linguistic relativity. In Gentner, D., and Goldin-Meadow, S. (Eds.). *Language in mind: Advances in the study of language and thought*, 157–191. Cambridge, MA: MIT Press.

Slobin, D. I. (2006). What makes manner of motion salient? Explorations in linguistic typology, discourse, and cognition. In Hickmann, M., and Robert, S. (Eds.). *Space in languages: Linguistic systems and cognitive categories*, 59–81. Amsterdam/Philadelphia: John Benjamins.

Slobin, D. I., and Bever, T. G. (1982). Children use canonical sentence schemas: A crosslinguistic study of word order and inflections. *Cognition*, 12(3), 229–265. https://doi.org/10.1016/0010-0277(82)90033-6.

Smith, M., and Wheeldon, L. (1999). High level processing scope in spoken sentence production. *Cognition*, 73(3), 205–246. https://doi.org/10.1016/S0010-0277(99)00053-0.

Sportiche, D. (1988). A theory of floating quantifiers and its corollaries for constituent structure. *Linguistic Inquiry*, 19, 425–449. https://doi.org/10.2307/25164903.

Sugisaki, K., Otaki, K., Yusa, N., et al. (2012). The acquisition of word order and its constraints in Kaqchikel: A preliminary study. In Chu, C.-Y., et al. (Ed.). *Selected*

Proceedings of the 5th Conference on Generative Approaches to Language Acquisition North America (GALANA 2012), 72–78. Somerville, MA: Cascadilla Proceedings Project.

Symeonidou, I., Dumontheil, C. W., and Breheny, R. (2016). Development of online use of theory of mind during adolescence: An eye-tracking study. *Journal of Experimental Child Psychology*, 149, 81–97. https://doi.org/10.1016/j.jecp.2015.11.007.

Tada, H. (1993). *A/A-bar partition in derivation. Doctoral dissertation*, Massachusetts Institute of Technology, Cambridge, MA.

Takeshima, Y., Tachibana, R., Asaoka, R., et al. (2014). Processing loads related to word order preference during sentence production in Japanese: An NIRS and eye tracking study. *Tohoku Psychologica Folia*, 73, 36–45.

Tamaoka, K., Asano, M., Miyaoka, Y., et al. (2014). Pre- and post-head processing for single- and double-scrambled sentences of a head-final language as measured by the eye tracking method. *Journal of Psycholinguistic Research*, 43, 167–185. https://doi.org/10.1007/s10936-013-9244-8.

Tamaoka, K., Kanduboda, P. B. A., and Sakai, H. (2011). Effects of word order alternation on the sentence processing of Sinhalese written and spoken forms. *Open Journal of Modern Linguistics*, 1(2), 24–32. https://doi.org/10.4236/ojml.2011.12004.

Tamaoka, K., Sakai, H., Kawahara, J., et al. (2003). The effects of phrase-length order and scrambling in the processing of visually presented Japanese sentences. *Journal of Psycholinguistic Research*, 32, 431–454. https://doi.org/10.1023/A:1024851729985.

Tamaoka, K., Sakai, H., Kawahara, J., et al. (2005). Priority information used for the processing of Japanese sentences: Thematic roles, case particles or grammatical functions? *Journal of Psycholinguistic Research*, 34, 281–332. https://doi.org/10.1007/s10936-005-3641-6.

Tamaoka, K., Zhang, J., Otsuka, Y., et al. (2021). *Derivation of VOS in Tongan: An experimental investigation. Architectures and Mechanisms for Language Processing (AMLaP 2021)*. September 2, 2021, Université de Paris, France.

Tanaka, M. N., Branigan, H. P., McLean, J. F., et al. (2011). Conceptual influences on word order and voice in sentence production: Evidence from Japanese. *Journal of Memory and Language*, 65(3), 318–330. https://doi.org/10.1016/j.jml.2011.04.009.

Tarallo, F., and Myhill, J. (1983). Interference and natural language processing in second language acquisition. *Language Learning*, 33(1), 55–76. https://doi.org/10.1111/j.1467-1770.1983.tb00986.x.

Tateishi, K. (1990). *The S-structure syntax of the subject and 'S-adjunctions. Doctoral dissertation*, University of Massachusetts, Amherst, MA.

Tay Coyoy, A. (1996). *Análisis de situación de la educación maya en Guatemala*. Guatemala: Cholsamaj.

Thompson, C. K., Bonakdarpour, B., and Fix, S. F. (2010). Neural mechanisms of verb argument structure processing in agrammatic aphasic and healthy age-matched listeners. *Journal of Cognitive Neuroscience*, 22(9), 1993–2011. https://doi.org/10.1162/jocn.2009.21334.

Tichoc Cumes, R., Ajsivinac Sian, J. E., Oscar García, L. P., et al. (2000). *Runuk'ul pa rub'eyal rutz'ib'axik ri Kaqchikel ch'ab' äl: Gramática normativa del idioma Maya Kaqchikel*. Chimaltenango: Comunidad Lingüística Kaqchikel de la Academia de las Lenguas Mayas de Guatemala.

Tomlin, R. S. (1986). *Basic word order: Functional principles*. London: Croom Helm.
Tomlin, R., and Rhodes, R. (1992). Information distribution in Ojibwa. In Payne, D. L. (Ed.). *Pragmatics of word order flexibility*, 117–135. Amsterdam: John Benjamins.
Traxler, M. J., Morris, R. K., and Seely, R. E. (2002). Processing subject and object relative clauses: Evidence from eye movements. *Journal of Memory and Language*, 47(1), 69–90. https://doi.org/10.1006/jmla.2001.2836.
Trueswell, J. C. (1996). The role of lexical frequency in syntactic ambiguity resolution. *Journal of Memory and Language*, 35(4), 566–585. https://doi.org/10.1006/jmla.1996.0030.
Trueswell, J. C., Tanenhaus, M. K., and Garnsey, S. M. (1994). Semantic influences on parsing: Use of thematic role information in syntactic ambiguity resolution. *Journal of Memory and Language*, 33(3), 285–318. https://doi.org/10.1006/jmla.1994.1014.
Trueswell, J. C., Tanenhaus, M. K., and Kello, C. (1993). Verb-specific constraints in sentence processing: Separating effects of lexical preference from garden-paths. *Journal of Experimental Psychology: Learning, Memory, and Cognition*, 19(3), 528. https://doi.org/10.1037/0278-7393.19.3.528.
Tsukida, N. (2009). *Sedekku-go (Taiwan)-no bunpoo [Grammar of Seediq (Taiwan)]*. Doctoral dissertation, The University of Tokyo, Tokyo, Japan.
Ueno, M., and Kluender, R. (2003). Event-related brain indices of Japanese scrambling. *Brain and Language*, 86(2), 243–271. https://doi.org/10.1016/S0093-934X(02)00543-6.
Vissers, C. T. W., Kolk, H. H., Van de Meerendonk, N., et al. (2008). Monitoring in language perception: Evidence from ERPs in a picture-sentence matching task. *Neuropsychologia*, 46(4), 967–982. https://doi.org/10.1016/j.neuropsychologia.2007.11.027.
Walenski, M., Europa, E., Caplan, D., et al. (2019). Neural networks for sentence comprehension and production: An ALE-based meta-analysis of neuroimaging studies. *Human Brain Mapping*, 40, 2275–2304. https://doi.org/10.1002/hbm.24523.
Wanner, E., and Maratsos, M. (1978). An ATN approach to comprehension. In Halle, M., Bresnan, J., and Miller, G. A. (Eds.). *Linguistic theory and psychological reality*, 119–161. Cambridge, MA: MIT Press.
Wassmann, J., and Dasen, P. R. (1998). Balinese spatial orientation: Some empirical evidence of moderate linguistic relativity. *Journal of the Royal Anthropological Institute*, 4(4), 689–711. https://doi.org/10.2307/3034828.
Watanabe, A. (2017). The division of labor between syntax and morphology in the Kichean agent-focus construction. *Morphology*, 27, 685–720. https://doi.org/10.1007/s11525-017-9312-0.
Waters, G., Caplan, D., Alpert, N., et al. (2003). Individual differences in rCBF correlates of syntactic processing in sentence comprehension: Effects of working memory and speed of processing. *NeuroImage*, 19(1), 101–112. https://doi.org/10.1016/S1053-8119(03)00007-7.
Whorf, B. L. (1956). *Language, thought and reality: Selected writings of Benjamin Lee Whorf (Edited by: J. B. Carroll)*. Cambridge, MA: MIT Press.
Yang, C. L., Charles, A. P., and Liu, Y. (2010). Sentence integration processes: An ERP study of Chinese sentence comprehension with relative clauses. *Brain and Language*, 112(2), 85–100. https://doi.org/10.1016/j.bandl.2009.10.005.
Yano, M., and Koizumi, M. (2018). Processing of non-canonical word orders in (in) felicitous contexts: Evidence from event-related brain potentials. *Language,*

Yano, M., and Koizumi, M. (2021). The role of discourse in long-distance dependency formation. *Language, Cognition and Neuroscience*, 2021, 711–729. https://doi.org/10.1080/23273798.2021.1883694.

Yano, M., Niikuni, K., Ono, H., et al. (2019). Syntax and processing in Seediq: An event-related potential study. *Journal of East Asian Linguistics*, 28(4), 395–419. https://doi.org/10.1007/s10831-019-09200-9.

Yano, M., Tateyama, Y., and Sakamoto, T. (2014). Processing of Japanese cleft constructions in context: Evidence from event-related brain potentials. *Journal of Psycholinguistic Research*, 44(3), 277–286. https://doi.org/10.1007/s10936-014-9294-6.

Yano, M., Yasunaga, D., and Koizumi, M. (2017). Event-related brain indices of gap-filling processing in Kaqchikel. In Harris, S. R. (Ed.). *Event-related potential (ERP): Methods, outcomes, research insights*, 89–122. Waltham, MA: NOVA Biomedical.

Yasugi, Y. (1996). Kaqchikel. In Kamei, T., Kono, R., and Chino, E. (Eds.). *Gengogaku daijiten dai 1 kan [A dictionary of linguistics, vol. 1]*, 1140–1142. Tokyo: Sanseido.

Yasugi, Y. (2005). Fronting of nondirect arguments and adverbial focus marking on the verb in Classical Yucatec. *International Journal of American Linguistics*, 71(1), 56–86.

Yasunaga, D., Yano, M., Yasugi, Y., et al. (2015). Is the subject-before-object preference universal? An event-related potential study in the Kaqchikel Mayan language. *Language, Cognition and Neuroscience*, 30(9), 1209–1229. https://doi.org/10.1080/23273798.2015.1080372.

Index

"thinking for speaking" hypothesis, 76, 81
"Tzotzil" Sign Language, 69

absolute frame of reference. *see* reference
absolutive case. *see* case
accuracy, 119, 142, 194, 195, 199, 202
accusative case. *see* case
Active Filler Strategy, 50
adjunct, 20, 132, 134
agent, 5, 12, 13, 39, 72, 101
Agent Focus, 21, 139, 140
agent voice. *see* voice
agent–action–patient, 70, 80, 116
agent–patient order, 5, 11, 75, 77, 165
Agent–Patient Preference in Thought, 75
agen–patient–action, 11, 70, 80
agreement, 8, 18, 126
Aissen, 12, 19, 21, 97, 129, 130, 188
Ajsivinac Sian, 8, 19, 21, 61, 91, 97, 188
Aldridge, 189, 190, 199
alignment, 16–19
allocentric coordinate. *see* coordinate
Al-Sayyid Bedouin Sign Language, 70
Altmann, 98
ambiguity, syntactic, 50, 91
American Sign Language, 69
Anand, 1, 188
animacy, 29–31, 98, 102, 113, 187
animal, 77, 89
animal recall task. *see* task
antecedent, 4
anterior negativity. *see* event-related potential (ERP)
anterior temporal lobe, 48
Aoshima, 185
articulation, 94
auditory semantic anomaly detection task. *see* task
Australia, 170
Avar, 203

Baayen, 195
Bader, 2, 185
Baker, 127
Balinese, 170
Barr, 109, 195
basic word order. *see* word order
Basque, 3, 24, 33, 50
Bates, 3, 75, 195
behavioral experiment, 9, 23, 34, 36, 164
Belize, 15, 170
Bennett, 21
Bever, 3, 6, 25, 78, 86
bilingualism, 115, 121
Binding Condition A, 127
Binding Condition C, 128
Boatman, 123
Bock, 6, 25, 76, 78, 95, 105, 107, 187
Bohnemeyer, 171
Bornkessel, 5, 143, 185, *see also* Bornkessel-Schlesewsky
Bornkessel-Schlesewsky, 5, 6, 25, 39, 54, 79, *see also* Bornkessel
brain activation, 9, 36, 41
Branigan, 6, 25, 79, 95, 187, 202
Brennan, 48, 161
Broca's area, 37, 39
Brown, C. H., 53, 171
Brown, J. M., 172
Brown, P., 170, 184
Brown, R. M., 15, 22
Brown-Schmidt, 96

Campbell, 16, 172
canonical word order. *see* word order
Caplan, 27, 39, 44, 47, 75, 193
Carnie, 22
case
  absolutive case, 17, 32, 138
  accusative case, 17, 32, 96, 104
  dative case, 34
  dependent case, 35
  ergative case, 17, 32, 138

225

case (cont.)
    marked case, 32
    nominative case, 17, 32, 96, 104
    unmarked case, 32
case marking, 17, 32, 72, 91
case-markedness hypothesis, 32, 33, 35
Caucasian, 203
Charles, 53
Chen, 27
Chinese, 53, 70, 75
chips recognition task. *see* task
Chol, 13, 126, 131, 135
Chomsky, 1, 127, 138, 164
Choo, 149
Christiansen, 142
Christianson, 96
Chujo, 2
Chung, 12
Clemens, 22, 25, 140
Clifton, 50
cognitive factor, 5, 7, 11, 25, 36, 76, 164
Cohn, 188
Collins, 149
comprehension, 23, 36, 114, 141, 164
    gesture comprehension, 70
Comrie, 5, 96
conceptual accessibility, 6, 81, 101, 187
conceptual processing. *see* processing
conceptual saliency, 12, 25, 95, 101, 112, 185, 187
conceptual-intentional system, 164
context, 19, 23, 61, 63, 96, 166, 169
Coon, 12, 21, 131, 137, 139, 140
coordinate
    allocentric coordinate, 169
    coordinate system, 167
    egocentric coordinate, 169
Coppola, 69
corpus, 3, 164
Croft, 5

Dasen, 170, 171
dative case. *see* case
Dayley, 139
De Smedt, 95
Dependency Locality Theory (DLT), 24, 141, 143, 155, 157, 161
    DLT simplified discourse processing cost, 143
    DLT storage costs, 144
    DLT structural integration cost, 143
dependent case. *see* case
dependent-marking, 17
Diesing, 139
discourse-given, 96

DLT. *see* Dependency Locality Theory (DLT)
dorsolateral prefrontal cortex, 43
Dryer, 6, 66, 67, 72
Dutch, 53, 170

Early Immediate Constituent (EIC), 24
Easy First, 95
Eberhard, 1, 173, 190
ecological validity, 194
egocentric coordinate, 167, *see* coordinate
electroencephalogram, 36, 38, 51
Elliot, 34
empathy, 6
empty category, 4
England, 15, 19, 21, 22, 91, 97, 172, 184, 188
English, 1, 3, 5, 39, 47, 70, 75, 170, 190
Erdocia, 3, 4, 24, 33, 50, 185
ergative case. *see* case
ergative(-absolutive) language. *see* language
Erlewine, 140
ERP. *see* event-related potential (ERP)
event, 9, 14, 35, 51, 61, 77, 78, 84
    nonreversible event, 71
    reversible event, 72, 81
event apprehension, 115
event representation, 74
event structure, 5, 25
event-related potential (ERP), 3, 9, 23, 38, 49, 115, 164
    anterior negativity, 3, 23, 38
    N400, 38
    P600, 3, 9, 23, 38, 49, 53, 55, 62, 64, 115, 189
Experience-Based Hypothesis, 142, 155, 157, 161, 162
eye-tracking, 2, 23, 103, 105, 108, 164, 187, 189

faculty of language
    faculty of language in the broad sense (FLB), 164
    faculty of language in the narrow sense (FLN), 164
faculty of language in the broad sense (FLB). *see* faculty of language
faculty of language in the narrow sense (FLN). *see* faculty of language
FALCOHN. *see* Field-Based Approaches to Language, Cognition, and Human Nature (FALCOHN) project
Feldman, 70
Feleki, 95
Fennig, 15, 173
Ferreira, 70, 71, 72, 73, 76, 77, 82, 89, 96, 99, 114, 194
Fiebach, 185

Index

Field-Based Approaches to Language, Cognition, and Human Nature (FALCOHN) project, 2, 166
field-based cross-linguistic cognitive neuroscientific research, 164
fieldwork, 21, 164
figure, 167
filler, 4
filler-gap dependency, 4, 50, 141, 159, 187
Filler-Gap Domain, 152
Finnish, 2, 3, 23, 86
Fischer, 69
Fisher, 68
Fitch, 164
fMRI. *see* functional magnetic resonance imaging (fMRI)
Foley, 190
Forster, 34
frame of reference (FoR). *see* reference
Frazier, 50, 185
frequency, 141, 156, 161, 165
Friederici, 37, 143
Fukui, 186
functional brain measurement, 1, 36, 37
functional magnetic resonance imaging (fMRI), 1, 2, 9, 23, 36, 122, 164
Futrell, 70, 75, 81

gap, 4
García Matzar, 8, 15, 19, 21, 22, 61, 97, 188
Garnsey, 142
Garzon, 22
Gell-Mann, 6, 10, 66, 68, 69
Gennari, 99, 102
geographical feature, 171
German, 1, 2, 3, 23, 39, 50, 185
gesture, 11, 70, 77
gesture comprehension. *see* comprehension
gesture production. *see* production
Gibson, 4, 5, 13, 24, 70, 71, 73, 75, 76, 77, 81, 89, 99, 114, 143, 194
Givón, 69
Gleitman, 105, 170, 171
goal voice. *see* voice
Goldin-Meadow, 70, 73, 75, 76
Golinkoff, 6, 25, 79
grammatical factor, 164
grammatical processing. *see* processing
grammatical relation, 98
Greek, 86
Greenberg, 1, 10, 66
Greenberg's Universal 1, 10, 66
Grewe, 2, 23, 39
Griffin, 105, 107
Grodner, 194

Grodzinsky, 37, 39, 44
ground, 167
Guatemala, 2, 15
Guerrera, 34
Guugu Yimithirr, 170

Hagiwara, 24, 44, 50, 185
Hagoort, 37, 53
Hakulinen, 2, 86
Hall, 70, 71, 72, 73, 76, 77, 82, 89, 99, 114
Harbusch, 143
Harley, 137
Harris, 25
Hauser, 164
Haviland, 70
Hawkins, 4, 24, 143, 149, 159, 163
head-marking, 8, 16, 18, 81, 85, 98, 101, 188
Heaton, 21
Hebrew, 84
Hemforth, 23
Henderson, 21, 139
Hickok, 47
hierarchical distance, 13, 156, 161
Hierarchical Distance Hypothesis, 156, 159, 161, 162
Hirsh-Pasek, 6, 25, 78
Hoenkamp, 95
Holcomb, 54
Holmer, 191
home sign, 69
Hualien, 192
Hujanen, 23
human, 77, 89
Hwang, 187
Hyönä, 23

iconicity, 5
IGV. *see* Individual Grammar View
Imamura, 3, 23, 65, 86, 96, 156, 166, 185
Imanishi, 21, 22, 126, 129, 137, 138, 139
incorporation, 137
Individual Grammar View, 7, 8, 24, 31, 44, 48, 54, 60, 115, 141
Individual Grammar View [Order of Thought], 75, 78
Individual Grammar View [Processing Load], 25, 31
Individual Grammar View [Word Order Selection], 87
Individual Grammar View [Order of Thought]. *see* Individual Grammar View
Individual Grammar View [Processing Load]. *see* Individual Grammar View
Individual Grammar View [Word Order Selection]. *see* Individual Grammar View

Indo-European language, 1
Indonesia, 170
inferior frontal gyrus (IFG), 2, 3, 5, 9, 23, 37, 39, 43, 47, 107, 110, 123
information structure, 23
Inoue, 167, 171, 184
integration, 143
International 10–20 system, 52, 103
intrinsic frame of reference. *see* reference
Irish, 75
Italian, 3, 75, 86
Itoh, 185

Jaeger, 25, 188, 195
Japan, 171
Japanese, 1, 2, 3, 4, 7, 13, 17, 18, 23, 32, 34, 39, 40, 50, 53, 75, 77, 78, 86, 96, 102, 156, 161, 167, 170, 175, 179, 181, 185, 190
Jarvis, 37
Jasper, 53
Johnson-Laird, 169

K'iche', 21
Kaan, 50, 53, 54
Kaburaki, 6
Kaiser, 2, 23, 194, 203
Kamide, 98
Kant, 169
Kaqchikel, 2, 7, 8, 18, 188, 201
Karlsson, 86
Kaufman, 16, 172
Kayne, 131, 137
Keenan, 5, 96
Kello, 98
Kemmerer, 5, 25, 39, 44, 187
Kempen, 95, 101, 143
Kim, 2, 23, 39, 40, 44, 46, 114, 122, 123, 185, 200
Kimmelman, 67
King, 75
Kinno, 2, 9, 23, 39
Kishimoto, 96, 160
Kitagawa, 96
Kiyama, 113, 118, 122, 188, 200
Kluender, 24, 50
Kobe, 171
Kochi, 171
Koizumi, 2, 3, 23, 27, 35, 46, 48, 50, 51, 53, 64, 65, 86, 94, 96, 109, 114, 115, 121, 122, 123, 156, 166, 185, 188, 189, 200, 203
Kondo, 185
Korean, 2, 23, 75, 187
Kronmüller, 109
Kubo, 77, 99, 100, 189
Kuno, 6, 23

Kuperberg, 54
Kuroda, 96
Kuznetsova, 195

Laka, 4
Langacker, 1, 5
language, 164
 (nominative-)accusative language, 17, 32, 34
 Austronesian language, 13, 33, 166, 170, 185, 190
 ergative(-absolutive) language, 8, 16, 17, 33
 Mayan language, 15, 126, 140, 165, 170
 Object-before-Subject (OS) language, 1
 OS language, 2, 77
 Pama-Nyungan language, 170
 pro-drop language, 19
 sign language, 67, 69
 SO language, 2, 75
 Subject-before-Object (SO) language, 1
language center, 43
Langus, 70, 75
Larsen, 18, 21
Lascaratou, 86
latency, 12, 102, 104, 108
lateral premotor cortex, 124
Lau, 123
Lee, 96, 149
Levelt, 76, 94
Levinson, 167, 169, 171, 184
lexical access, 123
lexical maze task. *see* task
Li, 167, 170, 171
Lindsley, 98
Linear Correspondence Axiom (LCA), 131
linear distance, 13, 143, 156, 161
Linear Distance Hypothesis, 157, 162
linguistic relativity, 167
Little, 15, 22, 172
Liu, 53
Loebell, 76

MacDonald, 95, 99, 102, 142
MacWhinney, 5, 6, 65, 187
magnetic resonance imaging (MRI), 39
 functional MRI. *see* functional magnetic resonance imaging (fMRI)
 structural MRI, 39
magnetoencephalogram (MEG), 38
magnetoencephalography (MEG), 1
Majid, 170, 171
Malchukov, 101
Maldonado, 21
Mapping Hypothesis, 139
Marantz, 4, 24, 35, 123
Matchin, 47

Matsumoto, 20, 171
Matzke, 50, 185
Maxwell, 15, 22, 172
Mayan language. *see* language
Mayberry, 70, 71, 72, 73, 76, 77, 82, 89, 99, 114
Mazuka, 2, 185
McDonald, 95, 187
Meir, 84
Meng, 185
Mexico, 15, 170
Meyer, 39
middle temporal gyrus, 123
Miller, 169
Minimize Domain, 152
Minimize Filler-Gap Domain, 141, 155, 159
Mirković, 99, 102
Mirror Principle, 127
Mishra, 171
Miyagawa, 186
Mobley, 54
Momma, 101
Mopan, 170, 174, 184
Moravcsik, 101
Morey, 76
Moseley, 164
Myachykov, 95
Myhill, 64
Mylander, 70

N400. *see* event-related potential (ERP)
Nakano, 185
Napoli, 67, 70
near-infrared spectroscopy, 12, 39, 103, 107, 110, 164
Nespor, 70, 75
Newmeyer, 69
Newport, 69
Nicaraguan Sign Language, 69
Nichols, 17, 18, 98
Niraula, 171
NIRS. *see* near-infrared spectroscopy
noisy channel hypothesis, 71, 77, 81, 99, 114
nominative case. *see* case
nominative-accusative languages. *see* language
nonreversible event. *see* event
nonreversible sentence. *see* sentence, event
nontopicalized subject. *see* subject
Norcliffe, 1, 25, 97, 107, 113, 188
Norman, 18, 21
noun phrase accessibility hierarchy, 95
Nuger, 18

O'Grady, 4, 13, 21, 24, 25, 141, 186
object, 13

Object-before-Subject (OS) language. *see* language
object-extracted relative clause. *see* relative clause
Ohta, 122
Oldfield, 40, 45, 51, 108
Olsthoorn, 101
Ono, 203
OS language, 164, *see* language
OS word order. *see* word order
Osaka, 171
Osterhout, 54
Otaki, 137
Otsuka, 17, 33

P600. *see* event-related potential (ERP)
Paczynski, 188
Palauan, 18
pantomime, 70, *see* gesture
passive, 90
passive sentence. *see* sentence
patient, 5, 14
patient–agent order, 5
Pearlmutter, 142
Pederson, 76, 169, 170, 171
perception, 94
perspective-taking, 6, 25, 101
Pesetsky, 149
Philippine, 187
Phillips, 101, 123, 185
Pickering, 6, 25, 79
picture description task. *see* task
picture–sentence matching task. *see* task
Pinker, 167, 171
Poeppel, 123
Polinsky, 203
Polish, 86
Postal, 138
posterior superior temporal cortex, 37
pragmatically determined word order. *see* word order
predicate fronting analysis, 12, 126, 131
Preminger, 21
Primus, 5, 6, 25, 32, 79, 187
Pritchett, 4, 24
processing
  conceptual processing, 94
  grammatical processing, 94, 115
pro-drop language. *see* language
production, 3, 11, 114, 164
  gesture production, 70, 75
  sentence production, 86, 101
Pye, 21
Pylkkänen, 37, 48, 123, 137

questionnaire, 164

Reali, 142
reference
  absolute frame of reference, 167, 168, 170, 171, 181
  frame of reference (FoR), 167
  intrinsic frame of reference, 169
  relative frame of reference, 167, 168, 170, 179, 181
  spatial frame of reference, 167
relative clause, 5, 186
  object-extracted relative clause, 3, 5, 149, 152
  subject-extracted relative clause, 3, 5, 144, 149, 152
relative frame of reference. *see* reference
response time, 115, 120, 194, 199
reversible event. *see* event
reversible sentence. *see* sentence
Richards, M., 15
Richards, N., 138
Riesberg, 190
right-specifier analysis, 12, 126, 128, 135, 137, 165
Rizzi, 138, 191
Robinson, 97
Rodríguez Guaján, 8, 19, 21, 22, 61, 97, 188
Rogalsky, 47
role conflict hypothesis, 71, 72, 77, 82, 99, 114
Rösler, 3, 23, 50
Ruhlen, 6, 10, 66, 68, 69
Russian, 2, 23

Saito, 186
Sakai, 44
Sakamoto, 65
saliency. *see* conceptual saliency
Sandler, 70
Santi, 39, 44
Sapir, 167
Sato, 65, 156
Sauppe, 187, 189, 202
Schlesewsky, 25, 39, 54, 79, 143, 185
Scott, 37
scrambling, 4, 96
Seediq, 13, 189, 190
Seidenberg, 142
Sekerina, 2, 23, 185
self-paced reading task. *see* task
Senghas, 69
sensory-motor system, 164
sentence
  nonreversible sentence, 26, 29

passive sentence, 90
reversible sentence, 29
subject-initial sentence, 101
verb-initial sentence, 91, 101
sentence plausibility judgment task. *see* task
sentence production. *see* production
sentence-assembly task. *see* task
Serbo-Croatian, 3, 86
Set A, 18
Set B, 18
Shain, 161
Shibata, 2
Shibatani, 96, 150
Siewierska, 86
sign language. *see* language
similarity-based competition, 99, 102, 113
Simons, 15, 173
Sinhalese, 23
Slobin, 3, 6, 25, 74, 76, 78, 81, 86
Smith, 98
SO Preference, 2–3
  SO Preference in Basic Word Order, 10, 66
  SO preference in ergative language, 33, 34
  SO Preference in Sentence Comprehension, 8, 24
  SO Preference in Sentence Production, 11, 86
SO Preference in Basic Word Order. *see* SO Preference
SO Preference in Sentence Comprehension. *see* SO Preference
SO Preference in Sentence Production. *see* SO Preference
SO word order. *see* word order
SO word order preference. *see* preference
SOV word order. *see* word order
Spanish, 12, 15, 21, 70, 75, 115, 120, 121, 125, 173, 184
spatial frame of reference, 13, *see* reference
speed–accuracy trade-off, 199
speeded grammaticality judgment task. *see* task
Sportiche, 191
Sprenger, 101
Stanczak, 39
starting point, 6
storage, 143
structural distance, 149
Structural Distance Hypothesis, 141, 149, 152, 155, 159
subject, 13
  nontopicalized subject, 96, 97, 165
  topicalized subject, 96, 97, 165
Subject-before-Object (SO) language. *see* language

Index

subject-extracted relative clause. *see* relative clause
Sugisaki, 21
Supalla, 69
superior temporal gyrus, 44, 123
Sutton-Spence, 67, 70
Swaab, 54
Symeonidou, 109
symmetrical voice. *see* voice
syntactic complexity, 102, 112, 185, 186, 202
syntactic complexity hypothesis, 31, 189, 199
syntactic structure, 12, 141, 165
syntactically determined word order. *see* word order

Tada, 21
Tagalog, 75, 187, 189
Taiwan, 13, 189
Takeshima, 105
Tamaoka, 2, 23, 34, 185
Tanaka, 5, 6, 25, 79, 95, 187, 202
Tanenhaus, 98, 142
Tarallo, 64
task
 animal recall task, 174, 175, 179
 auditory semantic anomaly detection task, 188
 chips recognition task, 176, 179
 lexical maze task, 34
 picture description task, 89, 102
 picture–sentence matching task, 44, 61
 self-paced reading task, 2, 23, 33
 sentence plausibility judgment task, 2, 9, 23, 27, 34, 41, 46, 193
 sentence-assembly task, 187
 sentence–picture matching task, 49, 51, 115
 speeded grammaticality judgment task, 186
 transitive inference task, 177, 179
Tateishi, 96
Tateyama, 65
Tay Coyoy, 15, 172
the faculty of language in the broad sense (FLB). *see* faculty of language
thematic role, 187
theoretical linguistics, 164
thinking, 74, 76, 105
Thompson, 39
thought, 2, 7, 10, 13, 14, 37, 71, 74, 77, 85, 95, 164, 167
Tichoc Cumes, 8, 19, 21, 61, 97, 188
time course, 38, 49, 61, 102, 105, 109, 194
Tomlin, 66, 95
Tongan, 17, 33
topic, 20, 61, 96, 97, 156, 160
topicalized subject. *see* subject

trace, 4
transitive inference task. *see* task
Traxler, 75
Trueswell, 23, 98, 142, 194, 203
Truku, 185, 189, 190
Tsukida, 189, 190, 202
Turkish, 3, 70, 75, 84, 86
Tzeltal, 113, 170, 171, 174, 184
Tzotzil, 129

UCV. *see* Universal Cognition View
Ueno, 24, 50
Universal Cognition View, 5–6, 7, 8, 24, 31, 44, 48, 55, 60, 141, 190
 Universal Cognition View [Order of Thought], 75, 78
 Universal Cognition View [Processing Load], 25
 Universal Cognition View [Word Order Selection], 88
Universal Cognition View [Order of Thought]. *see* Universal Cognition View
Universal Cognition View [Processing Load]. *see* Universal Cognition View
Universal Cognition View [Word Order Selection]. *see* Universal Cognition View
universal saliency hypothesis, 190

view point, 6
Vissers, 54
voice, 126, 185, 189, 192
 agent voice, 192, 196
 antipassive voice, 100, 139
 goal voice, 192, 196
 passive voice, 90, 93, 190, 202
 symmetrical voice, 14, 190, 202
von Cramon, 39

Wagers, 185
Walenski, 37, 47
Wanner, 66
Warren, 6, 25, 78, 95, 187
Wassmann, 170
Watanabe, 21
Waters, 27, 39, 47
Watson, 96
weak crossover, 138
Wernicke's area, 37
Wheeldon, 98
Whitman, 4, 24
Whorf, 167
word order
 basic word order, 1, 2, 5, 6, 8, 10, 19, 21, 24, 67, 75, 165, 200

word order (cont.)
　canonical word order, 41, 107, 148, 185, 186, 188, 200, 202
　OS word order, 2, 23, 185
　OSV word order, 2, 23, 74
　OVS word order, 2, 74
　pragmatically determined word order, 97
　SO word order, 2, 23, 66, 84, 185
　SOV word order, 2, 11, 67–70, 73
　SVO word order, 2, 73, 116, 192, 196
　syntactically basic word order, 25, 26, 33, 44, 48, 55, 88, 94, 113, 191
　syntactically determined word order, 97
　verb-initial word order, 81, 85
　VOS word order, 2, 7, 19, 26, 33, 35, 36, 49, 192, 196
　VSO word order, 2, 33

Yang, 53
Yano, 50, 51, 53, 64, 65, 115, 121, 166, 191, 199, 200, 201, 203
Yasugi, 20, 172
Yasunaga, 51, 53, 62, 64, 115, 121, 188, 200
Yucatec, 170, 174, 184

For EU product safety concerns, contact us at Calle de José Abascal, 56–1°, 28003 Madrid, Spain or eugpsr@cambridge.org.